# The Garden of Vegan

# The Garden of Vegan

TANYA BARNARD & SARAH KRAMER

ARSENAL PULP PRESS
VANCOUVER

EIGHTH PRINTING: 2009

ARSENAL PULP PRESS
200 - 341 Water Street
Vancouver, B.C.
Canada V6B 1B8
*arsenalpulp.com*

The publisher gratefully acknowledges the support of the Government of Canada through the Book Publishing Industry Development Program for its publishing activities.

Book and cover design by Lisa Eng-Lodge
Production assistance by Felicia Lo
Cover photo by Mulitin Gubash
Cover food styling by Eric Akis
Interior photos by Kaisha Goodacre, Wendy Clarke, Claire Westby, Chris Frey,
  Tanya Barnard, and Sarah Kramer
Cover author photo by Claire Westby
Printed and bound in Canada

The authors and publisher assert that the information contained in this book is true and complete to the best of their knowledge. All recommendations are made without guarantee on the part of the authors and Arsenal Pulp Press. The authors and publisher disclaim any liability in connection with the use of this information. For more information, contact the publisher.

NATIONAL LIBRARY OF CANADA CATALOGUING IN PUBLICATION DATA:
Barnard, Tanya 1972-
  The garden of vegan

  Includes index.
  ISBN 1-55152-128-8

  1968-  II. Title.
TX837.B278 2002   641.5'636   C2002-910926-4

  ISBN13 978-1-55152-128-2

# CONTENTS

DEDICATED TO

the memory of Riley and Black Bumps Kramer

# ACKNOWLEDGMENTS

These people kick ass and we need to thank them!

Special thanks to those of you who submitted recipes; we are honored that you shared them with us. It was fun testing them and we hope your new-found fame doesn't go to your head (!). We also need to thank Rachel and Christine who suggested *The Garden of Vegan* as a title. Thank you so much!

Thanks, also, to: Arsenal Pulp for being so good to us. Donna Wong-Juliani for her sage advice. The Younge-Grodin family for letting us use their backyard for the cover photo, and Auntie Bonnie for letting us use her kitchen. Vensanto Melina for all her advice. Marc, Holly, and Savonna for showing us such a good time. Li Eng-Lodge and Felicia Lo for the great book design. Mulitin Gubash for shooting the cover photo. Erik Akis for styling our food. Dave Shiskoff and the Murdock family for supporting us so enthusiastically. Kaisha Goodacre, Wendy Clarke, Claire Westby, and Chris Frey for taking photos used inside the book. Martin Wales and Yasmin Vickery for letting us use their house for photos. Martin Wales, Chris Cowley, and Dustin Rideout for looking so swanky in our photos. Zoe and Andy at AcheRecords.com. MooShoes.com for supporting our arches. HerbivoreClothing.com for keeping us clothed.

## SARAH

Tanya and I have been so blessed since *How It All Vegan!* came out in 1999. We have met so many amazing people, received endless encouraging e-mail and letters from fans, and have had an amazing time promoting the book. I still can't quite believe that I'm a cookbook author with two books under my belt!

There are so many friends and family that I need to thank, but first I want to thank you. That's right – I'm talking about YOU! Thank you for supporting us when *How It All Vegan!* first came out, and for buying multiple copies to give to your friends and family; for forwarding our web page (*GoVegan.net*) to people you thought might be interested; for showing up at our various cooking demos and laughing at our silly skits and for watching us on TV. I am touched and inspired by your encouragement every day. Without your support, we wouldn't have been able to write *The Garden of Vegan*.

I also have to thank my husband Gerry (*gerrykramer.com*), who rocks my world. He is always by my side through thick and thin and is the most patient, supportive, loving partner a girl could ever wish on a star for. He is a tireless supporter of me and my dreams and works hard so I can achieve them.

Hugs and snuffles to my fur-family, Sir Douglas-Fort and Fergus. You guys are always at my fingertips when I need you. To Riley and BB, to know you was to love you and to be loved by you was amazing. Snuggles and scratches to Frankie and Jupiter.

Thank you to everyone in the Kramer, Ball, Geiger, Reid, Anderson, and Kindrachuk family. They fully support everything I do and having that kind of support makes a girl stand taller. Especially my Dad and Denise, both of whom have an adventurous spirit when it comes to food, and thank Elvis it rubbed off on me. Your support and encouragement is priceless. Thanks to my brother Ben for all his chef advice. And to my niece Heidi and my nephew Eli: you are what dreams are made of.

Thanks also to: Maureen; your friendship is precious and I am blessed to have you in my life. To Jennifer, who is my rock, and her family, and Shoshana and her family (especially Gerry, who sends me horribly hilarious e-mail). Maury, Graham, Theresa, and Meagan. Todd for finding his way back into my life. Corri, Rob, Scott, all the old-school Regina gang, and the Springfield kids who still keep in touch. The gang at the Queen Street house (Ken, Joe, and especially Meghan, who left us too soon – she always had a smile on her face and a sparkle in her eye and I miss that). All the ladies at the Stitch N Bitch, Corri, Lisa, Greg, and lil' Charlie. Jana at Earth's Herbal Products. The gang at The Tattoo Zoo, especially Janine for being so supportive of Gerry and me. Everyone in the Capital City Scooter Club; I am so lucky to have a group of friends like you, especially all my ladies in the Wild Cherry Scooter Club. And those in the scooter scene in the Pacific Northwest; you guys rock!

Special thanks to Garry and Andree Hurl for finding me a portable dishwasher (they saved me from dishpan hands). To Cheryl at Toto's Pet Grooming for her sage doggie advice and for keeping Fergus looking so sharp. Thank you to Gail, Leeza, and Steve for making my back not hurt anymore.

Thanks to Danny Smith (*LaymanBooks.com*) who inspires me to write, and helps me to focus, and Becky for all her advice!

And again, I need to thank Tanya, who has been my "bestest" best friend for over ten years. We've never really had a fight (knock on wood) – well, okay, maybe a few grumpy words, but never a knock-down yelling match. Well, there was this one time where I was so mad at her I couldn't talk and I had to put the phone down ... oh, and then there's the time I hung up on her. But don't worry, we worked it out like we always do. I could hang out with her 24-7 and the only thing that would drive me crazy is that she doesn't like to plan ahead for what we're going to be eating later on in the day (!). We are almost always on the same page; she laughs at my stupid jokes, she doesn't think I'm a dork, and she supports every single choice I make. I love her to death. Yay, Tanya! Best friends rock!

Thank you to my late friend Peter Boyle. He inspired me in more ways than I can say with a few choice words. Not a day goes by that I don't think about him and miss him.

Lastly I'd like to leave you with one of my favorite quotes. In the immortal words of Lloyd Dobler here are some words of wisdom to live by:

> "I don't want to sell anything, buy anything or process anything as a career. I don't want to sell anything bought or processed...or buy anything sold or processed...or process anything sold, bought, or processed...or repair anything sold, bought, or processed. You know, as a career, I don't want to do that."

I think that says it all. Enjoy the book!

# TANYA

A publication this size is not possible without the help and support of many. I feel truly blessed to have such a wonderful community of friends and family that supports, nourishes, inspires, and loves me. I couldn't live without you and hope I never have to.

A great big thank you goes to my family. They are truly a supporting bunch and take excitement in all my adventures. Thank you, Mom, Bob, Kari, Dave, Brandon, Hayley, Trevor, Stephanie, Jordon, Nana, and Papa. These last three years my family has seen the addition of three new members: my sister and her husband blessed us with two lovely children, Brandon and Hayley, and Leanne and Bryan presented us with Breannah this last spring. I love the new babies and get great satisfaction spending time with them and getting to know them. It's a wonderful feeling when your family gets bigger and bigger.

A great big enormous thank you to my sweetie Matthew. You're such a wonderful friend and partner. It's nice to spend time with someone who loves to cook and eat as much as I do. We have so much fun perusing the fancy cooking stores dreaming and drooling over all the products like they're candy. I learn so much from you and your wonderful family. Thanks for being there to listen to all my tribulations and excitements, for holding my hand when the going gets tough, and sharing in all the laughter.

Thank you to my housemates Cory and Caleb. They survived my noisy late-night recipe testing, not to mention the recipes themselves! Nights will be quiet and calm again.

Thank you to my recipe testers: Matthew, Maureen, Cory, David, Marion, Brad, Andrew, Lindsey, Ken, and everyone at Fresh Piks. Your approval and honesty played a crucial role in determining which recipes made the book. Not only did you eat everything I made so I didn't have to throw it away, but your taste buds and criticism were essential to this project.

Thanks to my friends who live far away. You may not be near, but I hold you close. I get strength and love from you all and I want to thank you for that. Sarah T., Laura, Chris H. and father Ken, Holly, Todd, Rob, and Darja.

Thanks to all my friends who live close by. There have been many, many people over the last three years who have been wonderful and supportive. I wish I could thank every one of your personally, but unfortunately there is not enough space. You know who you are! But I do have to say a special thank you to my girl Mo. Being involved in groups like the Friday Nite S+C, Capital City Scooter Club, and Stitch N Bitch keeps me from being a boring person. Without all these fun people in my life, life would surely be a drag! Now that this project is finished it will be fun to attend these social events with regularity again. Let the fun begin!

I want to thank the vegan community from all over the world. Your support has provided me with encouragement to see this project to the end. But an even bigger thanks goes to the Victoria vegan community because if they don't like you at home, they won't like you anywhere else! Big thanks to Dave M., Jon, Sarah K., Brandon, Brooke, Tyrone, Trevor and Tammy M., David S., Brent, and Andy.

And lastly I have to say thanks to my wonderful friend and book partner Sarah. I'm so excited that we did it again! Ten or more years of laughter and tears, ups and downs, and still we're friends. It truly is remarkable. In case you didn't know, you're the wind beneath my wings!

Introduction

Welcome to *The Garden of Vegan*. In our last book, *How It All Vegan!*, we covered the basics of vegan life: how to set up an easy-to-use kitchen, where our vegan roots came from, and aspects of Veganism 101.

We hope that *How It All Vegan!* helped you to get your foot in the vegan door and that you're now having fun incorporating veganism into your life. Even if you're not 100 percent vegan, we wanted to tantalize your palate, make your belly feel full and satisfied, and perhaps open your mind to the idea that a vegan lifestyle doesn't always have to be about sprouts and sandals. Although, if that's what you're into ... yay!

*The Garden of Vegan* is an extension of *How It All Vegan!*: more yummy, easy-to-prepare recipes, plus some more ... dare we say ... gourmet recipes. Plus tips for throwing parties, tricks for when you screw up in the kitchen, and answers to frequently asked questions.

One of our favorite things in the first book was to include recipes submitted from our friends and family. This time around, not only has Auntie Bonnie, Cousin Tasha, Tanya's Na-Na Marg, and other friends and family members submitted more recipes, but we asked all of YOU to help out as well. We received countless recipes from as far as Australia, Texas, Kentucky, Ontario ... all over the place. It's been a blast testing them all, and adding them to the book. We can't thank you all enough for your support ... now we also have to thank you for your recipes. You guys rock!

We hope you enjoy the book and will visit us at *GoVegan.net*. Now get into your kitchen and start cooking!

# SARAH'S INTRODUCTION: THROW ME A CURVE

Nothing makes me feel better than a mouthful of delicious vegan food. There is something satisfying about starting with raw ingredients and with a few simple flicks of the knife and a blast of heat, creating a meal.

I eat for different reasons. Obviously, hunger is number one. There's also health, of course, and lastly, my favorite: for comfort. Certain foods and kitchen smells take me back to a place where nothing mattered but trying to stay up past your bedtime and convincing your parents into thinking that you brushed your teeth.

The kitchen is where I feel most connected to my past. My mum loved to cook and was ahead of her time with regard to vegetarianism. I think I was the only veggie-kid I knew growing up in Regina, Saskatchewan. All my friends were meat and potatoes while I was salad and soup.

I had a healthy relationship with food. Okay, sure, I went through kid phases when I would only eat grilled cheese sandwiches. Then there was the baked beans and bananas phase. I even remember wanting to be a cat, and my parents letting me eat soup out of a bowl on the floor.

My mum died when I was ten and my memories of her are fragmented at best and are more like snapshots in a photo album than a movie in my head. The most intense memories I have of her are in the kitchen: watching her make me play dough from scratch; helping her stir the cookie dough and anxiously waiting for the moment when she did her final scrape of the bowl and allowed me lick what was left. I remember banana chips and carrot sticks were my after-school snack. I remember being so excited when she'd bring out the carrot cake at my birthday parties. I remember the big jar of honey on the top shelf of the cupboard that was brought out for special occasions.

Yeah. Things were a little different at the Kramer house.

My dad and stepmum gave me the bowl my mum used to use to make bread and cookies in; a large ceramic bowl that is heavy and large enough for a triple batch of cookies. I had been begging them to give it to me for years. It's the one thing that reminds me the most of my mum. They finally relented when Gerry and I eloped to Vegas in 1996. They gave it to me as a wedding present and it is one of my most treasured objects.

Our family's relationship with food changed when my mum died. My dad was devastated and I remember eating a lot of pizzas. Inside I felt a shift occur; the joy of eating and sharing a meal with family had suddenly changed into something else. My dad, brother, and I were like zombies; just there, but not really. A little black rain cloud sat over top of me and stayed with me for a long, long time.

When my stepmum Denise moved in, I gave her a hard time. Oooh, that's an understatement: I was the devil. I was an eleven-year-old with the weight of the world on her shoulders and I didn't give Denise any slack. I was a horrible stepdaughter. I criticized her food, refused to eat what she offered. I had bile in my belly and I let everyone have a taste of it.

As I became a preteen and then a teenager, under the confusion of all that comes with puberty, food became something else yet again. My school was not in the same area I lived in, so I would go to friends' houses at lunchtime. I'd be armed with my veggie sandwich on brown bread and watched my friends devour fluorescent orange pasta and sip bubbly sugary drinks. Eventually I began dumping my lunch to eat what they were eating. I have this vivid memory of sitting in my friend Vanna's kitchen eating a giant bowl of cake icing for lunch and watching on TV the footage of President Reagan being shot.

Grades 7 and 8 were all about sleepovers at my girlfriends' houses. The food at my house seemed so bland compared to what they had: cakes, cookies, white sugar icing, potato chips, chocolate bars, and all the Pic-a-Pop you could drink. Not a carrot in sight. I was a skinny little kid and could consume half a cake and not even have my belly pooch out. I've always been a bit of a late bloomer and I didn't look like any of my friends. While they were all blossoming into women, I still looked like a little kid. My friends were envious; by that time they were all watching their weight.

As I entered high school I started worrying about my weight too. By then my girlfriends and I had decided that if you looked in a mirror, held your knees together, and couldn't see through your thighs, you were fat. According to our test, we all needed to go on diets.

In high school, food had no meaning to me. It was a waste of time. I only ate if I had to. I had cereal in the morning, and replaced lunch with a cigarette and a Slurpee. I had to eat dinner because we always ate

together as family, but I would do my darnedest to be sent to my room so I could skip out on eating.

I wanted to be able to see through my thighs. I hated my body. I thought my thighs were fat, that my stomach protruded too much. My arms were thick. I would be in tears if the scale hit ninety-five pounds. My goal was to be eighty-three pounds. I thought eighty-three would be perfect. Then I would be perfect.

When I graduated from high school (by the skin of my teeth), I moved out of the house and was on my own for the first time. Food was last on my list of priorities; it consisted of things out of boxes and cans. I wouldn't eat anything that was fresh unless I had to. Especially food that had veins; tomatoes and lettuce freaked me out. I didn't even want to touch them. Anything out of a package was all I could manage to swallow.

Being poor, I worked out a budget for food. After cigarettes and other necessities like hairspray for my Mohawk, punk rock shows, and beer (God, I was stupid) I had thirty-five dollars a week for food. That meant I could only eat once or twice a day. But by then, I could do that. I learned that cigarettes curb your appetite, so I smoked more. Almost a pack and a half a day. Anytime my stomach growled, I would light up a smoke.

I was in a bad place for a long time in Regina. I finally decided to make a change, so I packed up my stuff and hopped the train west to Victoria. I started to change my life in positive ways, but my food issues followed me. When my health began to deteriorate and I was diagnosed with Chronic Fatigue Syndrome (CFS), I could barely eat at all. I was so exhausted; it was an ordeal just to pick up a fork. I mostly ate cereal and on a good day could manage to make perogies. I think that's all I ate for a month. One day I stepped on the scale and I was eighty-three pounds.

I looked in the mirror and realized that I was killing myself. I need to fix things. I need to make myself better.

It was interesting, because while I was struggling to get my weight up, become healthy again, and learn to have a new relationship with food, I had people coming up to me and telling me I looked fantastic. They wanted to know how I stayed so skinny. They wished they had CFS so they could lose some weight (ha ha).

It freaked me out. I looked like a skeleton, I knew I looked bad, and yet people wanted to look like me.

As I struggled with my CFS and began leaning towards veganism, my relationship with food made a dramatic shift. Food became fuel. It gave me energy and filled me up and made me strong. Slowly I became friends with food again. I started to enjoy cooking for myself and memories of my mum and her joyful relationship with food came back to me.

This isn't to say I still don't have that voice in my head that tells me my thighs are too big. There is no stinking way you can see through my thighs anymore (!) but that's not a measure of a woman anyway.

Women are supposed to be soft. We're meant to be round. We are built for cuddling. Curvy waists, sloping thighs, round soft bellies. That's what's real. My body makes more sense to me now that it's at the weight it's supposed to be. Sure, it may be a little squishy and you may not be able to see my ribs anymore, but you're not *supposed* to see my ribs.

Tanya and I get lots of letters from girls who want to be vegan so they can lose weight and it breaks my heart. This is what I tell them:

First off, if you're under twenty years old, you're still in or coming out of puberty and your body is still growing. Even if you're not in puberty, and you are in your thirties like me, or whatever age you are, your body is always changing. It depends on you to keep it healthy. Just eat properly, and leave it alone. Mucking around with your weight only leads to trouble. Your body is what your body is, so try to enjoy it rather than make it look like something it's not.

But saying that, there are some healthy things you can do:

·   Never skip meals. Eat well-balanced meals full of all the nutrients you need in a day.

·   Drink lots of water. Not pop or juice or coffee ... water.

·   Exercise every day if you can. Not anything crazy but things like walking, hiking, running around with your dog, etc. ... as well as something exercise-like (yoga, weights, etc.) at least 3-5 times a week.

·   Don't eat after 8 pm.

·   Let your body become what it is and try enjoy it.

I still struggle every day with the negative voices in my head that tell me my belly is poochy and that my thighs are too big. I just turned thirty-four and I always thought that by the time I reached this age, I would be comfortable with what my body is. But I'm not. I'm never satisfied. It's a constant struggle that is slowly getting better but has yet to go away.

I occasionally have to remind myself that food is my friend. Remind myself that my CFS is finally under control now. I am a healthy, almost fully functioning human being again. I am no longer bedridden, no longer have to miss out on all the fun. I try to make sure that there is no denying myself anymore. Now I can relish the taste of a tomato; enjoy the smell of rolled oats and freshly baked bread. Fill my mouth with food and not stress about consequence. And most importantly, there is nothing I enjoy more than sitting at a table with my family and friends, enjoying each other and a good meal.

Food is life. Without it, we die.

I am constantly asked when I turned/decided/went vegan.

It wasn't a specific day, like my husband, who remembers the exact day and time. For me, everything in my life has been a step forward in a personal journey; every day I learn something new about myself. Every day I make tiny choices. What I do know is that my experiences with animals has changed my life forever. I am unabashedly in love with them and they have taught me so much about myself.

My life lessons come from all different kinds of sources. I don't ignore what's right in front of me anymore.

I've tried to turn my focus outward; to stop obsessing over little things and to just enjoy what's around me. For example, my cats BB and Riley came into my life when I needed them the most. I was twenty-one (God, was I really ever twenty-one?). Practically a baby myself. I was not very confident, not a nice person, selfish, manipulative. Living with cats changed me. I learned that the love you put out comes back to you ten times over. What a gift they gave me.

I recently lost both of them to illness. To say that I am devastated is an understatement. They showed me the pleasure of snuggling an afternoon away and to not sweat the little things. To be quiet and to revel in the things at my fingertips and not worry about the things I can't reach. My understanding of compassion came directly from my relationship with them.

My friend Ian R. sent me a quote by Robert A. Heinlein the day Riley died. It said: "There is no such thing as 'just a cat'." Ain't that the truth?

Why am I vegan? How can I not be? I can't love one animal and eat another. That seems stupid to me. Every single action we do and decision we make affects the world around us. For example:

- Fish all the salmon in the sea until they are almost extinct and then complain about the price of Coho. There's an obvious solution there.

- Dump toxic waste and then complain about birth defects. There's an obvious solution there.

- Drive your car to the corner store and complain about pollution. There's an obvious solution there.

- Waste away to eighty-three pounds and wonder why you're sick. There's an obvious solution there.

Compassion isn't sissy; it isn't hippie dippy. It's a way to change the world, and it can change you at the same time. If you think the tiny things you do every day (negative or positive) don't make a difference, think again. Compassion, caring, taking care of what's around you in a positive and pro-active way, is the only way things can change in a healthy way. And not only that, you might learn something about yourself. You might start showing yourself a little compassion.

Life lessons come with many different faces. Slow down and take a look at what you are experiencing every day. If you don't embrace that and learn something from what is happening to you at this exact moment... What's the point?

My desire with *How It All Vegan!* and now with *The Garden of Vegan* is to make veganism a fun and easy place to be. So that you can spend less time worrying about how to be vegan and spend more time just enjoying being vegan.

Have a good time, enjoy yourself. Love the things around you and more importantly, love yourself.

– SARAH

# TANYA'S INTRODUCTION: A PILE OF LEAVES

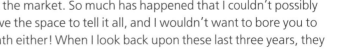

There is an old Japanese proverb: The wind will pick up the leaves scattered around and swirl them about. Then it will drop them, and they will form a pile. I think this is a powerful message. It speaks to me as I believe that's how communities are built; a group of like-minded individuals from different walks of life, having the same strong desires and passions, attracting one another. From this we form one huge community, like leaves in a pile. I couldn't live without my community of friends, and don't ever want to. There are many days when I'm buried in work, but I take a moment and smile, because I know my friends are there. However your community presents itself, love it and nurture it, as it's the glue that holds you together. I know that mine is, and I'm thankful everyday that I have it.

I can't believe it's been three years since *How It all Vegan!* first hit the market. So much has happened that I couldn't possibly have the space to tell it all, and I wouldn't want to bore you to death either! When I look back upon these last three years, they

seem remarkable, challenging, rewarding, and painful, because as you must know, a lot can happen in three years. I've grown a lot, and feel blessed daily by the gift of beautiful friends and family to share life with. I'm very excited to bring you *The Garden of Vegan*. This book has seen many sleepless nights up late in my kitchen trying to get recipes right, nights full of tears, laughing fits, you name it. The result of our efforts is what you now hold in your hands. So please, enjoy it and let us know what you think.

The most exciting thing about having a new cookbook published means a book tour! And if you've been good vegans we'll come to your town and visit you soon! One of the things that I love about writing cookbooks is traveling and meeting people who love what we do. It means so much to me, and gives me so much inspiration. Just knowing that people enjoy our work gives me the energy and passion to keep on doing it. Without you, there would be no book two, and I think the most important person to thank for that is you.

The last three years have taken Sarah and me on numerous adventures. We've had the opportunity to promote ourselves on radio, television, and in print. We've traveled far and wide to participate in cooking demonstrations and speaking engagements. We've gone to Toronto twice and down the west coast to Bellingham, Seattle, and Portland. We even went all the way to Louisville, Kentucky to do a cooking demonstration for Earthsave! I love to travel and explore new cities. Each trip was amazing because I came away with a number of new friends. It's nice to invite new people into your life. I hope that with this new cookbook I can do the same. All of you reading this are friends that I just haven't met yet!

Food is something that is always on my mind. Whenever I try and do a cleanse or fast, I never last long because I can't stop thinking about food. I love thinking about mealtimes and different ways to prepare them using alternative ingredients. I love mucking about in the kitchen trying different grains and vegetables and combining different textures and flavors. I think I'm lucky as cooking comes naturally to me. I find it hard to believe that some people think they can't cook. It seems so simple to me; get a little this, mix it with a little that, and you've got yourself a wonderful vegan dish. This book is tried and true testament that anyone with a stovetop and oven can make amazing quick and simple meals, even you!

When I think about food, I think about pleasure. I think about soul-nourishing satisfaction. I find that I eat really slowly so I can taste every morsel and contemplate why it's so pleasurable. Is it the taste? The texture? The company I'm dining with? Sometimes, especially when Matthew (my sweetheart) is over, we spend more than an hour eating dinner. It's such a wonderful time of eating, talking, and laughing that it's hard not to feel fully nourished afterwards, and not just in our bellies! It makes me sad when I think that not everyone eats in the same manner and thus misses out on the wonderful experience of eating. What kind of messages are we sending to children? Cultivating healthy bodies and minds starts with cultivating healthy mealtimes.

What does the word food mean to you? What associations, if any, do you have to it? Does it conjure up bad issues in you, thoughts of calorie counting and diet shakes? It's a loaded word for sure. Our fast food life and culture has definitely changed the way we think about food. It seems it has morphed into something that does not represent its original purpose, which is simply to nourish and sustain life, to keep us healthy and happy and connected to our families, friends, and environment. I fear that new generations of kids will have a different attitude towards food. They are going to believe that it only comes from a store, where you can get whatever you need and want all year round. They won't know and understand how an eggplant grows, or where bananas come from. They won't know how hard a farmer works and how they struggle to stay in business. Do

we know the ramifications this ignorance will have on our future? Food for thought, no doubt.

Educating ourselves about food and its positive and negative effects on bodies, families, and culture is essential. What else better defines a culture than its food? While it is important to maintain a positive outlook on our evolving contemporary world, some things should remain sacred, namely food. Every body is unique and different eating habits work for different bodies. I think that it's important to figure out what works best for your body and live and eat according to that. If meat is what makes your body truly feel good, I can live with that because that is you and your body's choice, while being vegan is mine. Sounds like a contradiction for sure, but you can purchase animal products in a thoughtful and ethical way, such as products raised organically, free-range and chemical-free. If you eat meat, just try to remember that a life was taken to give you life. Some would argue that vegetables do the same – give up their life without choice to nourish and sustain ours – but that's a whole other topic for another time.

There are people and organizations out there who strive to maintain a healthy balance between our contemporary world and the sacred act of eating and food cultivation. Some are close at hand and some are international. Many cities now have farmer's markets. Try supporting them; it's so nice to give your money directly to those who cultivate your food. The slow food movement is a great example of an international movement of individuals who want to see the idea of food and its intended use maintained and cultivated. Its proponents believe that food should be about enjoyment and nourishment. Mind you, this is not a vegetarian movement, but I think that there are strong lessons to be learned from it. They believe that our fast way of life threatens our environment and our landscapes and that as human beings we have to slow down our lifestyle before we make ourselves extinct. The slow food movement encapsulates almost everything that I believe about our contemporary world. But I too have a hectic lifestyle. I'm a full-time university student and a preacher of the vegan lifestyle. (Can I get an amen?) So I'm constantly trying to find a healthy balance between the two. It's difficult, but all I can do is try my best.

I know that a lot of what I think is idealistic. But as individuals we owe it to ourselves to do all that we can to make the world better. My wise friend Jamie once told me that if you strive for what you believe in and only see a small change, then that's good enough, because at least you know that you tried and were true to yourself. I really think that he is right. I believe that it's important to make your choices with dignity and thoughtfulness. Then when you look back on your life you will know that it was lived with grace and integrity. I believe that awareness and education is the key to opening all doors, then comes putting all that knowledge into practice. Practice makes perfect, so if all we do is a little each day, soon that's all you will know. If you can, slow down, sit with your family and friends, and enjoy their company. Tell them once in a while how much you enjoy them and take pleasure in having them in your life. You never know how that little act of kindness will change and make their day. Now enough about me and what I think. Grab your apron and cooking utensils and get in the kitchen. We have a book filled with new and exciting recipes for you to try and enjoy. I know that I enjoyed testing every one of them and I hope that you do too!

– TANYA

Kitchen
Wisdom

# FREQUENTLY ASKED QUESTIONS

Since the publication of *How It All Vegan!* in 1999, we've received wonderful, supportive e-mails and letters every day from all over the world, via our website (GoVegan.net). It's not a bad way to start the day! We try our best to answer every single letter.

We also receive tons of questions. We've compiled some of the ones that keep coming up over and over again. Read on; there might be something in here that you didn't know!

## Questions About Us

*Which one of you is Sarah and which one of you is Tanya?*
This is an easy one to answer! On the cover of this book, Tanya is the one holding the parasol. *When How It All Vegan!* was published, people were confused because on the cover Tanya's name appears below Sarah's picture, and vice versa. Oh well...there are worse things than being mistaken for your best friend....

*Are you sisters?*
We are not sisters...but best friends.... Oh and by the way, our grey hair is real. Everyone thinks we pay money for it, but we came by it honestly!

*My roommate has a crush on you two. Are you free?*
Tell them to get a grip! Sarah is married and Tanya is not taking applications at this time.

*Will you open a How It All Vegan restaurant?*
If you have the money and the time to run it....

*What if I find what I think is an error?*
We check and recheck every single page of a book before printing, but sometimes when you read the same thing over and over again, you miss stuff. With every edition we try to fix the mistakes that we (or you) find. If you see something that doesn't look right, drop us a note at *ifoundatypo@govegan.net*.

*How can I purchase wholesale copies of the book?*
If you run a store or another retail outlet, or wish to purchase 10 copies or more, you may qualify for a wholesale discount. Contact our publishers directly either at *arsenalpulp.com* or by phone: 1-888-600-PULP (North America only).

*Where can I send you a letter?*
You can write us via the website *hi@govegan.net* or snail mail via: Sarah Kramer & Tanya Barnard, P.O. Box 8727, Victoria, BC, V8W 3S3, Canada.

*The restaurants I frequent won't tell me the ingredients of their dishes. How do I know what I'm eating is vegan?*
All restaurants have ingredient books. Ask politely to speak to the manger and explain that there are certain foods you can't eat. They don't need to know if it's a lifestyle choice or an allergy. Just be firm that you can *not* have certain ingredients in your meal. Most restaurants are very accommodating. If not … remember, your money speaks volumes. Use it to support businesses that support your lifestyle.

*I'm a vegan attending college. Any tips?*
There are all sorts of things you can eat on a limited budget and with limited kitchen space. First, join or start a vegan/vegetarian club at your school. It's a great way to meet like-minded people and maybe you'll make some new friends! Second, if you have access to a microwave, see our chapter on microwavable meals (pg. 60). Keep up your strength, kids, you'll need it for exams!

*I'm the only vegan I know … I'm lonely!*
First off, just because you're vegan doesn't mean you can only hang out with vegans! But don't fret. You're not alone. You'd be surprised who's vegan/vegetarian these days.

There are now a gazillion vegan websites on the Internet. It seems we have started a trend! At *GoVegan.net*, we have a bulletin board where you can chat with other vegans. We try to answer any questions that are posted there.

But as for real, not virtual, friends: ask around where veggie-heads congregate. Health food stores are a good bet. You may find there is a vegan/vegetarian club or potluck group that you could hang out with. Or start your own club! Make posters and host potlucks. We have all sorts of potluck ideas in the Party chapter (pg.218).

*Are vitamins vegan?*
Some are and some aren't. You need to check the label for no-no ingredients (pg. 238).

*Do you have any advice for dealing with people who ask me to explain myself and my decision to be vegan?*
You don't have to explain anything. Life choices are personal and private. If you do want to say something, make sure that the person you are engaging in conversation actually wants to have an intelligent conversation about your choices and isn't just looking for an argument. You'll never get your point across with someone who just wants to argue.

*I'm 16 years old and my school wants me to dissect an animal! What should I do?*
You don't have to do that if you don't feel it's morally right. Explain your convictions to your teacher and ask them to give you an alternative assignment. It helps if your family supports your decision. Or talk to your teacher about doing your dissection on-line. Check out *Froguts.com* for ideas. It's freaking brilliant!

*I work for a restaurant that serves meat. Should I quit my job?*
Dude, that's totally up to you. Draw your own lines as to where your veganism begins and ends. We are not the vegan police … oh, and can I get a salad instead of fries with that?

*I'm 12 years old and my family won't support my going vegan. I don't work, so I don't have money to buy my own food. What can I do?*

That really sucks! It must make meal times very challenging. It's hard to live with people who don't share your same beliefs, especially when they're your parents. All we can suggest is trying to talk to them. Be really open and communicate with them about veganism as much as possible. Research and present them with factual information on the vegan diet and lifestyle. Try not to get defensive with them, but present your arguments in a clear, thoughtful, and concise manner. Work with them to find solutions that satisfy both you and your parents, and dedicate yourself to making mealtimes work. If they are worried about having to make extra dishes every night, get in the kitchen and show them how it's done! Seeing you make an effort might make them change their minds. Good luck.

## Health Questions

We are not nutritionists, so if you would like more information about these next three questions, we highly recommend you read *Becoming Vegan*, written by our wonderful friend and registered dietitian Vesanto Melina and her co-author Brenda Davis (published by the Book Publishing Company, 2000). Some of the information provided below was borrowed from their book.

*I don't think I'm getting enough nutrients from my vegan diet. How can I tell?*

There is a lot of information available on this subject. Educate yourself; remember, knowledge is power. Start by reading a good, comprehensive nutrition book like *Becoming Vegan*. Whether you've become vegan for reasons of ethics, animal rights, the environment, or simply to keep yourself healthy and fit, you'll accomplish your goals if you become more knowledgeable about nutrition!

*Why has my period has stopped since I became vegan?*

There is no nutrient missing in a well-balanced vegan diet that would cause this problem. Vegan diets can provide plenty of iron, protein, calories, and every other nutrient, including vitamin B12 (from fortified foods or supplements), that you need for normal menstruation and overall good health.

We don't feel comfortable diagnosing medical problems; that is something you need to discuss with your doctor. But sometimes insufficient calories are a possible cause of amenorrhoea (absence of menstruation). Take a look at your diet and make sure it is well balanced and contains everything you need.

*My hair is falling out. Is it because I am vegan?*

Go to any vegetarian festival and you'll see plenty of vegans with full heads of hair. Possible causes for your situation could be genetics, or it could be from a lack of protein and/or the mineral zinc. This can be remedied, allowing you to remain vegan without going bald.

The most powerful vegan food sources for iron and zinc are legumes: lentils and split peas can be made into delicious soups, and chickpeas are found in hummus, curries, and salads. Then there are all sorts of beans: red, white, black, pinto, lima, mung, cranberry, Anasazi, kidney, and many more. Soy foods are outstanding sources of protein and zinc (iron, too): tofu, tempeh, soy milk, and miso. Half the world's protein comes from grains; whole grains are rich in iron and zinc, too. So make the acquaintance of some new grains: barley, millet,

oatmeal, quinoa, rice, whole-wheat flour, and wheat germ. Almonds, cashews, hazelnuts, pine nuts, and various seeds can also provide some of what you need. We even get some protein and minerals from our veggies: green and yellow beans, peas, broccoli, kale, or mushrooms. Though they're low in calories, a significant proportion of those calories is protein. This list is by no means complete. Read chapters 3 and 6 in *Becoming Vegan* for more information. As you can see, if you have a well-rounded, complete diet, your body will be not be lacking what it needs to be healthy.

## Food Questions

*What do you mean by "dry sweetener" and "liquid sweetener"?*
There are so many different kinds of sweeteners on the market that we wanted to give you the opportunity to choose which one you would like to use. Dry and liquid seems like the easiest way to describe them. Examples of dry sweeteners are cane sugar and date sugar; examples of liquid sweeteners are maple syrup, stevia, and barley malt. Have fun and be adventurous when you cook. Try out new and unusual ingredients and you'll be pleasantly surprised by the results. We guarantee it!

*What is Braggs and where can I get it?*
Braggs is a tamari/soy sauce alternative. It's a product made by Patricia Bragg using a secret family recipe. It has only two ingredients: soy beans and water. There are no chemicals, colorings, or salt added and it's incredibly delicious. It's available in health food stores, some grocery stores, and on-line at Bragg.com. We love this stuff and so should you!

*I'm allergic to soy. What can I replace it with?*
We're so sorry to hear that! Soy is a staple product for most vegans. If you're looking to add a "meaty" texture to your dishes, try making seitan (pg. 208) and using it in place of soy. If it is protein that you need, it's easy to make complete proteins. Just combine beans with brown rice, corn, nuts, seeds, or wheat. Or combine brown rice with beans, nuts, seeds, or wheat. Not only is quinoa high in protein but it's delicious, too!

*Is salt vegan?*
It sure is! But regular table salt is sometimes treated with the additives magnesium carbonate, magnesium oxide, and calcium silicate. So we recommend using sea salt. This is salt obtained from the ocean, as opposed to land salt. It is either sun-baked or kiln-baked, is high in trace minerals, and contains no chemicals or sugar. Now get shakin'!

*Is sugar vegan?*
Actually it depends on how you look at it. Refined sugars do not contain any animal products, but most sugar refineries use animal charcoal filters. So by an ingredients-based definition of veganism, refined sugar is vegan. But due to the fact that most refined sugar is processed with animal bone char, we suggest you don't use them. You can purchase organic sugar, cane sugar, or turbinado sugar, which are vegan. If you're not sure if the sugar product your purchasing is vegan, call the company and ask. Remember, you're sending them a message with your dollars!

*Are beer and wine vegan?*
There are no fishes swimming in your drink, but there is definitely something fishy going on in some alcoholic beverages. Isinglass, a substance taken from the swim bladders of fish, is used to clarify some beers. Wine is sometimes clarified with animal products such as gelatin or albumin. If you gotta drink, your best bet is to contact the makers of your favorite brands and see how they make their brew, or simply make your own. Bottoms up!

*What vegan foods can I take with me when I go camping?*
Making food by a campfire is so much fun! Roasting tofu dogs over a open flame makes them taste so delicious. In order to eat well while camping, you have to plan ahead and take lots of healthy food with you. Fruits, veggies, trail mix, dips, and crackers are good to have on hand. Also, check out the recipes in Appies and Snacks (pg. 100). Most of them travel well and are good-for-you delicious treats for when you're away from your oven.

*Do airlines offer vegan meals?*
Yes. When booking your ticket, ask them if they have a "strict" vegetarian meal. Then two days before you fly, call the airline and confirm that your meal is being made. We can't count the number of times they've forgotten to make our requested special meals. Airplane food is usually pretty gross, and they have no clue as to what to feed vegans. We usually bring our own snacks and meals on board with us. As long as you don't bring fruits across the border, they don't mind if you bring your own food.

*If I'm in a strange city, where can I eat?*
The first place we check before we go on a trip is *HappyCow.net*. It's a wonderful comprehensive list of vegan/veggie-friendly places to eat around the world. If you don't have time to surf the Net, grab the local phone book and look for a health food store or some sort of health/veggie place. Ask the people who work there where to find a good place for vegan food. Usually they'll know all the good places to go.

*I can't seem to give up dairy (cheese, milk, etc.). How can I do it?*
You make a choice. Do you want to be vegan or not? No one forces you to eat cheese; you make that decision on your own. There are plenty of alternatives nowadays that mimic milk and cheese. Okay, so they don't taste *exactly* like what you're giving up, but they are pretty close! Look, you've gone this far. It's just one more tiny step towards becoming a full-fledged vegan warrior!

*Are chocolate chips vegan?*
Ohmygod *yes!* Yes, yes, yes. We get this question all the time. What you need to do is read the ingredients and avoid chocolate that has milk ingredients. Stick to "pure" chocolate chips. If you're looking for chocolate bars, there are some incredible vegan chocolate bars out there. Check your local health food store.

*I live at a high altitude. Should my baking times be different then the book?*
Well ... yes. If you live above 3,000 feet in altitude, the lower atmospheric pressure will affect your baking. This can usually be corrected by decreasing the amount of leavening agent and by increasing the baking temperature 15 degrees to 25 degrees. The amount of sweetener as well as liquid can also affect your baking. Some recipes may work fine, some may take some fine-tuning.

| Adjustment | 3,000 feet | 5,000 feet | 7,000 feet |
|---|---|---|---|
| Reduce baking powder, for each tsp | decrease ⅛ tsp | decrease ⅛-¼ tsp | decrease ¼ tsp |
| Reduce sweetener, for each cup | decrease 0-1 tbsp | 0-2 tbsp | 1-3 tbsp |
| Increase liquid, for each cup | add 1-2 tbsp | 2-4 tbsp | 3-4 tbsp |

*Are modified milk ingredients really made from milk?*
Yep, they sure are. Just because they are modified doesn't change what they really are! Stay far, far away.

## Vegan Shopping

*Where can I find shoes?*
Ahhh, shoes, Sarah's weakness! Vegan shoes can be found at most shoe stores. Shoes, like food, have ingredients listed. Check for a label on the sole, inside the shoe, or on the shoe box for symbols or words that state "Made from man-made materials." Ask the salesperson to show you shoes that are non-leather. Or you can get on-line and shop at stores like *MooShoes.com* or type "vegan shoes" into a search engine and pick and choose from a ton of different shoe sources.

*Is makeup vegan? What about shampoo and hair products?*
Well, it depends. Some companies don't use animal ingredients in their products, but they do test on animals. Some companies don't test on animals, but they do use animal ingredients. Then there are companies who don't use animal ingredients or test on animals at all – we like them the best. Go to your local health food store and check out the products available in your area, or check the Internet.

   You *can* have bouncing, well-behaved hair and paint your face with pretty colors, and be cruelty free at the same time.

## Saucy Questions

*Is oral sex vegan?*
Well ... if the cow says it's okay....

You have no idea how many times we have been asked this question.

Seriously ... being vegan is a choice. We choose not to use or consume animal products. Animals don't have a voice and we're pretty sure if they did, they would tell us to keep our hands to ourselves.

A cow doesn't want to be killed for food or clothing, but they don't have a voice. So we use our common sense and choose not to abuse our power. Our money speaks volumes, and every pair of non-leather shoes, every non-animal ingredient product we buy tells the "powers that be" that we don't want products with animal ingredients; as a vegan consumer, every cent we spend says, "We choose not to use animal products." That's a powerful statement.

Now, what does this have to do with oral sex? Look. It's all about consent. Animals can't give consent, but we can. If it's okay with you, and the other person is also consenting, go for it!

*Are condoms vegan?*
You would think that in this day and age there would be an easy, animal-friendly, vegan way to protect yourself from pregnancy and disease. These days it's almost impossible to be 100% vegan, but that doesn't mean you shouldn't try your hardest to be the best vegan you can be. There are a few choices out there.

Traditionally the processing of latex, used to make condoms, has involved the use of casein – a milk protein. In 1999, a new animal-friendly condom was introduced to the market. It has been officially approved by *VeganSociety.com*.

Available at *Condomi.com* and from other Internet sources, this condom contains no animal products and conducts no animal testing. The condoms are fully tested and surpass standards set by the British Standards Institute and the World Health Organization.

As for other contraceptives:

The Pill is full of animal ingredients. Lactose (milk sugar) and magnesium stearate (often animal derived) are found in virtually every contraceptive pill, and if they don't have animal ingredients, they are still tested on animals.

Spermicides are supposed to be used in combination with other methods of contraception. Generally, they do not contain any animal-derived ingredients, but are usually tested on animals.

Now get out there, have fun, and protect yourself!

# W H O O P S !

Did you futz something up? Is the smell of onions on your fingers driving you crazy? Here are a few tricks and tips to get you out of a jam or just make things easier. We have compiled a list of twenty-seven ingenious ways to help you perform kitchen magic!

1. Keep your mixing bowl still while you stir or beat in it by wrapping a damp, folded kitchen towel around the base of the bowl.

2. Keep green salads fresh for a longer time by sprinkling them with the juice of a lemon or lime.

3. Intensify the sweetness of any dish with a pinch of salt.

4. For a more delicate onion flavor in a dish, sauté the onions first.

5. Allow more time to bake two sheets of cookies in the same oven than one sheet. The same holds true for multiple batches of cakes, pies, or muffins.

6. Enhance the sweetness of corn by adding a tablespoon of corn syrup to the water in which you boil it.

7. Avoid burned or overbaked cookies by cooling the cookie sheet between bakings, or by alternating two sheets. It you put the cookie dough on a warm sheet, the dough will start to melt and spread before the cookies are placed in the oven.

8. Transfer rolled-out dough from the pastry board to the pie plate with the help of a rolling pin. Roll the dough up on the rolling pin; lift and place the dough end on one rim of the pie plate, then unroll the dough slowly.

9. Frost a cake without making a mess of the plate by placing four 2-inch wide strips of waxed paper around and partially under the cake. Spills and drips will fall on the paper. Pull the paper strips out when the cake is frosted; the plate stays sparkling clean.

10. If a soup is too salty, add a chopped potato or two. The potatoes will absorb some of the saltiness.

11. Remove a cake easily from its tin by letting it remain in the tin for five minutes after it has finished baking. This will give the cake time to shrink a bit.

12. Freeze fresh herbs, such as dill, chives, rosemary, and thyme. Put them in tiny freezer bags or containers and store them in the freezer until they are needed. Add them still frozen to any recipe that calls for them.

13. Maximize the flavor you get from dried herbs by soaking them for five minutes in a bit of the cooking liquid, then adding them with the liquid to the dish.

14. Intensify the flavor of chocolate in a recipe by adding a small amount of vanilla extract during cooking.

15. Loosen stubborn cookies from the cookie sheet by holding the sheet over direct heat for a few seconds, then moving the sheet around so the heat loosens the areas where the cookies cannot be removed.

16. Get more juice from citrus fruits by heating the lemons, oranges, or grapefruit in the oven for just a few minutes before extracting the juice.

17. A rule of thumb for cooking vegetables covered or uncovered: vegetables that grow underground should be cooked covered; those that grow above ground should be cooked uncovered.

18. Always tie whole seasonings, bay leaves, or whole cloves in a small square of cheese cloth before cooking. This way, when you go to remove them after cooking it won't be a problem to locate them. It's always unpleasant to bite into a whole clove unexpectedly.

19. Remove burnt edges from a cake with a fine grater, lightly applied. Use it to remove browned edges, too.

20. Liven up soups by serving with a sprig of fresh herb. Looks good, and tastes great.

21. Remove onion smell from your hands by holding a stainless steel spoon in your hand and running the spoon under cold tap water. It really works, try it!

22. Avoid storing different cakes, cookies, or bread in the same container. They affect each other and get stale faster.

23. Prepare "vanilla sugar" to use whenever a recipe calls for vanilla and sugar. The flavor is wonderful. Slit open one side of a vanilla bean, cut it into two-inch lengths, and bury the pieces in a jar of sugar. Allow three or four days for the sugar to absorb the vanilla. Refill the jar with sugar as needed, as the bean last for ages.

24. When you cut or chop sticky fruit, such as dates or raisins, prevent them from sticking to the knife by occasionally dipping the knife into boiling water....

25. Prevent your eyes from tearing up when slicing any member of the onion family by ensuring the onion, scallion, leek, or shallot is well-chilled before cutting.

26. If carrots have become limp, recrisp them in a bowl of ice water.

27. Get the smell of garlic off your hands by washing your hands in cold water and rubbing them with table salt, then washing in soap and warm water.

# FORTY-FIVE THINGS TO DO WITH BAKING SODA

In the first book we listed forty-five things to do with vinegar; now we're giving you forty-five things to do with baking soda. Enjoy!

1.   Wash the dirt, residue, and pesticides off of fruit and veggies in a bowl filled with water and 2-3 tablespoons of baking soda.

2.   Add a dash of baking soda to baked beans to help eliminate gaseous side effects...if you know what we mean....

3.   When making tomato-based soups, sauces, and chilis, add a pinch of baking soda to cut the acidity level of the tomatoes.

4.   If you've added too much vinegar to a recipe, add a pinch of baking soda. This helps to counteract the acidity.

5.   Keep counters free of stains from tea bags or juice spills by making a paste of baking soda and water. Apply, let sit, then wipe off.

6.   Give your cutting board a good cleaning by spreading baking soda over top and sprinkling with vinegar. Let the bubbles do their thing, and then rinse with water.

7.   Rid your hands of onion and garlic smells by sprinkling baking soda into the palm of one hand. Make a paste by adding water and rub between your two hands. Rinse with water.

8.   Polish chrome with a equal mixture of baking soda and creamy peanut butter. Rinse with water.

9.   Sprinkle baking soda inside rubber gloves. This keeps them dry, smelling good, and they'll slip on more easily, too.

10.  Before you leave on vacation, sprinkle baking soda down your kitchen drain to eliminate any odors that may creep up while you're away.

11.  Keep coffeemakers clean by regularly brewing 1 quart of warm water with ¼ cup baking soda.

12.  Sprinkle baking soda in the drip pans of stove elements. The baking soda will eliminate food odors and help minimize the possibility of fire.

13.  Clean a burnt pan by bringing two inches of water to a boil and adding ½ cup of baking soda. Leave overnight, and it should wipe up easily in the morning.

14. Remove rust from kitchen appliances and linoleum floors by scrubbing with a paste of baking soda and water.

15. Remove rust from nuts and bolts by covering them with baking soda, then pouring vinegar over top. Scrub with a brush once fizzing subsides.

16. Fight odors by placing a opened box of baking soda in the area. This goes for bathrooms, closets, fridges, garages, and under sinks. Do not re-use this soda for cooking.

17. Curb nasty odors in your kitchen garbage can by sprinkling baking soda in the bottom.

18. Apply baking soda to a wet sponge to remove marks off a wall. This includes crayon, grease, and pencil.

19. Wash a cup of baking soda down the toilet every week to help prevent clogging.

20. For a temporary fix of cracked plaster or nail holes, fill them with a paste of baking soda and water.

21. For a permanent fix of cracked plaster or nail holes, fill them with a paste of baking soda and glue.

22. To get smoke odors out of furniture, sprinkle it liberally with baking soda, let sit for twenty minutes, and vacuum away.

23. Remove wine or grease stains on carpets by immediately sprinkling them with baking soda. Leave on until stain is absorbed and vacuum away.

24. Remove black scuff marks on linoleum floors by scrubbing with a paste of baking soda and water.

25. For a monthly carpet cleaning, sprinkle baking soda over carpets and let sit overnight. Vacuum up in morning. Add a few drops of essential oil if you want to "pretty" up the room.

26. Clean dirty mops and rags by regularly soaking them in two quarts of warm water with ¼ cup baking soda. This helps eliminate odors and dirt build-up.

27. To fight damp and musty smells in basements and garages, fill old nylons with baking soda and hang them from the ceiling. Be careful not to put them in places where you would walk into them!

28. Keep musty odors out of rarely used suitcases and trunks by sprinkling baking soda in them before they are stored.

29. Sprinkle baking soda in smelly shoes after wearing them to help neutralize odors. Shake out the excess powder the next day.

30. Use ½ cup of baking soda along with usual cleaner in the washing machine for extra cleaning power.

31. Instead of fabric softener, use ½ cup of baking soda instead. This make clothes nice and soft and is also good for sensitive skin.

32. Treat ring-around-the-collar by rubbing a paste of baking soda and water to the troubled area.

33. Remove smoke odors from cloths by soaking them in baking soda and water before washing.

34. Remove gasoline and oil odors from clothes by placing clothes in a trash bag with 1 cup of baking soda. Let sit for 2 days before washing.

35. For maximum odor control, sprinkle baking soda into clean socks before putting them on.

36. Ran out of underarm deodorant? Sprinkle some on under your arms for odor protection and moisture absorption.

37. Clean dirty nails with a scrub brush dabbed with baking soda. Dirt dissolves and rinses away.

38. Soak toothbrushes overnight in a solution of baking soda and water for sparkling clean bristles.

39. Get relief from canker sores by rinsing mouth with a solution of baking soda and water. This neutralizes the acids in your mouth.

40. To sweeten and clean dentures, soak for 30 minutes in a mixture of baking soda and water.

41. Bring comfort to tender toes and feet by soaking them in a solution of ¼ cup baking soda and 1 quart warm water.

42. Remove foot calluses and dead skin easily by using a pumice stone after soaking in above solution.

43. For immediate relief from bee stings and insect bites, apply a paste of baking soda and water to the troubled area. Repeat again if necessary.

44. Feel relief from sunburns by soaking in a tub of tepid water, ¼ cup baking soda and ½ cup cornstarch.

45. Keep hands soft and attractive by sprinkling some baking soda in dish water when washing the dishes.

# F I R S T   A I D

Tanya and I bought new fancy knives when we started recipe testing for the new book. We were both tired of using crappy cheap knifes that don't really do the job. Well, guess what? I cut myself really badly and realized I had no idea what to do. So I went and bought myself *First Aid, First on the Scene: The Complete Guide to First Aid and CPR* from St. John Ambulance and learned some basics. (**S**)

## What to do if you cut yourself

Bleeding from a minor cut usually stops on its own within a few minutes with a bit of direct pressure and may only require a band-aid. If the bleeding does not stop after a few minutes or gets worse you will need to administer first aid. Wounds that need prompt medical attention include those that are deep, gaping, jagged or you cannot control the bleeding. Blech!

1. Swear like a sailor. If you've only got a minor wound and there is dirt in it, rinse it lightly with lukewarm running water.

2. Use a clean, non-stick dressing to apply direct pressure to the wound.

3. Once applied, do not keep checking it. Apply pressure for 15 minutes.

4. If blood soaks through the dressing, just apply another dressing over it and continue with direct pressure.

5. Raise the bleeding part above the level of the heart, keeping direct pressure over the dressing.

6. If bleeding is severe or does not stop after 15 minutes, seek medical attention.

7. Call a family member. Even if it is just to whine, a friendly voice will always make you feel better.

## What to do if you burn yourself

When treating any burn, DO NOT:

· apply grease or lotion.

· breathe or cough on the burn.

· use cotton or adhesive dressings.

· disturb blisters or dead skin.

· apply ice directly to a burn.

· do not remove clothing that is stuck to the burned area

*Minor Burns*

To consider the burn as minor only the first layer of skin will be affected. This is called a First Degree Burn. The skin colour will be pink to red, there will be slight swelling, the skin will be dry and there will be pain.

1.  Cool the burn right away by immersing in cool water. If you are unable to do this, pour cool water on the area or cover it with a clean wet cloth. Cool with water until the pain has lessoned.

2.  Gently pat the area dry with a clean cloth. Cover the burn with a dry, sterile, non-adhesive dressing.

3.  Elevate the area.

4.  Watch the burn area for infection

*Severe Burns*

If you suspect a severe burn look for any of the following signs:

*Second Degree:* skin is raw and red in colour; skin is moist and ranges in colour from white to cherry red, blisters, extreme pain.

*Third Degree:* charred black skin, skin is dry and leathery and little or no pain.

1.  Call "911" or your emergency medical number.

2.  Loosen or remove anything on the burned area that is tight. Remove rings and other constricting items.

3.  If the burn is 2nd degree and smaller than the person's chest, cover it with clean, cold, wet towels.

4.  If the burn is 3rd degree or larger than the person's chest, do not use cold compresses and do not immerse the burn in cold water.

5.  Cover the burn with a dry, sterile, non-adhesive dressing.

6.  Separate burned fingers or toes with dry, sterile, non-adhesive dressings.

7.  Treat for shock. Lay the person flat, cover with a blanket and elevate the feet.

8.  Reassure the person as you wait for medical attention.

*Reprinted with permission from St. John Ambulance © 2001.*

Breakfasts

Your grandma was right – breakfast is the most important meal of the day. Think about it – after sleeping for 7 or 8 hours, your body needs nourishment, and a quick bowl of sugary cereal and a cup of coffee ain't gonna cut it! You need fuel so you can have energy for your day.

In the hustle and bustle of getting ready in the morning, take an extra moment to make yourself something delicious. Breakfast doesn't have to be a complicated event, just a nice healthy start to your day. And a good breakfast can help boost your attention span, help you think more clearly, and problem solve faster!

# QUICK MUESLI

Ahh, nothing like a bowl of hippie food to satisfy your growling belly. This recipe is quick and easy and travels well.

**4 ½ cups rolled oat flakes**
**½ cup wheat germ**
**½ cup wheat bran**
**½ cup oat bran**

**1 cup raisins**
**½ cup walnuts, roughly chopped**
**¼ cup raw sunflower seeds**

In a large bowl, combine all ingredients and stir together until well mixed. Store in an airtight container. Makes approx. 8 cups.

# OVEN-BAKED MUESLI

A yummy alternative to store-bought cereals. This recipe is not only good for you, but tastes great too.

**3 cups rolled oat flakes**
**2 cups wheat germ**
**½ cup sesame seeds**
**¼ cup pumpkin seeds**
**½ cup cashews, roughly chopped**
**½ cup almonds, roughly chopped**
**½ cup shredded coconut**
**¼ cup olive oil**
**¼ cup maple syrup**
**1 cup dried fruit, your choice (e.g., raisins, apricot, etc.) (optional)**

Preheat oven to 225°F. In a large bowl, combine all ingredients and stir together until well mixed. On a lightly oiled 9x13 baking pan, spread mixture evenly and bake for 1 hour, stirring every 15 minutes. Let cool and stir in optional dried fruit. Store in an airtight container. Makes approx. 8 cups.

# BREAKFAST BARLEY

If you like barley and a hot breakfast that sticks to your ribs, this one is for you.

> **1 cup apple juice**
> **1 cup water**
> **½ cup dried pearl barley**
> **6-8 dried apricots, chopped into quarters**
> **¼ cup pecans, chopped (garnish)**

In a large saucepan, combine the juice, water, barley, and apricots. Bring to a boil, then reduce heat. Cover and let simmer for 45-50 minutes or until barley is cooked. Garnish with pecans and serve with soy milk. Makes 2 servings.

# CLAIRE'S COUSCOUS PORRIDGE

This recipe comes from our good friend Claire. Serve with a titch of maple syrup.

> **2 cups soy milk**
> **1 cup couscous**
> **¼ cup nuts (your choice; e.g., almonds, pecans, etc.), chopped**
> **¼ cup dried fruit (your choice; e.g., cranberries, raisins, etc.)**
> **2 tbsp coconut (optional)**

In a medium saucepan, bring the soy milk close to a boil, but not quite. Turn off heat, and stir in couscous, nuts, fruit, and optional coconut. Let stand covered for 5 minutes. Makes 1-2 servings.

# APPLES & OAT CEREAL

Apples and cinnamon and oats. Oh my!

> **4 cups water**
> **1 cup oat bran**
> **¼ cup raisins**
> **1 apple, chopped**
> **1 tbsp maple syrup**
> **½ tsp ground caraway seeds**
> **½ tsp cinnamon**
> **1 cup soymilk**

In a large saucepan, combine all the ingredients. Bring to a boil, then reduce heat. Cover and let simmer for 10-15 minutes. Makes 2 servings.

# BREAKFAST RICE

A lovely hot cereal that will keep you satisfied until it's time for lunch!

¼ cup oat bran
1 cup basmati rice
1 cup apple juice
1 ½ cups water
½ cup raisins
½ tsp cinnamon

In a large saucepan, combine all the ingredients. Bring to a boil, then reduce heat. Cover and let simmer for 15-20 minutes. Makes 2 servings.

# CINNAMON APPLE QUESADILLA

A quesadilla is a flour tortilla filled with goodies, then folded in half to form a turnover shape. The filling can include any combination of items. Here we've made a breakfast treat as good as apple pie.

2 tortilla shells
Quick and Easy Apples (pg. 42)
¼ cup grated soy cheese
4 tbsp soy yogurt (pg. 216)
Fruit salsa (pg. 130)

In a non-stick frying pan on medium heat, lay down tortilla shell. Place ½ of apple mixture to one half of the tortilla, top with cheese. Fold over shell and cover pan with lid. Let cook for 2-3 minutes, flip, and cook for an additional minute. Repeat with remaining tortilla. Serve with a large dollop of yogurt or fruit salsa. Makes 2 shells.

# NUMMY YUMMY WAFFLES

You can use any kind of flour in this recipe – chickpea, spelt, whole wheat. Whatever floats your boat.

1 cup rolled oat flakes
½ cup flour
1 ¼ cups soy milk
1 tbsp olive oil

2 tsp maple syrup
¼ tsp salt
½ tsp baking powder

In a food processor, grind the oat flakes until coarse. Add the remaining ingredients and blend until smooth. Spoon into a well oiled, hot waffle iron. Repeat until batter is gone. Makes 2-6 waffles, depending on size of waffle iron.

# BANANA WAFFLES

These naturally sweet waffles are a delight. Bananas, besides being scrumptious, are rich in potassium and vitamin C.

- **1 banana**
- **1 cup water**
- **1 cup soy milk**
- **1 tsp vanilla**
- **1 ½ cups flour**
- **½ cup rolled oat flakes**
- **2 tsp baking powder**
- **1 tsp cinnamon**
- **½ tsp nutmeg (optional)**

In a food processor, blend the banana and water until smooth. Add remaining ingredients and blend until well combined. Spoon into a well oiled, hot waffle iron. Repeat until batter is gone. Makes 4-8 waffles, depending on size of waffle iron.

# BLUEBERRY CORNMEAL PANCAKES

Blueberries have been around for thousands of years and were once called "star berries" because of the star-shaped calyx (scar) on the top of each berry. When buying or picking blueberries they must be ripe, as they do not continue to ripen after harvesting.

- **1 cup flour**
- **½ cup cornmeal**
- **1 tsp baking powder**
- **½ tsp baking soda**
- **¼ tsp salt**
- **1 cup soy milk**
- **¾ cup water**
- **1 cup blueberries**

In a medium bowl, stir together the flour, cornmeal, baking powder, baking soda, and salt. Add the soy milk, water, and blueberries and stir until "just mixed." Portion out about ¾ to 1 cup of the batter onto a hot non-stick pan or lightly oiled frying pan and cover with lid. Let sit on medium heat until the center starts to bubble and become sturdy. Flip pancake over and cook other side until golden brown. Repeat process until batter is gone. Make 2 or more servings.

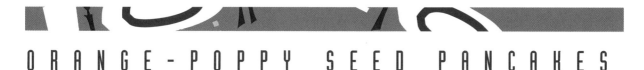

# ORANGE-POPPY SEED PANCAKES

Poppy seeds have a crunchy texture and a nutty flavor that add a little pop to these pancakes.

1 cup flour
½ tsp baking powder
½ tsp baking soda
¼ tsp salt
½ cup rolled oat flakes
1 tsp orange zest, grated

½ cup sunflower seeds
¼ cup poppy seeds
1 cup soy milk
⅓ cup orange juice

In a medium bowl, stir together the flour, baking powder, baking soda, salt, oat flakes, orange zest, sunflower seeds, and poppy seeds. Add the soy milk and juice and stir until "just mixed." Portion out about ¾ to 1 cup of the batter onto a hot non-stick pan or lightly oiled frying pan and cover with lid. Let sit on medium heat until the center starts to bubble and become sturdy. Flip pancake over and cook other side until golden brown. Repeat process until batter is gone. Make 2 or more servings.

# VEGAN BREAKFAST CREPES

Crepes are thin French pancakes that don't take any more effort to make than conventional pancakes, but they do require a delicate touch. They can be eaten at any time of the day. Check out dinner fillings on pg. 157.

Before you get started here are a few crepe tips:

· use a crepe pan or a good non-stick frying pan

· let your batter sit for ½-1 hour before cooking, as it will help make sturdier crepes

· the first crepe always sucks, so don't give up…try again!

powdered egg replacer to equal 2 eggs (pg. 212)
1 cup soy milk
⅓ cup water
1 cup flour
2 tbsp dry sweetener
1 tsp vanilla extract
2 tbsp margarine

In a blender or food processor, combine all ingredients and blend for 20 seconds. Be careful you don't blend too long, as the batter will end up gummy. Portion out 2-3 tbsp of the batter onto a hot non-stick pan over medium high heat. Lift and rotate the pan so the batter evenly coats the bottom. Cook until almost dry on top and lightly browned on the edges. Loosen the edges with a thin spatula and flip crepe over with your fingers, cooking for an additional 15 seconds. Adjust the heat as necessary. Place the crepe on a paper towel or cooling rack and set aside. Repeat process until batter is gone. Fill with desired ingredients (pg. 42), and roll up. Makes 8-12 crepes.

You can fill crepes with whatever you want. You can offer one kind of filling, or bowls of different fillings and let your guests decide. Here are a few to get you started.

# QUICK & EASY APPLE CREPE FILLING

**1 apple, sliced**
**¼ cup water**
**1 tbsp maple syrup**
**½ tsp cinnamon**

In a small saucepan, stir together all ingredients and bring to a boil. Reduce heat to medium-high and cook 2-5 minutes or until apples are tender. Set aside to cool. Makes approx ¾ cup.

# TANYA'S DECADENT CHOCOLATE CREPE FILLING

**½ cup chocolate chips**
**¼ cup soy milk**

In a small saucepan, melt all ingredients on medium heat until smooth. Make approx. ¾ cup.

# PINEAPPLE GINGER CREPE FILLING

**1 19-oz (540-ml) can unsweetened pineapple tidbits, drained**
**2 tsp fresh ginger, grated**
**¼ cup maple syrup**
**⅛ tsp cardamom**
**2 tbsp coconut, grated**

In a medium pot, cook the pineapple, ginger, maple syrup, and cardamom for 4-6 minutes on medium-high heat, stirring occasionally. Stir in grated coconut and remove from heat. In a blender or food processor, blend mixture for 5-10 seconds. Makes approx. 1 ½ cups.

*Other crepe filling ideas include the omelette or tofu scramble (pg. 45), topped with soy cheese, or the fruit salsa (pg. 130).*

# CONNIE'S OVERNIGHT APPLE FRENCH TOAST

My husband and I are often too busy for a hot breakfast during the week, so we make it a point to eat well on the weekends. I usually make this recipe Friday night and enjoy it for breakfast on a lazy Saturday morning.
– Connie, Houston, Texas

**2 Granny Smith apples, cored and sliced**
**3 tbsp margarine**
**2 tsp cinnamon**
**¼ cup dry sweetener**
**¼ cup maple syrup**
**1 cup apple juice**
**½ cup soy milk**
**½ cup soy yogurt (pg. 216)**
**½ tsp vanilla extract**
**4-6 thick slices of day-old French *or* regular bread**

In a medium saucepan, cook the apples in margarine on medium heat until apples start to soften. Add the cinnamon, sweetener, and maple syrup and cook until until apples are soft. Pour the ingredients into the bottom of a 8x8 baking pan. In a large bowl, whisk together the apple juice, soy milk, yogurt, and vanilla. Dip each slice of bread into the mixture until fully covered, and arrange on top of the apple mixture in the baking dish. (If you are using regular bread, make two layers of bread on top of the apples.) Pour remaining batter over the bread. Cover and refrigerate overnight.

Wake up, get out of bed ... drag a comb across your head. Then heat your oven to 350°F and bake for 35-40 minutes. Serve with fresh fruit and a strong cup of something hot!

# COUNTRY POTATO PATTIES

These simple potato patties are a scrumptious way to start your day. Serve with scrambled tofu (pg. 45) and fresh juice.

**3 large potatoes, chopped and boiled**
**½ small onion, minced**
**1 stalk celery, minced**
**½ small red bell pepper, minced**
**2 tbsp flour**
**1 tbsp parsley, minced**
**1 tbsp Braggs**

In a large bowl, mash the potatoes until smooth. Add the remaining ingredients and mix well. Shape the mixture into 4-6 patties. In a non-stick frying pan, fry on medium-high heat, flip, and cook until both sides are brown. Makes 2-4 servings.

# SARAH'S HEARTY HOME-FRY POTATOES

One of my favorite things about going on a road trip are greasy spoon home-fries. I think I've perfected them. Give them a go and let me know what you think! (S)

> **2 potatoes, cubed**
> **1 onion, roughly chopped**
> **1 tbsp olive oil**
> **1½-2 tsp all-purpose seasoning (pg. 210)**
> **¼ tsp pepper**
> **¼ tsp salt**
> **¼ cup fresh parsley, chopped**
> **1 hot chili, seeded and minced (optional)**

In a large non-stick frying pan on medium-high heat, sauté the potatoes and onion in oil for 8-10 minutes or until potatoes can be pierced easily with a fork. Stir in the remaining ingredients and sauté for an additional 2 minutes. Makes 2-4 servings.

# QUICK & EASY TOFU OMELETTE

Normally an omelette is derived from an egg mixture, but it's just as easy to use tofu. If you mess up flipping the omelette, just stir it all together and call it a tofu scramble!

> **½ lb medium tofu, mashed**
> **1 tbsp Braggs**
> **⅛ tsp turmeric**
> **1 tsp olive oil**
> **omelette filling (p. 45)**

In a small bowl, mash together the tofu, Braggs, and turmeric. In a medium frying pan on medium-high heat, sauté the tofu mixture in oil, pressing down with the back of a spatula. You want it to spread out flat on the bottom of the pan, while the bottom of the tofu is cooking. Cook for 6-8 minutes, until all the liquid has cooked off and the bottom of your omelette is starting to sear. Add your filling ingredients to half of the omelette, and flip the other half over to cover. Cover with lid, reduce heat to medium-low, and let sit for 2-4 minutes or until veggies are cooked. Makes 1 omelette.

Omelettes can be filled with whatever your heart desires. See page 44 for directions. Here are a few ideas:

# OLIVE OMELETTE

- ¼ cup basil olive pesto (pg. 137)

# SPINACH MUSHROOM OMELETTE

- ¼ cup spinach, chopped
- 2-3 mushrooms, chopped
- ¼ cup soy cheese, grated

# POTATO OMELETTE

- ¼ cup potato, grated and stirred in with the tofu mixture
- 1 tbsp red onion, minced
- ⅛ tsp black pepper

# TOMATO BASIL OMELETTE

- ¼ cup fresh basil
- ½ small tomato, seeds removed and chopped
- 1 tsp gomashio (pg. 209)

# SABROSO SCRAMBLED TOFU

Sabroso is Spanish for "tasty." That one word says it all....

- 1 small onion, chopped
- 4-5 mushrooms, sliced
- 1 tbsp olive oil
- ½ small green bell pepper, chopped
- 1 lb medium-firm tofu, crumbled
- 1 tbsp Braggs
- ½ tsp all-purpose seasoning (pg. 210)
- ⅓-½ cup salsa (you decide the heat) (pg. 131)

In a large saucepan on medium heat, sauté the onions and mushrooms in oil until the onions are translucent. Add the peppers and sauté for an additional minute. Add the remaining ingredients and sauté for 10-12 minutes on medium-high heat or until all the liquid has evaporated. Makes 4 servings.

# HUEVOS RANCHEROS

Spanish for "country style eggs," Huevos Rancheros can easily be imitated with tofu.

> **4 large tortilla shells**
> **1 cup refried beans (pg. 114)**
> **2 cups Sabroso Scrambled Tofu (pg. 45)**
> **1 cup soy cheese, grated**
> **1 avocado, sliced**
> **Salsa (pg. 131)**

Preheat oven to 350°F. On a baking sheet, lay tortilla shells down and spread on one half of the shell, a ¼ of the beans, tofu, and cheese. Fold over shell and bake for 15 minutes or until top is browned. Repeat with remaining ingredients. Serve with sliced avocado and salsa. Makes 4 servings.

# YUMMY BREAKFAST QUESADILLAS

Fold your tortilla shell over and make a kick-ass quesadilla or fold and wrap your tortilla shell around the ingredients to make a burrito. Either way your tummy will thank you!

> **1 small onion, chopped**
> **2 garlic cloves, minced**
> **1 tbsp olive oil**
> **4 mushrooms, sliced**
> **1 small red bell pepper, chopped**
> **½ tsp dried dill**
> **¼ tsp dried basil**
> **¼ tsp black pepper**
> **1 tbsp Braggs**
> **½ lb medium-firm tofu, crumbled *or* cubed**
> **2-4 tortilla shells**
> **½ cup soy cheese (optional)**

Preheat oven to 350°F. In a large saucepan on medium heat, sauté the onions and garlic in oil until the onions are translucent. Add the mushrooms, red pepper, dill, basil, pepper, and Braggs. Add tofu and sauté until the peppers are tender. On a baking sheet, lay tortilla shells down and on one half of the shell spread a portion of the tofu mixture and top with cheese. Fold over shell and bake for 15 minutes or until top is browned. Makes 2-4 servings.

# RASPBERRY FIG BREAKFAST BARS

Figs are a good source of iron and calcium as well as being tasty. These breakfast bars travel well and are great for a quick breakfast on the go.

| | |
|---|---|
| ¾ cup dried figs, cut in half | ¼ tsp salt |
| ½ cup water | ¼ tsp baking powder |
| 1 tbsp dry sweetener | ¼ tsp baking soda |
| 1 cup flour | ½ cup olive oil |
| 2 cups rolled oat flakes | 2 tbsp water |
| ½ cup dry sweetener (for crust mixture) | ½ cup raspberry jam (pg. 215) |

Preheat oven to 350°F. In a small pot, combine the figs, water, and sweetener. Bring to a boil, then reduce heat to medium-low and simmer for 20 minutes, or until the figs have softened. Set aside to cool. In a large bowl, combine the flour, rolled oats, sweetener, salt, baking powder, baking soda, oil, and water and stir together until well mixed. In a blender or food processor, blend the fig mixture and jam until smooth. Press half of the crust mixture onto the bottom of a lightly oiled 8x8 baking pan. Layer the fig mixture over top, spreading it out with the back of a large spoon. Press the remaining crust mixture over top. Bake for 25-30 minutes, or until the top is lightly browned. Set aside to cool. Makes 6-12 bars.

# DELIGHTFUL BANANA NUT MUFFINS

These lovely muffins are great if you're in a rush for the bus, or need an afternoon treat. The smell alone will get your tastebuds drooling.

1 ⅓ cups flour
½ cup dry sweetener
1 tsp baking powder
1 tsp baking soda
½ tsp salt
¾ cup oat bran
½ cup walnuts, chopped
2 bananas, mashed
⅓ cup olive oil
1 tsp vanilla extract
⅔ cup soy milk

Preheat oven to 375°F. In a large bowl, stir together the flour, sweetener, baking powder, baking soda, salt, oat bran, and walnuts. Add the mashed bananas, oil, vanilla, and soy milk and mix together gently until "just mixed." Spoon into a lightly oiled muffin pan and bake for 15-20 minutes. Makes 12 muffins.

# JUICES

Fresh juice is an excellent and healthy alternative to sugary, store-bought juice, coffee, and pop. Make sure you drink these immediately after juicing so you don't lose any of the nutrients. But this doesn't mean you're off the hook from eating eat fresh veggies and fruit. (Can you say fiber?) The combinations of juicing are as endless as your imagination. Here's a few to get your juices flowing!

## GOOD MORNING JUICE

This is a nice morning energy boost juice that will kick you in the pants and get you on your way.

**1 grapefruit**
**1 orange**

Run all the ingredients through a juicer. Pour into glass. Serve. Makes 1-2 servings.

## BRAIN FOG LIFTER

Forget where you left your pants last night? This will help.

**1 orange**
**1 grapefruit**
**1 apple**
**1 small yam**
**1 pear**

Run all the ingredients through a juicer. Pour into glass. Serve. Makes 1-2 servings.

## CARROT APPLE GINGER JUICE

My mum used to make this for me. Yum! (S)

**3-4 carrots**
**1 apple**
**1-2 inches fresh ginger**

Run all the ingredients through a juicer. Pour into glass. Serve. Makes 1-2 servings.

# RICH IN IRON JUICE

Roar! This juice will make you strong!!!

3 carrots
6 large spinach leaves
1 kale leaf
1 beet
1 handful parsley

Run all the ingredients through a juicer. Pour into glass. Serve. Makes 1-2 servings.

# GREEN-DAY JUICE

Check your teeth after you drink this!

6 large spinach
1 handful parsley
2 stalks celery
4 carrots

Run all the ingredients through a juicer. Pour into glass. Serve. Makes 1-2 servings.

# SMOOTHIES

Smoothies are a fast and scrumptious way to fill your belly in the morning. Depending on your combination of ingredients, they can be full of vitamins and minerals.

# NUT BUTTER & BANANA SMOOTHIE

Nuts and seeds are an important part of a healthful diet; they contain essential fatty acids, vitamin E, and many other important nutrients.

¼ cup apple juice
1 cup soy yogurt (pg. 216)
1 tbsp maple syrup
½ tsp vanilla extract
½ heaping tbsp nut butter (your choice)
½ banana

In a blender or food processor, purée all the ingredients until smooth and creamy. Serve chilled.
Makes 2 small or 1 large serving.

# STRAWBERRY CREAM PIE SMOOTHIE

Legend has it that if you break a double strawberry in half and share it with someone, you will fall in love with each other. We don't know if that's true or not ... besides, strawberries are too delicious to share.

**10 strawberries, stems removed**
**1 banana**
**1 cup soy milk**
**1 tbsp maple syrup**

In a blender or food processor, purée all the ingredients until smooth and creamy. Serve chilled.
Makes 2 small or 1 large serving.

# BLUEBERRY BLISS SMOOTHIE

A blissful state of being is only a gulp away with this delectable smoothie.

**1 cup blueberries**
**1 banana**
**½ cup coconut milk**
**½ cup soy milk**
**1 tsp spirulina**

In a blender or food processor, purée all the ingredients until smooth and creamy. Serve chilled.
Makes 2 small or 1 large serving.

# GET YOUR MOTOR RUNNING SMOOTHIE

I'm allergic to both caffeine and chocolate (sob) so instead of cocoa and coffee beans I substitute with 1 heaping tablespoon of my favourite instant grain beverage. Ⓢ

**2 bananas**
**1 cup soy milk**
**2-4 tsp whole coffee beans**
**2 tsp cocoa powder**
**2 tsp maple syrup**

In a blender or food processor, purée all the ingredients until smooth and creamy. Serve chilled.
Makes 2 small or 1 large serving.

# WISHFUL THINKING MANGO SMOOTHIE

Fresh mangos are packed with vitamins A, C, and D are a good source of potassium and beta carotene. The mango tree plays a sacred role in India; it is a symbol of love and some believe that it can grant wishes.

**1 large ripe mango**
**1 cup soy yogurt (pg. 216)**
**⅔ cup water**
**¼ tsp cinnamon**
**¼ tsp cardamom**

In a blender or food processor, purée all the ingredients until smooth and creamy. Serve chilled. Makes 2 small or 1 large serving.

# PINEAPPLE BANANA SMOOTHIE

Pineapples contain Vitamins A and C, but most importantly, they are a great source of an enzyme called bromelain, which helps the body's digestive system and also has anti-inflammatory properties.

**1 cup soy milk**
**2 cups pineapple**
**1 banana**
**½ papaya, seeds removed**
**2 tbsp coconut, shredded**
**1 tbsp maple syrup**

In a blender or food processor, purée all the ingredients until smooth and creamy. Serve chilled. Makes 2 small or 1 large serving.

# ZOE & ANDY'S MORNING SMOOTHIE

Our good friends at acherecords.com sent us this simple yet tasty smoothie. Give it a go!

**1 banana**
**½ cup berries (your choice; e.g., blackberries, strawberries, blueberries, etc.)**
**1 large *or* 2 small peaches, pit removed**
**1 cup soy milk**
**1 tbsp soy protein powder (optional)**

In a blender or food processor, purée all the ingredients until smooth and creamy. Serve chilled. Makes 2 small or 1 large serving.

Lunchbox

*Running out for a fast bite at lunchtime can be a speedy way to end your hunger pangs, but by mid-afternoon your body is taxed for fuel again and so is your pocketbook. So take an extra few minutes at home and make a lunch to take with you. Remember that eating isn't a nuisance; it should be your first priority. Food is the fuel that keeps your body going. Without it, you're a weak pile of skin and bones with a growling stomach, and that's not attractive.*

*Getting lunch ready for yourself or your family can be a big challenge, especially if you have picky eaters. One of the easiest ways to make sure everyone enjoys their lunches is to encourage them to be involved in the planning. Bring the whole brood along to the grocery store to pick and choose what items they want for lunch. That way each person can feel invested in his or her meal.*

*Here are a few lunchtime tips:*

1. **Get a lunch box**
   They're fun, they travel well, and you're not wasting paper brown bagging it to work. Put an abundance of choices inside. Have something warm, something filling, something fruity, something thirst quenching, something sweet. Then a snack for those mid-afternoon pangs.

2. **Don't forget a thermos**
   Who needs those wasteful little drink boxes! There's never enough juice and you can never get those tiny straws out of the packaging. Remember thermoses? They can provide you with a warm or cold drink to go with your lunch. Get two, and reserve one for soup!

3. **Lunch doesn't have to be boring!**
   Prepare any of the recipes in this chapter, partner it with some of your fabulous leftovers from the night before, and wow your co-workers with your homemade Garden of Vegan delights. Lunch never tasted so good.

# PITA SANDWICHES

*Pitas are great! This Middle Eastern flatbread travels well for lunch. Each pita round splits horizontally to form a pocket into which a wide variety of ingredients can be stuffed to make a sandwich. They also can be sliced into wedges and are great for dipping. Pitas can be easily made (pg. 170) or if you're short for time, are available at most health food stores and supermarkets.*

# QUICK & EASY PIZZA PIZZAZZ

There is almost no limit to the toppings that can be placed on a pizza crust. This is just a template for quick and easy pita pizzas, so feel free to use whatever toppings you desire, or whatever's hanging about in your fridge. The sun-dried tomato pesto recipe (pg. 137) would also make a delicious replacement for the tomato-based pizza sauce.

> **2 pitas (pg. 170)**
> **Pizza sauce (pg. 138)**
> **2-3 mushrooms, chopped**
> **1 small bell pepper (your choice), chopped**
> **1 stalk green onion, chopped**
> **2 tbsp olives (your choice), chopped**
> **2-4 sun-dried tomatoes, chopped**
> **1 cup spinach, chopped**
> **1 cup soy cheese, grated**

Preheat over to 375°F. On a lightly oiled baking sheet or lasagna pan, lay out the pitas and spread out half the pizza sauce on each. Layer with mushrooms, peppers, onions, olives, tomatoes, spinach, and cheese, in that order. Bake for 20-25 minutes, or until cheese has melted. Makes 2 servings.

# GREEK SALAD PITA SANDWICHES

A salad and a sandwich all in one.

> **3 cups romaine lettuce, chopped**
> **¼ cup olives (your choice)**
> **1 small tomato, seeded and chopped**
> **½ cup cucumber, seeded and cubed**
> **1 cup Fake Feta (pg. 211)**
> **2 tbsp marinade from Fake Feta**
> **4 pitas (pg. 170)**

In a medium bowl, toss together the lettuce, olives, tomato, cucumber, feta, and feta marinade. Slit open pita and fill each with mixture, or roll up ingredients in pita to make a wrap. Makes 4 servings.

# SAUTÉED VEGGIE PITA POCKETS

You can serve up these pockets hot or cold, depending on the weather. Hint: wait for veggies to cool before transferring mixture to pitas, that way they won't get soggy.

> **1 ½ tbsp tahini**
> **1 tbsp olive oil**
> **1 ½ tsp lemon juice *or* apple cider vinegar**
> **1 ½ tsp liquid sweetener**
> **1 tsp miso**
> **1 tsp water**
> **½ small onion, sliced**
> **2 cloves garlic, sliced**
> **1 tsp olive oil (for sauté)**
> **1 cup eggplant, salted, peeled and chopped (see Baba-Ganoush recipe, pg. 127)**
> **1 small bell pepper (your choice), sliced**
> **2-3 mushrooms, sliced**
> **½ medium tomato, chopped**
> **2 pitas (pg. 170)**

In a small bowl, whisk together the tahini, oil, lemon juice, sweetener, miso, and water. Set aside. In a large saucepan on medium heat, sauté the onion and garlic in oil until the onions are translucent. Add the eggplant, peppers, mushrooms, and tomatoes. Sauté until the vegetables are tender but firm to the bite. Add tahini mixture and mix well. Slit open pita and fill each one with half the veggie mixture. Makes 2 servings.

# PORTOBELLO MUSHROOM SANDWICH

The portobello mushroom is a large, fully mature version of the ordinary classic white mushroom. It has a denser and more substantial texture. In other words, it's delicious!

½ small onion, sliced
1 ½ tsp olive oil
1 tsp balsamic vinegar
2 portobello mushrooms, stem removed
1 tbsp olive oil

4 slices sourdough bread, toasted
2 tsp Dijon mustard
2 lettuce leaves
4 tomato slices
4 tbsp Caesar's Wife Dressing (pg. 97)

In a small saucepan on medium heat, sauté the onions in oil and vinegar until the onions are translucent. Set aside. In a large saucepan on medium heat, sauté the mushrooms in oil until they are tender, about 5-6 minutes. On one piece of toasted bread, spread half the mustard, layer with half the lettuce, tomatoes, and onions and top with one mushroom. Pour 2 tbsp of dressing over mushroom and cover with another toasted bread slice. Repeat with remaining ingredients. Makes 2 sandwiches.

# FRIED "EGG" SANDWICH

This delectable sandwich can also be served on toasted bread for a sturdier sandwich.

1 tbsp nutritional yeast
⅛ tsp salt
⅛ tsp black pepper
2 slices firm tofu (about the size of your bread)
1 tsp olive oil
2-4 slices whole grain bread
Mayonnaise (pg. 211)
Sprouts *or* lettuce
Tomato, thinly sliced

On a small plate, stir together the nutritional yeast, salt, and pepper. Dip both sides of the tofu slices in the nutritional yeast to coat. In a large frying pan on medium-high heat, sauté the tofu in oil until browned. Flip and cook other side. Assemble sandwich using bread, mayo, tofu, sprouts, and tomato. Serve open faced or sandwich style. Makes 2 sandwiches.

# DELICIOUS FRIED TOFU SANDWICH

This sandwich comes from Angela in Ottawa, Ontario. It can also be served on toasted bread for a sturdier sandwich.

**2 thin slices firm tofu (about the size of your bread)**
**½ tbsp dark sesame oil**
**1 tbsp Braggs**
**½ tsp all-purpose spice (pg. 210)**
**2-4 slices whole grain bread**
**Mayonnaise (pg. 211)**
**Sprouts** *or* **lettuce**
**Tomato, thinly sliced**

In a large frying pan on medium-high heat, sauté the tofu in oil and Braggs until browned. Flip, sprinkle each slice with all-purpose seasoning, and cook other side until browned. Assemble sandwich using bread, mayonnaise, tofu, sprouts, and tomato. Serve open faced or sandwich style. Makes 2 sandwiches.

# HUMMUS & VEGGIE SANDWICH

A delicious and nutritious sandwich that will have you raring to go!

**2-4 tbsp hummus (pg. 134)**
**4 slices bread**
**¼ cup sprouts (your choice)**
**1 small carrot, grated**
**4 rings red onion**
**½ avocado, sliced**
**2 tsp gomashio**

Spread hummus on each slice of bread. Assemble sandwiches by layering remaining ingredients between 2 slices of bread. Makes 2 sandwiches.

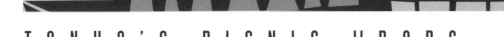

# T A N Y A ' S   P I C N I C   W R A P S

This is a great alternative to the everyday sandwich. I make sure to take this one to picnics, but it can be enjoyed on any occasion. (T)

**4 tortilla shells**
**1 cup refried beans (pg. 114)**
**½ cup carrot, grated**
**½ cup beet, grated**
**2 stalks green onion, chopped**
**4 tbsp sunflower seeds**
**1 cup sunflower sprouts**
**½ cup salsa (pg. 131)**

Lay one tortilla shell down and place one quarter of all ingredients on top, starting with the refried beans. Wrap up and lay seam-side down on plate. Repeat process with other tortilla shells. Makes 4 wraps.

# J O E L ' S   C A L Z O N E S

This amazing recipe comes from Joel in Guelph, Ontario.

**Calzone dough (pg. 175)**
**1 lb medium-firm tofu**
**1 tsp dried basil**
**3 tsp dried oregano**
**1 tsp salt**
**1 tsp black pepper**
**2 tbsp lemon juice**
**4 cloves garlic, roughly chopped**
**1 small onion, roughly chopped**
**2 cups mozzarella soy cheese, grated**
**4 cups spinach, roughly chopped**
**8 mushrooms, chopped**

Preheat oven to 450°F. In a blender or food processor, blend together the tofu, basil, oregano, salt, pepper, lemon juice, garlic, and onion. Pour into a large bowl and stir in soy cheese, spinach, and mushrooms. Divide dough into 6. On a lightly floured surface, roll out ball into a 6-inch circle. Place one cup of filling in middle of circle, fold over, and press edges with finger, then crimp edge with fork. Arrange on baking sheet and bake for 15-20 minutes. Makes 6 calzones.

Microwave Meals

These recipes are especially for all you crazy college kids living in dorms. But just so you know, Tanya wants nothing to do with this chapter. She thinks microwaves are creepy and doesn't want you to use them. With that in mind, you can consider these recipes for emergency purposes only! Use only if you are without proper cooking facilities.

Before you begin, you'll need to tap into your student loan to buy a few utensils and pieces of equipment (before you use it all up on beer and tattoos). Some of these items may not be allowed in your dorm, but if the school isn't going to provide you with vegan meals, then you need to do what you have to in order to stay healthy!

Here's what you'll need:

- Microwave oven
- Large microwave rice cooker or stand alone rice cooker (watch out for steam burns!)
- Various sized mixing bowls (microwave safe)
- Set of measuring cups and spoons
- Wooden spoon
- Cutting board
- Knife & vegetable peeler
- Various microwavable cookware
     8x8x2 pan
     Loaf pan
     Other microwave/storable containers
- Plates and eating utensils (duh)
- Large sealable containers for storing your non-perishable food items

Things to hit your parents up for:

- Beer refrigerator (not for beer ... for food)
- Vegetable steamer
- Electric wok
- Toaster (or even better ... a toaster oven!)
- Blender (see pg. 49-51 for smoothies)
- Juicer (there's nothing better then fresh juice) (see pg. 48-49 for juices)

**Remember that everyone's microwave is different, so cooking times may vary slightly.**

Chances are you'll have a grocery store nearby where you can buy what you need. Most of the ingredients in this chapter are canned or dried, but you need to incorporate fresh fruits and vegetables into your meals every day or you'll get scurvy and die!

In the event you don't live near a store, bring a bag with you to the school cafeteria and pocket some of the ingredients you need to make meals in your room. Like I said before, if they're not going to provide you with vegan meals, you're going to have to get resourceful. It's not stealing if you've paid your tuition! Besides, if you're paying to live in the dorm, the cost usually includes meals!

Be resourceful. Fresh items like cilantro, parsley, basil, lettuce, and tomatoes can be easily grown in a pot by the window. Try meeting other vegans/vegetarians like you by putting up posters and host a vegan potluck. Maybe you can "plot" together and start a guerrilla garden somewhere on campus. I always say grass is overrated; dig it up and plant something useful!

If you can get all your new friends organized, try to start a vegan/vegetarian food club. You'll meet like-minded people. Try to get local businesses or the school to donate food so you can offer a free vegan lunch to members once or twice a week. You might even get extra credit for your hard work!

Food Not Bombs is an excellent organization that recovers vegetarian food that might be discarded to create meals for hungry people. They have years and years of organizing experience getting food out to those who need it. Check out their website for ideas: FoodNotBombs.net.

Most schools also have food-banks for those who need a little extra help. Only use the food-bank if you yourself are financially strapped, and offer to volunteer some of your time in exchange. They are always in need of more help.

Now get studying, I can't do everything for you!

Remember to study hard and just say no!

– Sarah

# BREAKFAST

*I've said it before and I'll say it again! Breakfast is the most important meal of the day. So wake up, lazy-head … get up fifteen minutes early and make yourself something solid for breakfast. Coffee and a donut ain't gonna cut it. You need brain food!*

## MICROWAVE OATMEAL

**¾ cup rolled oat flakes**
**2 tbsp oat bran**
**2 tbsp wheat bran**
**2 tbsp wheat germ**
**3 tbsp raisins (optional)**
**1 cup cold water**

In a microwave-safe bowl, combine all the ingredients. Cook on high in the microwave for 1½-2 minutes. Add soy milk and top with sliced fresh fruit and maple syrup. Makes one large serving.

## FAUX EGG BREAKFAST MUFFINS

Forget the fast food version. These rival any Mc-death product!

**English muffin, halved**
**Nummy Yummy Scrambled Tofu (pg. 64)**
**Faux ham, chopped**
**Thin slice of soy cheese**

Scramble tofu with faux ham. Assemble muffin with scrambled tofu and soy cheese. Cook on medium high in the microwave for 1 minute to warm it up. Then, eat up, 'cause you deserve a break today!

You can add anything you want to these tofu recipes. Tofu is a sponge (not literally!) that will soak up whatever flavors you add to it. Here are three ideas to get you going! If you decide to use firm veggies such as carrots, cook them with the tofu so they have a chance to cook through.

# SPINACH, MUSHROOM, & TOMATO SCRAMBLED TOFU

½ lb firm tofu, mashed
2 tbsp Braggs
1 tbsp all-purpose spice (pg. 210)
¼ cup spinach
4 mushrooms, chopped
1 tomato, chopped

In a microwave rice cooker, combine the tofu, Braggs, and seasoning mix. Cook on high in the microwave for 2 minutes. Add the spinach, mushrooms, and tomato and cook for an additional 2 minutes. Serve with toast and juice. Makes 1 serving.

# ZUCCHINI, SPINACH, & OLIVE SCRAMBLED TOFU

½ lb firm tofu, mashed
2 tbsp Braggs
1 tbsp curry powder
¼ cup zucchini
¼ cup spinach
4 olives (your choice), chopped

In a microwave rice cooker, combine the tofu, Braggs, and curry powder. Cook on high in the microwave for 2 minutes. Add the zucchini, spinach, and olives and cook for an additional 2 minutes. Serve with toast and juice. Makes 1 serving.

# SARAH'S NUMMY YUMMY SCRAMBLED TOFU

½ lb firm tofu, mashed
2 tbsp Braggs
1 tsp turmeric
½ tbsp chili powder
1 small onion, minced
1 tomato, chopped

In a microwave rice cooker, combine the tofu, Braggs, turmeric, and chili powder. Cook on high in the microwave for 2 minutes. Add the onion and tomato and cook for an additional 2 minutes. Serve with toast and juice. Makes 1 serving.

# ENTRÉES

*Here are some easy meals you can make in the microwave that will help keep your energy up for all those late-night study sessions.*

## MICROWAVE OR TOASTER OVEN PIZZA

**English muffin (halved),** *or* **slice of bread, toasted**
**1 tbsp of all purpose tomato sauce (pg. 65) for each slice**

*Topping ideas:*
- **Faux pepperoni and mushrooms with soy cheese**
- **Sun-dried tomatoes, artichoke hearts, and fresh basil**
- **Hot peppers and leftover refried beans (pg. 114)**
- **Faux ham and pineapple with soy cheese**
- **Mushroom and olive with soy cheese**

Spoon tomato sauce onto muffin or toast. Add desired ingredients on top. Cook on high in the microwave or toaster oven for 2 minutes. Makes as many servings as you want.

## NO-COOK ALL-PURPOSE TOMATO SAUCE

This recipe is great for pizza sauce, over noodles, or added to beans and rice. Get creative!

**1 14-oz (396-ml) can tomato sauce**
**1 5-oz (156-ml) can tomato paste**
**1 tsp salt**
**1 tsp dry sweetener**
**2 tsp dried oregano**
**½ tsp black pepper**

In a bowl or jar, combine the tomato sauce, tomato paste, salt, sweetener, oregano, and pepper. Mix together well. Store in a container with a tight-fitting lid and refrigerate. Will keep for 5-7 days. Makes approx. 2 cups.

# BASIC BEANS & RICE

Here are some cheap and easy meals that combine rice and beans to make a perfect protein. You may fart, but you'll be smart!

**¾ cup white rice**
**1 ¼ cups water**
**1 19-oz (538-ml) can beans (your choice; e.g., kidney, black, mixed), drained and rinsed**
**2 cloves garlic, chopped**
**1 tsp black pepper**
**1 tsp salt**
**1 small carrot, chopped**
**1 small tomato, chopped**
**Braggs (optional)**
**Flax oil (optional)**

In a microwave rice cooker, combine the rice, water, beans, garlic, salt, pepper, and carrots. Cook on high in the microwave for 10-15 minutes or until rice is cooked. Stir in tomatoes and cook for an additional 2 minutes. Garnish with a dash of Braggs and flax oil. Makes 2 servings.

# CURRIED BEANS & RICE

Make your roommates' stomachs jealous with this aromatic and delicous recipe.

**¾ cup white rice**
**1 ¼ cups water**
**1 19-oz (538-ml) can beans (your choice; e.g., red, black, mixed), drained and rinsed**
**1 tbsp all-purpose spice (pg. 210)**
**1 tbsp curry powder**
**1 small carrot, chopped**
**4 mushrooms, chopped**
**¼ cup spinach, chopped**
**1 small tomato, chopped**
**Braggs (optional)**
**Flax oil (optional)**

In a microwave rice cooker, combine the rice, water, beans, all-purpose seasoning, curry powder, and carrots. Cook on high in the microwave for 10-15 minutes or until rice is cooked. Stir in mushrooms, spinach, and tomatoes and cook for an additional 2 minutes. Garnish with a dash of Braggs and flax oil. Makes 2 servings.

# LENTILS & RICE

Mmm, lentils! Lentils have a fair amount of calcium and vitamins A and B, and are a good source of iron.

**¾ cup white rice (your choice; e.g., jasmine, basmati)**
**1 ¼ cups water**
**1 19-oz (536-ml) can lentils, drained and rinsed**
**2 cloves garlic, chopped**
**1 small onion, chopped**
**1 carrot, chopped**
**1 tsp thyme**
**1 tsp cumin**
**1 tsp black pepper**
**½ tsp salt**
**1 tomato, chopped**

In a microwave rice cooker, combine the rice, water, lentils, garlic, onions, carrots, thyme, cumin, salt, and pepper. Cook on high in the microwave for 10-15 minutes or until rice is cooked. Stir in the tomatoes and cook for an additional 2 minutes. Garnish with a dash of Braggs and flax oil. Makes 2 servings.

# BEANS & RICE WITH TOMATOES, OLIVES, & CILANTRO

I used to think that cilantro was weird, but now I love it. Sometimes it's called Chinese parsley or coriander, depending on where you live.

**¾ cup white rice**
**1 ¼ cups water**
**1 19-oz (536-ml) can beans (your choice; e.g., red, black, mixed), drained and rinsed**
**1 tbsp oregano**
**1 tsp basil**
**6 jumbo olives (your choice), chopped**
**¼ cup zucchini**
**1 tomato, chopped**
**¼ cup fresh cilantro, chopped**

In a microwave rice cooker, combine the rice, water, beans, oregano, and basil. Cook on high in the microwave for 10-11 minutes or until rice is cooked. Stir in olives and zucchini and cook for an additional 2 minutes. Stir in tomato and cilantro. Garnish with a dash of Braggs and flax oil. Makes 2 servings.

# TAMALE PIE

Feel like showing off your culinary skills? This yummy recipe is a little more time-consuming than the others, but is still really easy to make.

**¾ cup uncooked cornmeal**
**1 tsp salt**
**2 cups water**
**2 cups canned beans (your choice; e.g., red, black, mixed), drained and rinsed**
**1 cup corn**
**1 small green bell pepper, seeded and chopped**
**¼ cup olives (your choice), sliced**
**1 cup All-Purpose Tomato Sauce (pg. 65)**
**½ tsp cumin**
**1 tsp chili powder**
**1 tsp dried oregano**

In a large bowl, combine cornmeal, salt, and water. Cook on high in the microwave, uncovered, for 6 minutes. Remove from microwave and stir well. In a large microwave-safe casserole dish, combine the beans, corn, green pepper, and olives. In a small bowl, combine the tomato sauce, cumin, chili powder, and oregano. Pour over bean mixture. Spread cornmeal over bean mixture evenly; cover and cook on high in the microwave for 8-10 minutes. Let cool slightly before serving.

# S O U P S

*Soups are easy to prepare in a microwave; they all follow a basic formula (see below). But in case you don't have time to figure out what goes where, I've included 3 microwave soup recipes.*

*You will need a large microwave-safe pot or large microwave rice cooker for them.*

# S O U P   I N   5   E A S Y   S T E P S

1. Microwave your firm veggies (such as potatoes, carrots, and squash) in a splash of oil for 2-4 minutes.

2. Add vegetable stock and spices, stir.

3. Microwave 2 minutes more.

4. Add other softer veggies (tomatoes, spinach, zucchini, etc. only need a little cooking).

5. Microwave 2 minutes more.

Eat up, buttercup!

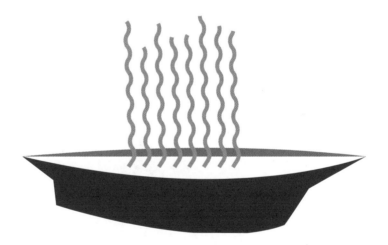

# BIG BOWL OF MISO NOODLE SOUP

Miso comes from fermented soybean paste, but don't let that scare you. It's a great flavor enhancer and has a reputation for boosting the immune system. If you don't have a bowl big enough, just eat out of the pot!

**2 ½ cups water**
**1 carrot, chopped**
**dry rice noodles for one person** *or* **1 pkg Japanese instant noodles (but discard the flavoring package – blech!)**
**½ lb firm tofu, cubed**
**8-10 sweet peas** *or* **snow peas**
**½ cup greens (spinach, kale, etc.), torn**
**1-2 stalks green onion, chopped**
**1 tbsp Braggs**
**pinch of black pepper**
**1-2 tbsp miso paste (depending on how strong you want your broth)**
**gomashio (optional) (pg. 209)**
**dark sesame oil** *or* **flax oil (optional)**

In a large microwave-safe pot or large microwave rice cooker, combine water, carrots, and noodles. You may have to break the noodles a little so they fit under the water. Cover and cook on high for 5 minutes. Stir in tofu and sweet peas and cook for an additional minute. Stir in greens, green onions, Braggs, pepper, and miso. Let sit covered for 1 minute. Garnish with Gomashio and a splash of dark sesame oil or flax oil.
Makes 1 large serving.

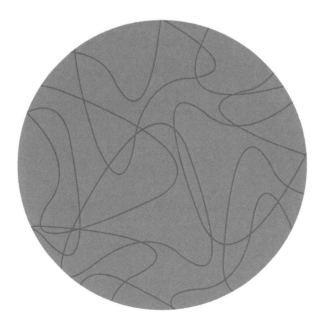

# CURRIED CHICKPEA POTATO SOUP

Chickpeas are also called garbanzo beans for some reason.... If you know why, please e-mail me at *garbanzo_chickpea_mystery@govegan.net.*

**1 tbsp oil**
**1 small onion, chopped**
**1 large potato, chopped**
**1 cup vegetable stock**
**2 tsp curry powder**
**½ tsp cumin**
**⅛ tsp black pepper**
**1 19-oz (538-ml) can chickpeas (garbanzo beans), drained**
**½ cup soy milk**
**1 cup spinach**

In a large microwave-safe pot or large microwave rice cooker, combine the oil, onion, and potato and cook on high in the microwave for 2 minutes. Stir and microwave for an additional 2-3 minutes or until potatoes can be poked easily with a fork. Stir in vegetable stock, curry, cumin, pepper, and chickpeas. Cook on high in the microwave for an additional 2 minutes. Add soy milk and spinach and stir. Let sit for 1 minute before serving. Makes 2 servings.

# VOLUPTIOUS VEGETABLE SOUP

You can add any veggies you want to this recipe. The more, the merrier!

**1 tsp oil**
**1 small onion, chopped**
**1 stalk celery, chopped**
**4 mushrooms, chopped**
**½ cup broccoli, chopped**
**½ cup zucchini, chopped**
**½ red bell pepper, chopped**

**1 large tomato, chopped**
**¾ cup water**
**1 tsp basil**
**1 tsp dried oregano**
**½ tsp black pepper**
**½ tsp salt**
**1 small can of beans (e.g., red, chickpea, kidney, etc.)**

In a large microwave-safe pot or large microwave rice cooker, combine the oil , onion, celery, mushrooms, and broccoli and cook on high in the microwave for 4 minutes. Stir and add the zucchini, red pepper, and tomato. Microwave on high for an additional 4 minutes. Stir in the water, spices, and beans. Microwave on high for an additional 4 minutes. Makes 2 servings

# TREATS

*Tired of your smelly roommate? Overwhelmed with term papers? Everyone needs a junk food fix, especially if you're burning the midnight oil studying.*

# APPLE CRISP

Are you dying for a piece of Grandma's apple pie? This easy apple crisp will transport you back to your family's kitchen when life was easier. If you have other fruit you'd like to add, just omit equal parts of apple for the fruit you are adding. Serve with vegan ice cream (pg. 201-205) or soy milk.

> **2 apples (your choice), cored and chopped**
> **3 tbsp margarine**
> **¼ cup dry sweetener**
> **4 tbsp flour**
> **1 tsp cinammon**
> **½ tsp ground nutmeg**
> **½ cup oatmeal**

Arrange apple pieces in an 8x8 microwave-safe dish. In a bowl, combine the margarine, sweetener, flour, cinammon, nutmeg, and oatmeal. Sprinkle mixture evenly over apples. Cook on high in the microwave for 10-12 minutes. Let stand 2 minutes before serving.

# BLESS-ED BROWNIES

There's nothing like chocolate brownies to kick-start a long night of studying. See page 199 for frosting ideas.

> **1 banana, mashed**
> **¾ cup dry sweetener**
> **⅓ cup margarine**
> **1 tsp vanilla extract**
> **⅓ cup soy milk**
> **1 cup flour**
> **4 tbsp cocoa**
> **½ tsp salt**
> **½ cup chocolate chips**
> **½ cup chopped nuts (optional)**

In a large bowl, mash the banana. Stir in the sweetener, margarine, vanilla, and soy milk and mix well. Add the flour, cocoa, and salt and mix well. Spread evenly in a lightly oiled microwave-safe loaf pan. Sprinkle chocolate chips and nuts on top. Cook on high in the microwave for 4 minutes. Let cool before cutting and serving.

# BANANA OATMEAL CHOCOLATE CHIP BARS

The good news is that you can make this recipe in a few minutes. The aroma alone will have you drooling... but the bad news is you have to wait for it to cool before you can eat it.

½ **banana, mashed**
½ **cup dry sweetener**
¼ **cup margarine**
1 **tsp vanilla extract**
¼ **cup soy milk**
½ **cup flour**
½ **oats**
1 **tsp baking powder**
¼ **tsp salt**
⅓ **cup chocolate chips**

In a large bowl, mash the banana. Stir in the sweetener, margarine, vanilla, and soy milk and mix well. Add the flour, oats, baking powder, and salt and mix well. Spread evenly in a lightly oiled microwave-safe loaf pan. Sprinkle chocolate chips on top. Cook on high in the microwave for 4-5 minutes. Let cool before cutting and serving.

# MICROWAVE PARTY MIX

A great nibbly recipe for the midnight muncher! Every microwave is a little different, so be careful not to burn your party mix.

2 **cups Chex-type cereal**
2 **cup Cheerios-type cereal**
1 **cup mixed nuts (your choice)**
1 **cup pretzels**
¼ **cup oil**
1 **tbsp Braggs**
½ **tsp garlic powder**
½ **tsp onion powder**
½ **tsp salt**
4 **tsp vegetarian Worcestershire sauce (pg. 207)**

In a large freezer bag, combine the cereals, nuts, and pretzels. Set aside. In a small bowl, stir together the oil, Braggs, garlic powder, onion powder, salt, and Worcestershire and pour into the bag. Close the bag tight and shake together until everything is well mixed. Pour into a large microwave-safe bowl and cook on medium in the microwave for 4-6 minutes, stirring every 2 minutes. Let cool before serving. Makes approx. 4 cups.

# ODDS & SODS

## MICROWAVE BEER BREAD

Spend all your dough on beer instead of bread? Have no fear, Sarah is here!

**3 cups flour**
**2 tsp baking powder**
**1 tsp salt**
**3 tbsp dry sweetener**
**1 ¼ cups beer (fresh ... not leftover from the night before!)**
**1 tbsp oil**

In a large bowl, combine the flour, baking powder, salt, and sweetener and whisk until well incorporated. Use ½ tbsp of oil to coat the microwave-safe bread pan. Stir in beer to flour mixture. Spoon together gently until everything is well mixed. (If you overmix, your bread will end up flat.) Pour into bread pan and press down. Use remaining oil to moisten the top of the dough. Cook on medium in the microwave for 9 minutes, then on high for an additional 2-3 minutes. Check after 2 minutes to see if done. Poke a knife or fork into bread and if it comes out clean ... you're ready! Let cool before slicing. Cheers!

# S O Y   Y O G U R T

Make this while you're in your room studying. It takes a few hours to make, but with not much effort. It will give you a good excuse to get away from the computer for a minute to stretch. If you make soy yogurt every week, you can use some of last week's batch as starter.

**2 cups soy milk**
**1 tsp active non-dairy acidophilus (found at health food stores)** *or* **2 tbsp plain soy yogurt with "live active cultures" (check label)**
**powdered agar** *or* **cornstarch (optional)**

In a microwave-safe bowl, heat the soy milk on high in the microwave for approximately 9 minutes or until it reaches 175°F. (You'll need a thermometer, but of course do not microwave the thermometer!) Remove from microwave and let cool until milk reaches about 100°F. Add the acidophilus or "starter yogurt" and whisk together well. Cover the bowl with plastic wrap or cover with lid and wrap bowl in small towel. You need to give the yogurt a nice warm place to do its thing. Return to microwave and heat on low for an additional 30 seconds. Let stand for 30 minutes. Reheat on low for 30 seconds every half hour for 4 hours. Leave it in the microwave during this time and don't open the microwave door. The yogurt may not be as thick as you're used to, so if you want you can add a touch of agar or cornstarch to thicken. For flavor, that's up to you. Add maple syrup or vanilla extract … whatever tickles your fancy. Remember to set aside some of the yogurt before you add your flavoring so you have a starter for your next batch. Makes approx. 2 cups. (If you have access to an oven, check out pg. 216 for oven-made yogurt.)

Soups

*Sipped or slurped, there is nothing quite as comforting as a bowl of soup.*

*Where did the word soup come from? From what we could find, before there was soup, there was broth. Back in the day (sometime around the 12th century), people used to pour broth over a piece of bread in a bowl. That bread was known as sop, and from sop came the word soup. No matter what you call it, there are lots of variations on the basic theme of soup.*

*A soup can be any combination of vegetables and other ingredients cooked in a liquid. Generally, soup is served as an appetizer before the main course, but sometimes a nice big bowl of comforting soup and a slice of bread or side salad is all you need as a meal.*

*And like Napolean Bonaparte once said: "An army travels on its stomach. Soup makes the soldier." So join the Vegan Army and get cooking!*

# SARAH'S HOT & SOUR GINGER SOUP

This fun and flavorful soup packs a powerful punch. I especially love this soup when I'm feeling a little under the weather. Ⓢ

**3 tbsp ginger, grated**
**½ cup shiitake *or* oyster mushrooms, chopped**
**1 ½ tbsp dark sesame oil**
**4 cups vegetable stock (pg. 217)**
**dry rice noodles *or* noodles of your choice (e.g., udon, buckwheat)**
**½ tsp red pepper flakes**
**3 tbsp rice vinegar**
**1 tbsp Braggs**
**1 lb firm tofu, cut into cubes**
**20 snow peas, ends removed**

In a large soup pot on medium-low heat, sauté the ginger and mushrooms in oil for 1-2 minutes, stirring often to prevent burning. Add the stock, rice noodles, and red pepper flakes. Bring to a boil, then reduce heat to medium-low. Simmer for 3-5 minutes or until noodles are cooked. Turn off heat, add vinegar, Braggs, tofu, and snow peas. Let stand covered for 5 minutes before serving. Makes 4-6 servings.

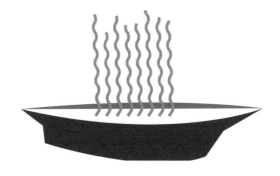

# WILD MUSHROOM SOUP WITH THYME

This full-bodied soup is a perfect way to chase the chill of a nasty autumn day. For a heartier soup, serve over ½ cup of cooked wild rice.

**3 tbsp shallots, minced**
**¾ lb assorted wild mushrooms (e.g., shiitake, oyster), chopped**
**⅛ tsp salt**
**1 tbsp olive oil**
**⅛ tsp black pepper**
**½ tsp dried thyme**
**2 cloves garlic, minced**
**4 cups vegetable stock (pg. 217)**
**1 medium potato, roughly chopped**

In a large soup pot on medium heat, sauté the shallots, mushrooms, and salt in oil until mushrooms are tender. Add the pepper, thyme, and garlic. Sauté for an additional 2 minutes. Add the stock and potatoes. Bring to a boil, then reduce heat to medium-low. Simmer for 15-20 minutes or until potatoes are tender. Remove from heat and transfer soup into a blender or food processor and blend until smooth (be careful when blending hot liquids). Makes 4 servings.

# BODACIOUS BEAN & BARLEY SOUP

This hearty and wonderful soup is a perfect way to get through those cold rainy days when you think you'll never see blue sky again.

**1 small onion, chopped**
**6 cloves garlic, minced**
**2 tbsp olive oil**
**⅔ cup uncooked pearl barley**
**3-4 cups vegetable stock (pg. 217)**
**1 cup cooked *or* canned chickpeas (garbanzo beans)**
**1 tsp cumin**
**1 tsp turmeric**
**1 cup soy yogurt (pg. 216)**
**½ cup fresh cilantro, chopped**
**1 tsp dried mint (*or* 1 tbsp fresh mint)**
**⅛ tsp salt**
**⅛ tsp pepper**

In a large soup pot on medium heat, sauté the onions and garlic in oil until the onions are translucent. Add the barley and sauté for an additional minute. Add the stock, chickpeas, cumin, and turmeric. Bring to a boil then reduce heat to medium-low. Simmer for about 45 minutes, or until barley is tender. Stir in yogurt, cilantro, mint, salt, and pepper. Remove from heat and let sit for 5 minutes before serving. Makes 4 servings.

# SPICY ASIAN NOODLE SOUP

Sarah likes to use udon noodles in this recipe, but Tanya likes to use rice noodles. Who do you like better …
we mean, which do you prefer?

**1 medium onion, chopped**
**1 medium carrot, chopped**
**1 stalk lemongrass, quartered and lightly bruised**
**2 tbsp fresh ginger, grated**
**4 cloves garlic, minced**
**1 tsp anise seed**
**2 tbsp sesame oil**
**8 cups vegetable stock (pg. 217)**
**2 tbsp Braggs**
**3 tsp Asian chili sauce**
**1 lb medium tofu, cubed**
**noodles of your choice (e.g., rice, udon)**
**1 cup bean sprouts**
**4 radishes, thinly sliced**
**2 stalks green onions, chopped**
**2 tbsp fresh cilantro, chopped**

In a large soup pot on medium heat, sauté the onions, carrots, lemongrass, ginger, garlic, and anise in oil until the onions are translucent. Add the stock, Braggs, chili sauce, and tofu. Bring to a boil, then reduce heat to low. Add the noodles, bean sprouts, and radishes. Simmer for 3-6 minutes or until noodles are cooked. Remove lemongrass and stir in the green onions and cilantro just before serving. Make 4-6 servings.

# SENSATIONAL SUN-DRIED TOMATO & CHICKPEA SOUP

This soup is amazing! Sun-dried tomatoes add a rich, intense flavor to any dish. They are found in most grocery or health food stores. You can find them in bulk, or in jars packed in oil, or you can make your own (pg. 208).

1 medium onion, chopped
2-3 garlic cloves, chopped
1 large carrot, chopped
1 tbsp dark sesame oil
3 ½ cups cooked *or* canned chickpeas
1 14-oz (420 mL) can crushed tomatoes
5-6 sun-dried tomatoes, chopped
1 tsp cumin

1 tsp dry mustard
⅛ tsp cayenne
⅛ tsp black pepper
½ tbsp apple cider vinegar
1 tbsp Braggs
2 cups vegetable stock (pg. 217)
2 tbsp tahini
¼ cup fresh parsley, minced

In a large soup pot on medium heat, sauté the onions, garlic, and carrots in oil until the onions are translucent. Add the chickpeas, tomatoes, cumin, mustard, cayenne, pepper, vinegar, Braggs, and stock. Bring to a boil, then reduce heat to medium-low. Simmer for 15-20 minutes or until carrots become tender. In a blender or food processor, blend ½ of the soup and the tahini until smooth (be careful when blending hot liquids); return to pot. Stir in parsley and serve. Makes 4 servings.

# SQUASH & SWEET POTATO SOUP WITH CHIPOTLE SAUCE

This savory potato soup will wow you with its bite!

1 medium onion, chopped
1 tbsp olive oil
1 leek, thinly sliced (white and pale green parts only)
2 tbsp fresh ginger, grated
2 cups yams, roughly chopped
3 cups squash (e.g., butternut, acorn, buttercup), roughly chopped
4 cups vegetable stock (pg. 217)
⅛ tsp black pepper
½-1 tsp chipotle sauce
½ cup soy yogurt (pg. 216)

In a large soup pot on medium heat, sauté the onions in oil until the onions are translucent. Add the leeks, ginger, yams, and squash and sauté for an additional 5 minutes. Add the stock and pepper. Bring to a boil, then reduce heat to medium-low. Simmer for 15-20 minutes or until vegetables are tender. In a blender or food processor, blend ½ or all of the soup until smooth (be careful when blending hot liquids); return to pot, and reheat. Add a generous dollop of yogurt to each portion of soup just before serving. Makes 4 servings.

# COUNTRY TURNIP CARROT SOUP

Turnips are a versatile vegetable and a good source of vitamin C. Don't be afraid of them; they can be boiled or steamed, mashed or puréed. You can even eat them raw. In this recipe, the turnips lend a lovely, gentle flavor to this rustic, down home soup.

**1 small onion, chopped**
**1 leek, thinly sliced (white and pale green parts only)**
**1 tbsp olive oil**
**2 cups turnips, chopped**
**1 large carrot, chopped**
**1 medium potato, roughly chopped**
**2 cups vegetable stock (pg. 217)**
**⅛ tsp nutmeg**
**⅛ tsp black pepper**
**1 tsp dried dill**
**1 cup soy milk**
**salt to taste**

In a large soup pot on medium heat, sauté the onions and leeks in oil until the onions are translucent. Add the turnips, carrots, potatoes, stock, nutmeg, pepper, and dill. Bring to a boil, then reduce heat to medium-low. Simmer for 15-20 minutes or until vegetables are tender. In a blender or food processor, blend ½ or all of the soup until smooth with the soy milk (be careful when blending hot liquids); return to pot and reheat. Season with salt to taste. Makes 6 servings.

# DELIGHTFUL BROCCOLI & RED PEPPER SOUP

Delightful. Need we say more?

**1 medium onion, chopped**
**2 cloves garlic, chopped**
**1 tbsp olive oil**
**4 cups broccoli, chopped**
**1 medium red pepper, chopped**
**3-4 cups vegetable stock (pg. 217)**
**1 tsp Braggs**
**½ tsp dried tarragon**
**¼ tsp dried thyme**
**⅛ tsp black pepper**

In a large soup pot on medium heat, sauté the onions and garlic in oil until the onions are translucent. Add the broccoli, red pepper, stock, Braggs, tarragon, thyme, and pepper. Bring to a boil, then reduce heat to medium-low. Simmer for 15 minutes or until vegetables are tender. In a blender or food processor, blend ½ or all of the soup until smooth (be careful when blending hot liquids); return to pot and reheat. Makes 4-6 servings.

# HOME-STYLE GREEN PEA SOUP

Nothing gives you the creature comfort feeling of "home" more than a beautiful bowl of Green Pea Soup. Optional: in a blender or food processor, blend ½ or all of the soup until smooth (be careful when blending hot liquids); return to pot and reheat.

**1 medium onion, chopped**
**2 cloves garlic, minced**
**1 tbsp olive oil**
**2 medium potatoes, chopped**
**1 medium carrot, chopped**
**4 cups vegetable stock (pg. 217)**
**1 cup dried green split peas**
**1 tbsp Braggs**
**3 bay leaves**
**1 tsp dried oregano**
**½ tsp cumin**
**⅛ tsp black pepper**
**⅛ tsp salt**

In a large soup pot on medium heat, sauté the onions and garlic in oil until the onions are translucent. Add the potatoes, carrots, stock, peas, Braggs, bay leaves, oregano, cumin, pepper, and salt. Bring to a boil, then reduce heat to medium-low. Simmer for 25-30 minutes or until peas are cooked. Makes 4-6 servings.

# GLORIOUS ROASTED GARLIC SOUP

Yum yum! This soup keeps the vampires away. Unfortunately, my boyfriend, too! Ⓣ

**1 medium onion, chopped**
**¼ cup shallots, chopped**
**1 large potato, chopped**
**1 tbsp olive oil**
**3 cups vegetable stock (pg. 217)**
**1 tbsp fresh thyme (*or* 1 tsp dried thyme)**
**3 heads roasted garlic (pg. 207)**
**1 cup soy milk**
**2 tbsp fresh parsley, minced**

In a large soup pot on medium heat, sauté the onions, shallots, and potatoes in oil until the onions are translucent. Add the stock, thyme, and roasted garlic. Bring to a boil, then reduce heat to low. Simmer for 10-15 minutes. In a blender or food processor, blend ½ or all of the soup until smooth (be careful when blending hot liquids); return to pot, and reheat. Add the soy milk and parsley. Stir and serve. Makes 4-6 servings.

# TANYA'S CURRIED SQUASH SOUP

I take this scrumptious creation to potlucks because it's always a hit. (T)

> 1 medium onion, chopped
> 2 tbsp olive oil
> 3 cups cauliflower, chopped
> 2 cups yams, chopped
> 2 cups squash(e.g., butternut, acorn, buttercup), chopped
> 1 medium potato, chopped
> 1 leek, sliced (white and pale green parts only)
> 4 cups vegetable stock (pg. 217)
> 1 180-oz (398-ml) can coconut milk
> 1 tbsp curry powder
> 1 tsp turmeric
> 1 tbsp Braggs

In a large soup pot on medium heat, sauté the onions in oil until translucent. Add the cauliflower, yams, squash, potatoes, and leeks and simmer for an additional 3 minutes. Add the stock, coconut milk, curry, turmeric, and Braggs. Bring to a boil, then reduce heat to low. Simmer for 10-15 minutes or until vegetables are cooked. In a blender or food processor, blend ½ or all of the soup until smooth (be careful when blending hot liquids); return to pot and reheat. Makes 4-6 servings.

# AUNTIE BONNIE'S BLACK BEAN SOUP

Every recipe my Auntie Bonnie shares with me is a blessing. This one rocks my world. Ⓢ

| | |
|---|---|
| 1 small onion, chopped | 1 ½ cups yams, peeled and cubed |
| 2 cloves garlic, minced | 1 tsp black pepper |
| 1 tbsp olive oil | 1 tsp salt |
| 1 stalk celery, chopped | 1 tsp red wine vinegar |
| 1 small red bell pepper, chopped | ¼ tsp chili powder |
| 1 small jalapeño pepper, seeded and minced | ⅛ tsp ground cloves |
| 2 cups vegetable stock (pg. 217) | ½ cup fresh cilantro, roughly chopped (garnish) |
| 2 cups cooked *or* canned black beans | |

In a large soup pot on medium heat, sauté the onions and garlic in oil until the onions are translucent. Add the celery, red pepper, and jalapeño, and simmer for an additional 3 minutes. Add the stock, beans, yams, pepper, salt, vinegar, chili powder, and cloves. Bring to a boil then reduce heat to low. Simmer for 10-15 minutes or until vegetables are cooked. In a blender or food processor, blend ½ or all of the soup until smooth (be careful when blending hot liquids); return to pot and reheat. Garnish with cilantro. Makes 4 servings.

# AUNTIE BONNIE'S BEAN & OLIVE SOUP

The Kramer women in my family love olives. Here is another wonderful recipe from my Auntie Bonnie. Ⓢ

| | |
|---|---|
| 1 medium onion, chopped | 1 tsp salt |
| 3-4 cloves garlic, minced | 1 tsp dried oregano |
| 2 tbsp olive oil | 1 ½ tsp dried basil |
| 1 stalk celery, diced | ⅛ tsp black pepper |
| 1 medium carrot, diced | 3 tbsp tomato paste |
| 4 cups vegetable stock (pg. 217) | ¼ cup dry red wine *or* 2 tbsp red wine vinegar |
| 1 small zucchini, diced | 1 tbsp lemon juice |
| 1 small green bell pepper, seeded and diced | ½ cup fresh parsley, minced (garnish) |
| 2 cups cooked *or* canned white navy beans | 1 small tomato, diced (garnish) |
| 1 cup Kalamata olives, pitted and sliced | |

In a large soup pot on medium heat, sauté the onions and garlic in oil until the onions are translucent. Add the celery and carrots and simmer for an additional 3 minutes. Add the stock, zucchini, green pepper, beans, olives, salt, oregano, basil, pepper, tomato paste, wine, and lemon juice. Bring to a boil, then reduce heat to low. Simmer for 10-15 minutes or until vegetables are cooked. Garnish with the parsley and tomato. Makes 4-6 servings.

# TANYA & MATTHEW'S THAI COCONUT MILK SOUP

Some of the ingredients in this soup can only be found in Asian markets, but we recommend going the extra mile. My sweetie Matthew says this soup is delicious all year round; in the winter because it's nice and spicy, and in the summer because the lime and ginger are refreshing. (T)

Make sure you wear gloves when you chop the chilies, otherwise your fingers will become deadly weapons that can burn your eyes or skin...for days. Hot water and soap helps, but wearing gloves is the key.

> **3 180-oz (396-ml) cans coconut milk**
> **1 ½ cups vegetable stock (pg. 217)**
> **3 pieces galangal (found in Asian markets)**
> **4 stalks lemongrass, cut into thirds and lightly bruised**
> **5 dried lime leaves (found in Asian markets)**
> **¼ cup shallots, minced**
> **1 lb firm tofu, cubed**
> **1 tbsp sesame oil**
> **2 tsp Asian chili sauce**
> **2 tbsp lime juice**
> **1 small carrot, chopped**
> **6 medium mushrooms, chopped**
> **2-3 serrano chilies, seeded and minced**
> **1 cup bok choy, roughly chopped**
> **2 tbsp fresh cilantro, chopped**

In a large soup pot on medium heat, combine the coconut milk, stock, galangal, lemongrass, and lime leaves. Bring to a boil, and then reduce heat to low. Simmer for 10-15 minutes. While soup is simmering, in a small saucepan on medium-high heat, sauté the shallots and tofu in oil until tofu is evenly browned. Remove the lime leaves and lemongrass from the soup, then add the sautéed shallots and tofu, chili sauce, lime juice, carrots, mushrooms, and chilies. Cook on medium-low heat for 10-15 minutes until vegetables are tender. Remove from heat and add bok choy and cilantro. Let sit for 5 minutes before serving. Makes 4-6 servings.

# WHOLESOME TOMATO RICE SOUP

This soup is just like Grandma's, only better! Sarah likes to blend half of the soup in a blender or food processor before adding the fresh tomatoes and basil (be careful when blending hot liquids).

> **1 medium onion, chopped**
> **3 cloves garlic, minced**
> **1 tbsp olive oil**
> **2-3 stalks celery, chopped**
> **1 carrot, chopped**
> **1 28-oz (796-ml) can diced tomatoes**
> **3 cups vegetable stock (pg. 217)**
> **½ cup uncooked white rice (your choice, e.g., jasmine, basmati)**
> **1 tbsp Braggs**
> **1 tsp black pepper**
> **¼ tsp red pepper flakes**
> **2 medium tomatoes, diced**
> **3 tbsp fresh basil, chopped**

In a large soup pot on medium heat, sauté the onions and garlic in oil until the onions are translucent. Add the celery and carrots and sauté for an additional minute. Add the tomatoes, stock, rice, Braggs, pepper, and red pepper flakes. Bring to a boil, then reduce heat to low. Simmer for 15 minutes or until rice is cooked. Stir in the tomatoes and basil just before serving. Makes 4 servings.

# GARDEN CARROT SOUP WITH FRESH GINGER

High in Vitamin A, carrots are a member of the parsley family. Who knew? This tempting soup will have you praising Mother Earth for her bounty.

> **4 large carrots, chopped**
> **1 leek, sliced (white and pale green parts only)**
> **2 tbsp dark sesame oil**
> **1 small yam, chopped**
> **1 tbsp fresh ginger, grated**
>
> **½ tsp salt**
> **½ tsp black pepper**
> **¼ tsp ground nutmeg**
> **2 cups vegetable stock (pg. 217)**

In a large soup pot on medium heat, sauté the carrots and leeks in oil for 3 minutes. Add the yam, cover, and cook for an additional 2 minutes. Add the ginger, salt, pepper, nutmeg, and stock. Bring to a boil then reduce heat to low. Simmer for 15-20 minutes or until vegetables are cooked. In a blender or food processor, blend ½ or all of the soup until smooth; return to pot and reheat. Makes 4 servings.

# HUNGRY PERSON STEW

This politically correct stew is as chunky as it is meaty, but in an animal-friendly sort of way. Seitan (wheat gluten) has a firm and meat-like texture that reminds us we don't have to be cruel to be kind.

| | |
|---|---|
| 1 small onion, chopped | ½ tsp dried thyme |
| 5 medium mushrooms, chopped | ¼ tsp red pepper flakes |
| 1 tbsp olive oil | ⅛ tsp black pepper |
| 2 medium carrots, chopped | 1 5½-oz (156-ml) can tomato paste |
| 1 large potato, chopped | 1 cup seitan, chopped (pg. 208) |
| 2 cups vegetable stock (pg. 217) | 1 cup fresh or frozen peas |

In a large soup pot on medium heat, sauté the onions and mushrooms in oil until the onions are translucent. Add the carrots and sauté for an additional minute. Add the potato, stock, thyme, red pepper flakes, pepper, and tomato paste. Bring to a boil, then reduce heat to low. Simmer for 15 minutes or until potatoes are cooked. Turn off heat and stir in the seitan and peas. Let stand for 5 minutes before serving. Makes 4 servings.

# CHRIS'S ALOO CHANA SOUP

Our good friends Chris and Jen, who run *FansOfBadProductions.com*, sent us this wicked soup recipe. Garam masala is blend of dry-roasted, ground spices. There are many different variations of this spice that you can find it at Indian markets and most supermarkets, or you can check out our version (pg. 210).

| | |
|---|---|
| 1 small onion, chopped | 1 14-oz (411-g) can diced tomatoes |
| 1 stalk celery, chopped | ¼ tsp turmeric |
| ½ tsp mustard seeds | ¼ tsp cumin |
| 1 tbsp olive oil | ¼ tsp cardamom |
| 1 tbsp fresh ginger, grated | ¼ tsp garam masala (pg. 210) |
| 2 cloves garlic, minced | ¼ tsp salt |
| 2-2 ½ cups vegetable stock (pg. 217) | ⅛ tsp cayenne pepper |
| 2 medium potatoes, cubed | 1 tbsp fresh mint, minced |
| 1 large carrot, chopped | 1 tbsp fresh fennel, minced |
| 1 cup cooked or canned chickpeas (garbanzo beans) | 1 cup spinach, chopped |

In a large soup pot on medium heat, sauté the onion, celery, and mustard seeds in oil until the onions are translucent. Add the ginger and garlic and sauté for an additional minute. Add the stock, potatoes, carrot, chickpeas, tomatoes, and stir in the turmeric, cumin, cardamom, garam masala, salt, and cayenne. Bring to a boil, then reduce heat to low. Simmer for 20-30 minutes or until potatoes are cooked. Remove from heat and stir in the mint, fennel, and spinach. Let stand covered for 5 minutes before serving. Makes 4-6 servings.

Salads
& Dressings

*Do the words "Eat your greens!" ring in your ears and conjure up bad thoughts when you think of salad? Fear no more. We've turned those dreaded thoughts into mouth-watering, tantalizing recipes. Salads can complement a variety of dishes, stand on their own as meals, or look good in a picnic basket. However you decide to indulge, bask in wonders of salad. Not only will they appease the palate but they will also provide a nutritious note to your diet. As for salad dressings ... well, they're like the icing on the cake, aren't they? Yum!*

# SALADS

## TANTALIZING TOFU & SPINACH SALAD

Sweet and Sour. Just like Tanya and Sarah!

> **1 lb medium tofu, sliced into strips or cubed**
> **1 tbsp dark sesame oil**
> **¼ cup rice vinegar**
> **1 tbsp Braggs**
> **2 tbsp miso**
> **1 tbsp Asian chili sauce**
> **1 ½ tsp maple syrup**
> **2 tbsp fresh ginger, grated or pickled ginger, chopped**
> **½ cup olive oil**
> **3 stalks green onions, chopped**
> **4 cups spinach, washed and stems removed**
> **1 tbsp gomashio (pg. 209)**

In a saucepan on medium-high heat, sauté the tofu in oil on medium high heat until browned. Set aside to cool. In a blender or food processor, blend the vinegar, Braggs, miso, chili sauce, maple syrup, ginger, and oil until smooth. In a large bowl, combine the green onions and spinach. Top with dressing, tofu, and gomashio. Make 2-4 servings.

# DELIGHTFUL RICE SALAD WITH OLIVES & SUN-DRIED TOMATOES

Rice salad never tasted so good! Sun-dried tomatoes have a chewy, intense flavor that is a perfect counterpart for any olive.

> **1 tbsp apple cider vinegar**
> **1 tbsp balsamic vinegar**
> **4 tbsp olive oil**
> **3 tbsp fresh parsley, chopped**
> **¼ cup rehydrated sun-dried tomatoes (pg. 208)**
> **⅛ tsp salt**
> **⅛ tsp black pepper**
> **2 cups cooked rice (your choice), cooled**
> **½ cup olives (your choice), chopped**
> **2 stalks green onions, chopped**

In a blender or food processor, blend the vinegars, oil, parsley, tomatoes, salt, and pepper. In a large bowl, combine the cooled rice, olives, green onions, and dressing. Toss together and serve. Make 2-4 servings.

# SWEET PEPPER BALSAMIC BEAN SALAD

This tart, tantalizing salad is a must-have for any picnic or potluck.

> **1 medium yellow bell pepper, chopped**
> **1 12-oz (370-ml) jar roasted red peppers, chopped**
> **2 cups cooked or canned black beans**
> **12 cherry tomatoes, halved**
> **2 tbsp fresh parsley, chopped**
> **3 tbsp balsamic vinegar**
> **1 tbsp Worcestershire sauce (pg. 207)**
> **1 tsp dry sweetener**
> **1 tsp dried basil**
> **2 cloves garlic, minced**

In a large bowl, combine the peppers, beans, tomatoes, and parsley. In a small bowl, whisk together the vinegar, Worcestershire sauce, sweetener, basil, and garlic. Pour over salad and toss well. Makes 4-6 servings.

# FANTASTIC DIJON POTATO SALAD

This delicate yet hardy salad is a perfect dish for any picnic or potluck.

- **14 small new potatoes, halved**
- **⅓ cup red wine vinegar**
- **¾ cup olive oil**
- **2 tsp Dijon mustard**
- **1 clove garlic, minced**
- **⅛ tsp black pepper**
- **2 tbsp fresh parsley, chopped**
- **2 tbsp fresh dill, chopped**
- **2 stalks green onion, chopped**
- **1 medium red bell pepper, chopped**

In a medium saucepan, boil potatoes until just tender. Drain and rinse under cold water. Set aside to cool. In a small bowl, whisk together the vinegar, oil, mustard, garlic, and pepper. Set aside. In a medium bowl, gently toss together the potatoes, parsley, dill, green onions, peppers, and dressing. Makes 2-4 servings.

# CLAIRE'S RED & RACY POTATO SALAD

"I always found the generic potato salad very unappetizing, so I invented my own years ago. It's a blend of sweet and spicy tastes. It's always a hit at picnics and now I am passing it on to you so you too can be a potato salad diva." – Claire, Los Angeles, California

- **20 small red pototoes, quartered**
- **½ cup red onions, minced**
- **1 cup seedless red grapes, cut in half**
- **¼ cup fresh cilantro, chopped**
- **¼ cup mayonnaise (pg. 211)**
- **3 tsp Dijon mustard**
- **⅛ tsp black pepper**

In a medium saucepan, boil potatoes until just tender. Drain and rinse under cold water. Set aside to cool. Once potatoes are cooled, combine them in a medium bowl with the onions, grapes, cilantro, mayonnaise, mustard, and pepper. Toss together gently. Makes 4-6 servings.

# AWESOME ASIAN NOODLE SALAD

Too delicious to talk about. Make it now!

**Enough noodles to serve 4 (e.g., rice, buckwheat, udon)**
**½ lb medium-firm tofu, cubed**
**1 tbsp dark sesame oil**
**1 cup mushrooms, chopped (e.g., portabello, shiitake, oyster)**
**1 medium red bell pepper, chopped**
**¼ cup rice wine vinegar**
**3 tbsp Braggs**
**1 tbsp dark sesame oil**
**1 tsp fresh ginger, grated**
**1 tbsp fresh parsley, chopped**

In a large pot of boiling water, cook noodles. Drain and rinse under cold water. Set aside. In a saucepan on medium-high heat, sauté the tofu in oil until tofu starts to brown. Add the mushrooms and sauté for 4 minutes. Stir in red pepper, remove from heat, and set aside to cool. In a small bowl, whisk together the vinegar, Braggs, oil, ginger, and parsley. In a medium bowl, combine the noodles and dressing. Toss with tofu mixture and serve immediately. Makes 2-4 servings.

# AUNTIE BONNIE'S CHICKPEA SALAD

It's a well-known fact that Kramer women love chickpeas and olives! My Auntie Bonnie has managed to merge the two in this unbelievable salad. (S)

**1 lb green beans, cut into 1-inch strips**
**2 cups broccoli, cut into small pieces**
**2 tbsp olive oil**
**2 tbsp balsamic vinegar**
**2 tbsp Braggs**
**1 tbsp lemon juice**
**1 tbsp Dijon mustard**
**1 clove garlic, minced**
**⅛ tsp salt**
**⅛ tsp black pepper**
**2 cups cooked *or* canned chickpeas**
**1 large tomato, diced**
**2 stalks green onion, chopped**
**1 jalapeño pepper, seeded and finely chopped**
**10 pitted olives (your choice), sliced *or* whole**

In a medium saucepan on medium heat, steam beans and broccoli until slightly tender. Rinse under cold water and set aside. In a small bowl, whisk together the oil, vinegar, Braggs, lemon juice, mustard, garlic, salt, and pepper. Set aside. In a large bowl, combine the chickpeas, tomato, onions, jalapeno, olives, green beans, and broccoli. Toss with the dressing and serve immediately. Makes 2-4 servings.

# PERFECTLY AMAZING PASTA SALAD

This is the perfect pasta salad. Once you've had it, you'll wonder how you ever went without!

**3-4 cups cooked pasta (your choice)**
**½ cup rehydrated sun-dried tomatoes, chopped (pg. 208)**
**½ cup olives (your choice), chopped**
**1 small red bell pepper, chopped**
**1 small green bell pepper, chopped**
**¼ cup fresh parsley, chopped**
**1 6-oz (180-ml) jar marinated artichoke hearts, chopped**
**½ cup olive oil**
**2 cloves garlic, minced**
**1 tbsp Dijon mustard**
**2 tbsp apple cider vinegar**
**2 tbsp balsamic vinegar**
**1 tbsp Braggs**
**1 tbsp dry sweetener**
**1 tbsp dried oregano**
**1 tsp dried basil**
**¼ tsp salt**
**¼ tsp black pepper**
**½-1 cup soy cheese, grated (optional)**

In a large bowl, combine the cooked pasta, tomatoes, olives, peppers, parsley, and artichokes. Set aside. In a small bowl, whisk together the oil, garlic, mustard, vinegars, Braggs, sweetener, oregano, basil, salt, and pepper until smooth. Add to the pasta mixture and toss well. Sprinkle with optional soy cheese and serve immediately. Makes 4-6 servings.

# ROASTED BEET, SHALLOT, & PECAN SALAD

Roasting veggies when you're hungry can seem like a step that you can skip. But trust us ... this recipe is worth the wait.

- **4 small beets, peeled and chopped**
- **½ cup shallots, chopped**
- **2 tbsp olive oil**
- **¼ cup olive oil (for dressing)**
- **2 tbsp red wine vinegar**
- **1 large clove garlic, minced**
- **1 head radicchio lettuce, torn**
- **⅔ cup pecans, dry roasted (pg. 209)**
- **⅔ cup soy cheese, optional**

Preheat oven to 450°F. In an 8x8 baking dish, combine the beets and shallots. Drizzle the 2 tbsp oil on top and mix well. Roast for 30 minutes. Set aside. In a small bowl, whisk together the oil, vinegar, and garlic. In a large bowl, add beets, lettuce, pecans, and dressing. Top with optional soy cheese, toss well, and serve immediately. Make 4-6 servings.

# SPINACH SALAD WITH GRILLED TOFU & APPLES

Simply scrumptious!

- **1 lb medium-firm tofu, sliced into strips or cubed**
- **1 tbsp dark sesame oil**
- **5 tbsp olive oil (for dressing)**
- **2 tbsp apple cider vinegar**
- **2 tsp Dijon mustard**
- **2 tsp maple syrup**
- **½ tsp salt**
- **¼ tsp black pepper**
- **4 cups spinach leaves, washed and drained**
- **1 Granny Smith apple, chopped**
- **1 cup fennel, grated**

In a saucepan on medium-high heat, sauté the tofu in sesame oil until browned. Set aside to cool. In a small bowl, whisk together the oil, vinegar, mustard, maple syrup, salt, and pepper. Blend until smooth. In a large bowl, together the spinach, apple, and fennel. Top with dressing and tofu and toss well. Serve ... Make 2-4 servings.

# RUSTIC QUINOA & YAM SALAD

In North America, yams are sometimes called sweet potatoes, and while they are similar, they are from different plant species. If you're confused, ask your grocer. They'll point you in the right direction.

| | |
|---|---|
| 1 cup quinoa | 1 medium red bell pepper, chopped |
| 2 cups water | 1 tsp cumin |
| 1 medium onion, chopped | ¼ fresh cilantro, chopped |
| 2 cloves garlic, minced | 2 tbsp lemon juice |
| 1 ½ cups yams, chopped | 1 tbsp Braggs |
| 2 tbsp olive oil | 1 tbsp maple syrup |

In a medium saucepan, stir together the quinoa and water. Bring to a boil, cover and reduce heat to medium-low. Simmer for 15 minutes or until cooked. Fluff with a fork and set aside to cool. In a large frying pan on medium heat, sauté the onions, garlic, and yams in oil until the yams are tender but firm to the bite. Add the peppers and cumin and sauté for an additional 2 minutes. Set aside until cool. In a large bowl, combine the quinoa, yam mixture, cilantro, lemon juice, Braggs, and maple syrup. Mix well and cool in refrigerator. Serve chilled. Makes 6 servings.

# EXTRAORDINARY QUINOA TABBOULEH

Deliciously tart and refreshing. After trying this tabbouleh with quinoa, you'll never go back to couscous!

- 1 cup quinoa
- 2 cups water
- 3 small tomatoes, chopped
- 1 ½ cups cucumber, seeded and chopped
- 2 stalks green onion, chopped
- 2 medium carrots, chopped
- 6 medium radishes, chopped
- 2 cloves garlic, minced
- ½ cup fresh parsley, chopped
- ¼ cup olive oil
- ¼ cup lemon juice
- 2 tbsp Braggs

In a medium saucepan, stir together the quinoa and water. Bring to a boil, cover and reduce heat to medium-low. Simmer for 15 minutes or until cooked. Fluff with a fork and set aside to cool. In a large bowl, combine tomatoes, cucumber, green onions, carrots, radishes, garlic, parsley, oil, lemon juice, Braggs, and quinoa. Mix well and cool in refrigerator. Serve chilled. Makes 6 servings.

# EXOTIC FRUIT SALAD WITH FRESH MINT SAUCE

Grab your grass skirt and coconut bra and let's get lei'd!

> 1 ½ cups papaya, seeded and roughly chopped
> ¼ cup dry sweetener
> 3 tbsp lime juice
> 1 ½ tbsp fresh mint, chopped
> 4 cups mango, chopped
> 2 cups pineapple, chopped
> ½ cup dried cranberries
> ½ cup flaked unsweetened coconut

In a blender or food processor, blend the papaya, sweetener, lime juice, and mint until smooth. In a large bowl, combine the mango, pineapple, cranberries, and coconut. Top with papaya sauce, mix well, and refrigerate. Serve chilled. Makes 2-4 servings.

# AMAZING GRACE PASTA SALAD

We both fell in love with this pasta salad when we tried it at the Amazing Grace Health Food Store in Louisville, Kentucky. We tried our best to duplicate it ... and we think we came pretty close. Go visit them if you're in the area.

> 5 large stalks asparagus, trimmed and cut into thirds
> 4-5 cups cooked spiral pasta
> 2 tbsp fresh basil, minced
> 1 tbsp Braggs
> 1 small red bell pepper, chopped
> ½ cup snow peas, cut into thirds
> 6-10 cherry tomatoes, whole or halved
> ¾ cup tofu mayonnaise (pg. 211)

In a medium saucepan, steam the asparagus until slightly tender. Rinse under cold water and set aside. In a large bowl, stir together the cooked pasta, asparagus, basil, Braggs, red pepper, snow peas, cherry tomatoes, and mayonnaise and toss well. Make 4-6 servings.

# DRESSINGS

## CAESAR'S WIFE'S DRESSING

Michelle sent in this recipe to us. She says: "This is the best vegan version of Caesar salad dressing I ever had. Good on salads, sandwiches, and great for dipping veggies in."

½ cup soft or silken tofu
2 tbsp miso
1 ½ tbsp lemon juice
1 clove garlic, minced
2 tsp nutritional yeast
¾ cup olive oil
Tabasco to taste
½ tbsp Braggs
1 ½ tsp red wine vinegar

In a blender or food processor, blend all ingredients until smooth and creamy. Makes approx. 1 cup.

## CREAMY DILL DRESSING

This tasty creamy dressing is also good as a veggie dip!

¾ cup soft or silken tofu
3 tbsp apple cider vinegar
2 tbsp fresh dill (*or* 2 tsp dried)
1 tsp salt
pinch of black pepper
1 tsp maple syrup

In a blender or food processor, blend all ingredients until smooth and creamy. Makes approx. 1 cup.

# TOMATO BASIL DRESSING

There is nothing like the fragrance of fresh basil to get your taste buds smacking!

- 1 cup tomato juice
- 2 tbsp apple cider vinegar
- 1 tbsp maple syrup
- 2 tbsp olive oil
- 2 tbsp fresh basil
- 1 tsp Dijon mustard
- ¼ tsp salt
- ⅛ tsp black pepper

In a blender or food processor, blend all ingredients until smooth and creamy. Makes approx. 1 cup.

# BALSAMIC VINAIGRETTE

Quick and easy but oh so good.

- ⅔ cup olive oil
- ¼ cup lemon juice
- 2 tbsp balsamic vinegar
- 2 cloves garlic, minced
- 1 tsp Braggs

In a blender or food processor, blend all ingredients until smooth. Makes approx. 1 cup.

# MAPLE DIJON FLAX OIL DRESSING

Flax contains several essential nutrients including calcium, iron, niacin, phosphorous, and vitamin E. It's also a rich source of Omega-3 fatty acids ... but forget all that. It makes things taste good. That's all you need to know.

- ½ cup flax oil
- 3 tbsp apple cider vinegar
- 2 tbsp water
- 2 tsp maple syrup
- 1 tbsp Dijon mustard
- 1 clove garlic, minced
- 1 tbsp fresh parsley

In a blender or food processor, blend all ingredients until smooth and creamy. Makes approx. ¾ cup.

# ORANGE-SHALLOT VINAIGRETTE

This will add a tangy zip to any salad.

- **6 tbsp fresh orange juice**
- **2 tbsp apple cider vinegar**
- **2 tbsp shallots, minced**
- **1 clove garlic, minced**
- **½ tsp salt**
- **½ cup olive oil**
- **2 tbsp maple syrup**

In a blender or food processor, blend all ingredients until smooth. Makes approx. 1 cup.

# SESAME GINGER DRESSING

This yummy, thick dressing will add flair to any salad!

- **4 tbsp sesame seeds**
- **4 tsp fresh ginger, grated**
- **6 tbsp olive oil**
- **2 tbsp Braggs**
- **2 tbsp rice vinegar**
- **⅛ tsp black pepper**

In a blender or food processor, grind the sesame seeds for 1 minute. Add the ginger, oil, Braggs, vinegar, and pepper. Blend until smooth. Makes approx. ¾ cup.

# SARAH & TANYA'S YOU-MUST-MAKE-THIS DRESSING

Just do what the title tells ya!

- **1 stalk green onion, roughly chopped**
- **2 cloves garlic, minced**
- **2 tbsp maple syrup**
- **4 tbsp apple cider vinegar**
- **1 tsp Dijon mustard**
- **1 tsp fresh chives**
- **1 tsp fresh dill**
- **1 tsp fresh parsley**
- **½ cup olive oil**
- **½ tsp salt**

In a blender or food processor, blend all ingredients until smooth. Makes approx. ¾ cup.

# CREAMY CUCUMBER DILL DRESSING

A fresh and surprising dressing that will put the yum back into yummy.

> **1 medium cucumber, peeled, seeded, and chopped**
> **2 tbsp fresh dill (*or* 2 tsp dry)**
> **¼ cup olive oil**
> **2 cloves garlic, minced**
> **½ tsp salt**
> **⅛ tsp black pepper**

In a blender or food processor, blend all ingredients until smooth. Makes approx. 1 cup.

# LEMON POPPY SEED DRESSING

Poppy seeds have a crunchy, nutty flavor that make this dressing a perfect accompaniment to any salad.

> **¾ cup soft or silken tofu**
> **3 tbsp lemon juice**
> **1 tbsp apple cider vinegar**
> **2 tbsp olive oil**
> **1 tbsp maple syrup**
> **2 tsp poppy seeds**
> **½ tsp salt**
> **⅛ tsp black pepper**

In a blender or food processor, blend all ingredients until smooth. Makes approx. 1 cup.

# SARAH'S SESAME DRESSING

After many months of working feverishly in the Garden of Vegan lab combining ingredients, I think I have invented the perfect dressing. Dr. Frankenstein would be proud. (S)

> **4 tbsp tahini**
> **2 tbsp rice vinegar**
> **2 tbsp Braggs**
> **2 tbsp dark sesame oil**
> **2 cloves garlic, minced**
> **¼ cup olive oil**
> **½ tsp black pepper**
> **2 tbsp fresh parsley, minced**

In a blender or food processor, blend all ingredients until smooth. Makes approx. 1 cup.

# MO KELLY'S [PAT KELLY'S SISTER] SALAD DRESSING

Our good friend Maureen makes an amazing salad dressing that we begged her to share with you. She doesn't use measurements in her recipes, but for us, she did. We love you, Mo!

> **½ cup olive oil (*or* flax oil *or* ½ olive and ½ flax)**
> **¼ cup balsamic vinegar (*or* apple cider vinegar *or* lemon juice)**
> **⅛ cup Braggs**
> **1 tsp Dijon mustard**
> **2-3 cloves garlic**
> **pinch of black pepper**
> **2 tbsp fresh herbs, minced (basil, oregano, mint, *or* a combination)**

In a blender or food processor, blend all ingredients until smooth. Makes approx. 1 cup.

Appies &
Snacks

# APPETIZERS

*Appetizers are great way to start a meal, as long as you don't eat too many and ruin your appetite. Appies are also great for potlucks (pg. 233), lunchboxes (pg. 52), and picnic hampers. The sky is the limit with appies from The Garden of Vegan!*

## HOT ARTICHOKE BAKE

This delectable recipe will have you reaching for more, but make sure to grab a new chip, don't double dip!

> **2 6-oz (156-ml) jars of artichoke hearts, drained and roughly chopped**
> **½ cup mayonnaise (pg. 211)**
> **½ cup non-dairy cream cheese**
> **¼ tsp salt**
> **¼ tsp black pepper**
> **4 tbsp soy Parmesan cheese**

Preheat oven to 350°F. In a large bowl, combine the artichoke hearts, mayonnaise, cream cheese, salt, pepper, and 2 tbsp of soy Parmesan. Mix together well and spoon into an 8x8 baking dish. Sprinkle top with remaining soy Parmesan and bake for 25-30 minutes or until top begins to brown.

## SARAH KRAMER'S STUFFED MUSHROOMS

This recipe comes from Sarah Kramer. No, not me, but my beautiful sister in-law. It's scrumptious and yummy...much like Sarah herself! Ⓢ

> **15 large mushrooms**
> **2 small carrots, roughly chopped**
> **1 small zucchini, roughly chopped**
> **4 tbsp margarine**
> **4 cloves garlic, minced**
> **1 ½ tbsp fresh parsley, minced**
> **⅛ tsp salt**
> **⅛ tsp black pepper**
> **2 tbsp soy Parmesan cheese (optional)**

Preheat oven to 350°F. Remove stems from mushrooms. Set stems aside. In a blender or food processor, combine the mushroom stems, carrots, and zucchini until they are finely chopped. In a large saucepan on medium heat, sauté the vegetable mixture in margarine for 2 minutes. Add the garlic and parsley and cook for an additional minute. Season with salt and pepper. Set aside to cool. Place the mushroom caps on a 9x13 baking dish. Fill caps with the vegetable mixture, and sprinkle with soy Parmesan. Bake for 15 minutes, or until mushooms are browned. Cool before serving.

# TOMATO BASIL BRUSCHETTA

Bruschetta is Italian for "to roast over coals"; this traditional garlic bread can be made before hand but is best when heated and served warm. The fresh flavors of basil and tomato make this appie "top notch" and a real crowd pleaser.

> **2 cups fresh tomatoes, chopped**
> **1 cup fresh basil, chopped**
> **½ small red onion, minced**
> **⅛ tsp black pepper**
> **3 cloves garlic, grated *or* finely chopped**
> **1 tbsp olive oil**
> **1 French baguette, halved and sliced (pg. 167)**
> **2 tbsp flax oil**

Preheat oven to 400°F. In a small bowl, combine the tomato, basil, onion, and pepper, and mix well. Set aside. In a small bowl, stir together the garlic and olive oil. With a knife, spread garlic mixture over each slice and arrange bread on baking sheet. Place in oven and bake until lightly toasted (approx 5-7 minutes). Place bread on serving tray and spoon tomato mixture on top. Drizzle with flax oil before serving. Serve immediately.

# ANTIPASTO

Antipasto (a.k.a. single dish of antipasti) is very easy to make because all the ingredients go into one pot. The variety of vegetable flavors combine to make a tasty dish, and it's also a great way to make the most use of the garden. This dish also freezes easily so you can keep it on hand all year around, making it great for impromptu get-togethers! Serve with crackers or bread.

> **1 cup red wine vinegar**
> **1 5.5-oz (156-ml) tin of tomato paste**
> **½ cup maple syrup**
> **2 tbsp Worcestershire sauce (pg. 207)**
> **1 tbsp salt**
> **1 tsp hot sauce (your choice)**
> **20 green beans, chopped**
> **1 cup cauliflower, chopped**
>
> **½ small zucchini, chopped**
> **1 small onion, chopped**
> **1 small red bell pepper, chopped**
> **4-6 mushrooms, chopped**
> **½ medium carrot, chopped**
> **½ cup olives (your choice), chopped**
> **4 cloves garlic, chopped**
> **1 tbsp fresh basil, chopped (*or* 1 tsp dried basil)**

In a large soup pot on high heat, combine the vinegar, tomato paste, maple syrup, Worcestershire sauce, salt, and hot sauce and bring to a boil. Add the beans, cauliflower, zucchini, onion, red pepper, mushrooms, carrots, olives, and garlic. Reduce heat to medium-low and simmer uncovered until vegetables are extremely tender, about 15-20 minutes. Remove from heat. Stir in basil. Let cool. Serve well chilled.
Makes approx. 6 cups.

# NOT PIGS IN A BLANKET

Okay, so the title of this recipe probably makes you cringe a little and conjures up bad memories of hot dogs that made your tummy ache, but we couldn't think of a better name.

> **Biscuit dough (pg. 174)**
> **6 tofu hot dogs, cut into thirds**

Preheat oven to 475°F. Roll out flat half of the biscuit dough on a lightly floured surface and cut into strips 2x4 inches. Roll hot dog piece in dough and lay on lightly oiled baking sheet. Repeat with remaining ingredients. Bake for 8-10 minutes or until browned. Makes 18 pigs.

# MILLER'S MAGNIFICENT 5-LAYER DIP

One of the dishes I bring out to impress my non-vegan friends and family is this 5-layer bean dip with faux sour cream. I think it shows that vegans can enjoy some of the foods that were once thought of as beyond our culinary capabilities. – David Miller, Victoria, BC

> **1 small onion, chopped**
> **2 garlic cloves, minced**
> **1 tbsp olive oil**
> **1 small red bell pepper, chopped**
> **1 ½ cups refried beans (pg. 114)**
> **¾ cup salsa**
> **¾ cup soy sour cream**
> **¼ cup soy cheese, grated**

In a medium saucepan on medium heat, sauté the onion and garlic in oil until the onions are translucent. Add the red pepper and sauté for 1 minute more. Add the beans and mix until well combined. Cook for 5 minutes on medium-low heat. In a medium bowl, spread out half the bean mixture. Layer with salsa, sour cream, remaining bean mixture, and cheese (in that order). Serve with tortilla chips for dipping. Makes approx. 4 cups.

# DOLMADES

These classic Greek appetizers are grape leaves stuffed with a tantalizing mixture of rice and herbs. The brine the grapes leaves are packed in is quite strong and salty, so be sure to rinse the leaves under cold water before using. Once you make these, you'll never go back to store-bought.

**1 small onion, chopped**
**1 tsp dried dill**
**1 tsp dried mint**
**1 tbsp olive oil**
**2 cups cooked rice**
**3-4 tbsp lemon juice *or* apple cider vinegar**
**2 tbsp olive oil (for mixture)**
**½ tsp salt**
**20 grape leaves, rinsed**

In a small saucepan on medium heat, sauté the onions, dill, and mint in oil until the onions are translucent. Set aside to cool. In a large bowl, combine the rice, lemon juice, oil, salt, and onion mixture. Mix well. On a flat surface, lay out one grape leaf. Place approx. two tablespoons of the rice mixture in the middle towards stem end. Fold sides over filling. Starting at stem end of leaf, roll up tightly. Make 20 rolls.

# TANYA'S LAZY QUESADILLA

The best thing about being a lazy vegan is that you can be a lazy cook too! Traditionally, a quesadilla is a flour tortilla filled with a savoury mixture and folded in half to form a turnover. But I usually just put filling in between two tortillas and cook it that way. Either method is sure to please. Serve with salsa (pg. 131) and soy sour cream. Ⓣ

**4 tortillas**
**1 ½-2 cups soy cheese, grated**
**1 medium bell pepper (your choice), sliced**
**2 stalks green onion, chipped**
**⅓ cup sundried tomatoes, chopped**

In a medium saucepan, place one tortilla flat down and top with half the cheese, pepper, green onion, and tomatoes. Lay another tortilla on top. Cook on medium/low heat until both sides are browned and soy cheese is melted. Repeat same process with remaining ingredients. Makes 2-4 servings.

# SONIA'S FALAFELS

This lovely recipe comes from Sonia in Vancouver. You can make falafel balls or squash them down to make patties. Either way, they're delish.

**2 cups cooked *or* canned chickpeas**
**2-4 cloves garlic, minced**
**2 tbsp fresh cilantro *or* parsley**
**1 tsp dried mint**
**½ tsp cumin**
**2 tbsp flour**
**½ cup medium-firm tofu**
**1 tsp salt**
**⅛ tsp black pepper**
**1 tbsp olive oil**

In a blender or food processor, combine all the ingredients and blend until well mixed. Roll mixture with wet hands into balls. In a medium frying pan, sauté balls on medium-high heat in oil until browned on all sides. Makes 10 large or 18 small balls.

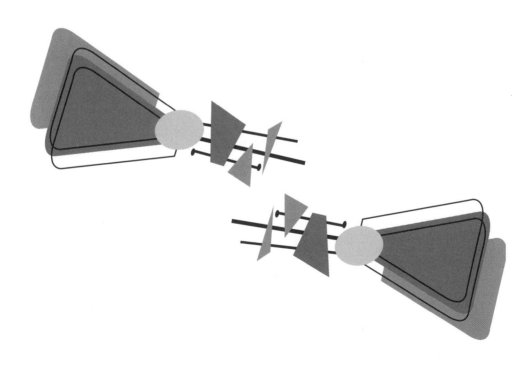

# SNACKS

*Store-bought junk food can be gross – most are packed with ingredients you can't pronounce and often contain animal ingredients. I mean, do you really need beef tallow to make a donut? We don't think so. Feast your eyes on some of the best vegan snack food recipes ever invented!*

## NANA MARG'S NUTS AND BOLTS

When I told my Nana that her recipe was going to be available for the world to enjoy, she blushed! Now, go and make my Nana proud. (T)

**4 tbsp olive oil**
**4 tsp lemon juice *or* apple cider vinegar**
**2 tbsp Braggs**
**½ tsp garlic powder**
**½ tsp onion powder**
**1 tsp salt**

**1 cup nuts (your choice, e.g., almonds, cashews, etc.)**
**1 cup pretzels**
**½ cup raw pumpkin seeds**
**1 cup sesame sticks**
**3 cups Rice Chex-style cereal**
**3 cups Cheerios-style cereal**

Preheat oven to 250°F. In a small bowl, whisk together the oil, lemon juice, Braggs, garlic powder, onion powder, and salt. In a large bowl, combine the nuts, pretzels, pumpkin seeds, sesame sticks, and cereals. Stir in the sauce and toss well. Pour onto a large cookie sheet or lasagna pan. Bake for 45 minutes, stirring every 15 minutes. Makes aproximately 9 cups.

## CRACKER JANES POPCORN

We don't want to get in trouble with your dentist, so make sure you floss your teeth after you eat this creation!

**8 cups popcorn**
**2 cups peanuts (*or* 1 cup peanuts and 1 cup various nuts)**
**½ cup margarine**
**1 cup dry sweetener**
**½ cup dark corn syrup**
**½ tsp salt**
**½ tsp baking powder**

Preheat oven to 250°F. In a large bowl, combine the popcorn and peanuts. Set aside. In a medium saucepan, bring the margarine, sweetener, corn syrup, and salt to a boil. Reduce heat and simmer for 5 minutes, stirring occasionally. Whisk in baking powder until smooth. Pour over popcorn and stir until well mixed. Pour into lightly oiled 9x13 lasagana pan. Bake for one hour, stirring occasionally. Cool and break up into small chunks. Makes approx. 6 cups.

# SPICY PARMESAN POPCORN

The aroma of this spicy concoction will have you drooling like Pavlov's dog.

¼ cup flax oil
2 tsp all-purpose spice (pg. 210)
⅓ cup soy Parmesan cheese
large bowl of popped popcorn

In a small bowl, stir together the flax oil and spice. Stir into popcorn. Add Parmesan and mix well. Serve.

# TROPICAL CRUNCH

A crunchy and exotic change from the usual trail mix.

3 cups Rice Chex-style cereal
1 cup various nuts, your choice
1 cup dried banana chips (pg. 110)
2 tbsp olive oil
2 tbsp maple syrup
½ tsp cinnamon

¼ tsp salt
½ cup raisins
¼ cup dried pineapple
¼ cup dried papaya
4 cups popped popcorn
1 cup grated coconut

Preheat oven to 300°F. In a large baking dish, combine the cereal, nuts, and banana chips. In a small bowl, stir together the oil, maple syrup, cinnamon, and salt. Pour mixture over cereal mix and toss until evenly coated. Bake for 8-10 minutes, stirring once. Let cool. In a large bowl, combine the cooled cereal mixture, raisins, pineapple, papaya, popcorn, and coconut and mix well. Makes approx. 10 cups.

# BANANA CHIPS

These are a delicious, chewy version of what you can buy in the store. If you get store-bought, check the ingredients, because some banana chips are NOT vegan.

**2 tbsp lemon juice**
**3 tbsp maple syrup**
**2 bananas, sliced into coin-sized pieces**

Preheat oven to 200°F. In a small bowl, stir together the lemon juice and maple syrup. Dip each banana slice in the lemon juice mixture and place on a lightly oiled cookie sheet. Bake for two to three hours, flipping occasionally to prevent burning. Makes approx. 1 cup.

# SPICY MAPLE NUTS

These three spiced nut recipes can be used on top of salads, desserts or taken to the movies as a snack.

**¼ cup maple syrup**
**½ tsp salt**
**½ tsp cayenne pepper**
**½ tsp cinnamon**
**1 ½ cups nuts (your choice, e.g., walnuts, pecans, almonds, etc.)**

In a small bowl, stir the maple syrup, salt, cayenne, and cinnamon. In a large fry pan, stir the nuts over medium-high heat for 2-5 minutes, or until they begin to look toasted. Stir in the maple syrup mixture and cook 15-30 seconds, or until liquid is evaporated. Remove from heat and let cool. Makes 2 cups.

# ALL-PURPOSE SPICE NUTS

**2 cup nuts (your choice, e.g., walnuts, pecans, almonds, etc.)**
**2 tbsp Braggs**
**2-3 tsp all-purpose spice (pg. 210)**

In a large frying pan, stir the nuts over medium-high heat for 2-5 minutes, or until they begin to look toasted. Stir in the Braggs and all-purpose seasoning and cook 15-30 seconds, or until liquid is evaporated. Remove from heat and let cool. Makes 2 cups.

# BBQ NUTS

**2 cup nuts (your choice, e.g., walnuts, pecans, almonds, etc.)**
**½ cup barbecue sauce (pg. 141)**
**dash cayenne pepper**

In a large frying pan, stir the nuts over medium-high heat for 2-5 minutes, or until they begin to look toasted. Stir in the barbecue sauce and cayenne and cook 15-30 seconds, or until sauce is evaporated. Remove from heat and let cool. Makes 2 cups.

Side Dishes

*Side dishes are a fun way to add pizzazz to your meal. While planning out your dinner, sit back and try to figure out what element might be missing. Choose something that will complement and accentuate your meal, and make it complete!*

# ZOE'S GRANDMA'S ROASTED NEW POTATOES

Zoe at *acherecords.com* sent us her grandma's recipe for Roasted New Potatoes. Yum yum yum!

**10 small new potatoes, quartered**
**5 cloves garlic, halved**
**1 small onion, diced**
**1 tbsp olive oil**
**1 tsp lemon juice**
**1 tsp dried dill**
**1 tsp dried rosemary**
**⅛ tsp salt**
**⅛ tsp black pepper**

Preheat oven to 375°F. In a large bowl, combine all the ingredients and toss well until potatoes are well covered. Spread out onto a 9x13 baking pan. Roast for 35-45 minutes. Stir occasionally to prevent burning. Makes 2-4 servings.

# BALSAMIC ROASTED SWEET POTATOES & SQUASH

Sweet potatoes are easy to prepare, extremely versatile, highly nutritious in vitamin A, and a good source of potassium and vitamins C and B6.

**2 large sweet potatoes, chopped**
**1 medium squash (your choice), chopped**
**2-3 tbsp olive oil**
**1 ½ tbsp balsamic vinegar**
**1 tbsp fresh rosemary, minced**
**1 tsp salt**
**1 tsp black pepper**

Preheat oven to 400°F. In a large bowl, combine all the ingredients and toss. Spread out on a 9x13 baking pan and roast in oven for 40-50 minutes or until vegetables can be pierced easily with fork and top is golden brown. Makes 4-6 servings.

# REFRIED BEANS

A simply delicious recipe sent in to us by Kelly from somewhere in cyberspace.

**2 tbsp margarine**
**2 cups cooked** *or* **canned pinto beans**
**1 small onion, chopped**
**¼ tsp salt**
**¼ tsp black pepper**

In a medium saucepan on medium-high heat, melt the margarine until it's bubbling. Add the beans and let cook for 3 minutes. Add the onions, salt, and pepper, but do not stir. Reduce heat to medium and cook until onions have softened. Mash the beans with a potato masher or the back of a spoon. Makes approx. 2 cups.

# BABY CARROTS IN DILL-CHIVE SAUCE

Folklore has it that burning dill leaves will clear away thunderstorms. We don't know if that's true, but we do know that fresh dill will lose its fragrance during cooking, so be sure to follow the recipe and add it after you have removed the sauce from heat.

**1 lb baby carrots (approx. 3 cups)**
**2 tbsp olive oil**
**1 tbsp flour**
**⅔ cup soy milk**
**1 ½ tbsp fresh dill, minced**
**1 tbsp fresh chives, minced**
**¼ tsp salt**

In a steamer, steam the carrots until just tender. In a small saucepan on medium heat, whisk together the oil and flour for one minute, stirring constantly. Add the soy milk and bring to a boil, stirring frequently until sauce thickens. Remove from heat and stir in the dill, chives, and salt. Place carrots in serving bowl and top with sauce. Makes 4-6 servings.

# SAUTÉED CAULIFLOWER & CILANTRO

Cauliflower is a member of the cabbage family. The entire vegetable can be consumed, including the leaves, so throw the whole shebang in there. Waste not, want not!

**2 cloves garlic, minced**
**2 tbsp dark sesame oil**
**½ large cauliflower, separated into tiny florets**
**½ cup fresh cilantro, chopped**

In a large saucepan on medium-low heat, sauté the garlic in oil until it starts to soften. Add the cauliflower and saute on medium-high heat, tossing until well coated with oil. Cover and let cook until cauliflower can be pierced easily with a fork, about 4-5 minutes. Stir in the cilantro, cover, and remove from heat. Let sit for 1 minute before serving. Makes 2-4 servings.

# GREEN BEAN & FENNEL TOSS

This is a wonderful Asian-inspired dish that combines the necessary daily greens with wonderful flavors. Bet you never thought that eating good could be so delicious.

**1 tbsp fresh ginger, grated**
**2 tbsp dark sesame oil**
**3 green onions, sliced**
**1 cup snow peas, cut into thirds**
**½ cup green beans, cut into thirds**
**½ cup fennel, finely chopped**
**1 cup bok choy, chopped**
**1 tbsp Braggs**
**1 tsp white wine vinegar**
**2 tbsp gomashio (pg. 209)**

In a large saucepan, sauté the ginger in oil on medium-low heat for 2 minutes. Add the onions, snow peas, green beans, fennel, and bok choy and cook on medium high, for 3-4 minutes or until fennel is cooked. Add the Braggs, vinegar, and gomashio. Cook for an additional minute and serve. Makes 2-4 servings.

# NEW POTATOES WITH FRESH ROSEMARY & THYME

Everyone loves the taste of nutrient-rich potatoes, so it's easy to prepare healthy dishes that both adults and kids will eat. We suggest going back for seconds!

> **20 new potatoes, halved**
> **1 medium onion, chopped**
> **1 tbsp olive oil**
> **2 cloves garlic, sliced**
> **1 tbsp fresh rosemary**
> **1 tbsp fresh thyme**
> **⅛ tsp salt**
> **⅛ tsp black pepper**

In a large frying pan on medium-high heat, sauté the potatoes and onions in oil until the potatoes can be pierced easily with a fork. Add the garlic, rosemary, thyme, salt, and pepper and sauté for an additional 2-5 minutes until potatoes are golden brown. Makes 2-4 servings.

# CARAMELIZED ONION & FENNEL MASHED POTATOES

It's a good thing that potatoes are classified as a vegetable; they contribute to your daily recommended intake of fruits and vegetables. Smother this one in gravy (pg. 140) and dig in!

> **3-4 medium potatoes, cubed**
> **1 medium onion, chopped**
> **1 small fennel bulb, finely chopped**
> **1 tsp dry sweetener**
> **1 tsp salt**
> **½ tsp pepper**
> **2 tbsp olive oil**
> **½ cup soy milk**
> **2 tbsp flax oil**

In a large pot on high heat, boil the potatoes in water until they can be pierced easily with a fork. While potatoes are cooking, in a large saucepan on medium heat, sauté the onion, fennel, sweetener, salt, and pepper in oil until onions are translucent. Set aside. Mash potatoes with soy milk and flax oil. Stir in onion mixture and mix well. Make 4 servings.

# CHICKPEAS & SWISS CHARD

This yummy recipe makes an excellent side dish, or it can be served over rice garnished with flax oil and Braggs.

**1 small onion, chopped**
**2-3 cloves garlic, minced**
**1 ½ tbsp dark sesame oil**
**1 large tomato, chopped**
**2 cups cooked** *or* **canned chickpeas**
**¼ tsp salt**
**¼ tsp black pepper**
**½ tbsp lemon juice**
**3-4 cups Swiss chard, roughly chopped**

In a large saucepan on medium heat, sauté the onion and garlic in oil until the onions are translucent. Add the tomato, chickpeas, salt, and pepper and let simmer for 5 minutes. Stir in the lemon juice and lay the chard on top. Turn off heat; cover and let sit for 2 minutes. Makes 2-4 servings.

# FRIED PINEAPPLE RICE

Let us fill you in on an ancient secret: really delicious fried rice lies in the use of cooled, cooked rice. Freshly cooked rice will only produce a sticky mess. Tropical pineapple gives this dish the aroma and taste of paradise! It's delish served hot or cold.

**1 small onion, chopped**
**1 tbsp sesame oil**
**1 tbsp Braggs**
**2-3 cups cooked rice, cooled**
**½-¾ cup pineapple, chopped**
**1 small tomato, chopped**
**2 tbsp raisins**
**1 tsp curry**
**½ tsp turmeric**
**⅛ tsp salt**
**⅛ tsp black pepper**
**2 tbsp fresh cilantro, chopped**

In a large saucepan on medium heat, sauté the onions in oil until the onions are translucent. Add the Braggs, cooked rice, pineapple, tomato, raisins, curry, and turmeric. Mix thoroughly and cook for 6-8 minutes or until all ingredients are heated throughout. Season with salt and pepper, and garnish with cilantro.
Makes 4-6 servings.

# FANTASTIC FRAGRANT RICE

If you're in a hurry you can also use basmati or jasmine rice, just make sure you adjust the cooking time accordingly.

**1 cup brown rice**
**2 cups water**
**1 tsp turmeric**
**1 tsp five-spice powder (pg. 210)**
**2 tbsp Braggs**

In a medium pot on high heat, combine all the ingredients and bring to a boil. Cover with lid, reduce heat, and simmer for 40-45 minutes or until rice is cooked. Makes 2-4 servings.

# ZUCCHINI WITH TOMATOES & MARJORAM

This is a simple but rewarding dish. Zucchinis are easy to grow, as they can thrive in most climates. They're also extremely versatile. From entrées to cakes, you can put them in almost any dish.

**3 cups zucchini, chopped**
**2-3 cloves garlic, minced**
**1 tbsp olive oil**
**3 medium Roma tomatoes, chopped**
**1 tsp dried marjoram**
**1 tsp dried oregano**
**¼ tsp salt**
**¼ tsp black pepper**
**2 tbsp soy parmesan (optional)**

In a large saucepan on medium heat, sauté the zucchini and garlic in oil until zucchini is tender but firm to the bite. Add the tomato, marjoram, oregano, salt, and pepper and cook an additional 1-2 minutes. Garnish with soy parmesan. Makes 2-4 servings.

# SWISS CHARD & GARLIC

Swiss chard is a versatile and often overlooked green. A member of the beet family, it's a good source of vitamins A and C, as well as iron. You can substitute kale for the chard in this recipe.

**2-3 cloves garlic, minced**
**1 tbsp dark sesame oil**
**3 cups Swiss chard, chopped**

In large saucepan on medium-low heat, sauté the garlic in oil until it's tender. Lay the chard on top. Turn off heat; cover with lid and let sit for 2 minutes. Toss and serve. Makes 2-4 servings.

# CHARMING FENNEL ROASTED VEGETABLES

Roasting vegetables is an easy way to bring out their intense flavor. You can roast all kinds of vegetables, either alone or in combination with others.

> **1 large red onion, roughly chopped**
> **2 small zucchinis (approx 4 cups), roughly chopped**
> **10-12 mushrooms, chopped**
> **10 stalks asparagus, trimmed and cut into thirds**
> **1 red bell pepper, seeded and roughly chopped**
> **6-10 cloves garlic**
> **¼ cup olive oil**
> **1 tsp fennel seeds**
> **½ tsp red pepper flakes**
> **⅛ tsp salt**
> **⅛ tsp black pepper**
> **2 tbsp red wine vinegar**

Preheat oven to 400°F. In a large bowl, combine all the vegetables. Add oil, fennel seeds, red pepper flakes, salt, and pepper, and toss until vegetables are well coated. Spread vegetables out onto a large baking sheet and roast for 25-30 minutes. Stir vegetables occasionally to prevent burning. Once cooked, place back into bowl and stir in vinegar. Toss together and serve. Makes 4-6 servings.

# GARLIC ASPARAGUS

Asparagus is best when bought fresh, but it can be refrigerated for two or three days. Wrap stem ends in damp paper towels, then cover entire bunch with plastic wrap, or stand straight up in a container of water.

> **15 stalks asparagus, trimmed and cut into thirds**
> **2 tbsp olive oil**
> **4 cloves garlic, minced**
> **1 tbsp parsley, chopped**
> **⅛ tsp salt**
> **⅛ tsp black pepper**

In a steamer, steam asparagus until "just" tender. In a large saucepan on medium-low heat, sauté the garlic, parsley, salt, and pepper in oil until garlic is softened. Add the asparagus and sauté for an additional minute. Makes 2-4 servings.

# SAUTEED SHIITAKE & RED PEPPERS

This delish dish comes from our good friend Chris Harris. Shiitake stems are very tough and should be removed before cooking, but don't throw them out; they can be used to flavor stocks or soups.

**8-10 shiitake mushrooms, sliced**
**2 whole bay leaves**
**1 tbsp olive oil**
**1 medium red bell pepper, sliced**
**1 tsp-½ tbsp cracked black pepper (you decide the heat)**

In a medium saucepan on medium-high heat, sauté the shiitake mushrooms and bay leaves in oil until the mushrooms have browned. Add the red peppers and sauté until tender, about 3-5 minutes. Remove bay leaves, stir in pepper, and serve. Makes 2 servings.

# MATTHEW'S DELICIOUS TOFU

Just like Matthew, this dish is spicy, sweet, and salty. In other words, delectable!

**1 lb medium-firm tofu, chopped**
**2 tbsp olive oil**
**3 cloves garlic, minced**
**1 tbsp fresh ginger, grated**
**¼ tsp dried chili, _or_ 1 tsp Asian chili sauce**
**⅛ cup maple syrup**
**⅛ cup Braggs**
**1 tsp lemon juice**
**¼ cup dry roasted almonds, chopped (garnish) (pg. 209)**

In a medium saucepan on medium-high heat, sauté the tofu in oil until browned. Reduce heat to medium-low and add the garlic, ginger, and chili. Sauté for 5 minutes. Add the maple syrup, Braggs, and lemon juice. Cover and cook until the liquid has evaporated. Garnish with almonds. Make 2-4 servings.

# SHAKE'N FRY

An easy and scrumptious breading recipe.

- **½ cup Cornflake-like cereal**
- **¼ cup flour**
- **1 tsp salt**
- **¼ tsp paprika**
- **¼ tsp dry sweetener**
- **¼ tsp garlic powder**
- **¼ tsp onion powder**
- **½ lb medium-firm tofu, sliced *or* cubed**
- **1 tbsp olive oil**

In a blender or food processor, combine the cereal, flour, salt, paprika, sweetener, garlic, and onion powder, and blend until well combined. In a medium-sized plastic bag (with no holes), combine the tofu and the cereal mixture and shake until well coated. In a medium saucepan on medium heat, sauté the tofu mixture in oil until browned. Makes 1-2 servings.

# BREADED & FRIED TOFU

"This is a breading recipe I've been having some fun with. It's for those times that I want something sort of greasy and fried, but not all that bad for me. I use firm tofu that has been frozen and then thawed." – Jane, Ann Arbor, Michigan

- **½ cup flour**
- **2 tbsp nutritional yeast**
- **2 tsp all-purpose seasoning (pg. 210)**
- **1 lb firm tofu, sliced *or* cubed**
- **2 tbsp olive oil**

In a medium-sized plastic bag, combine the flour, yeast, and seasoning. Add the tofu and shake until well coated. In a medium saucepan on medium heat, sauté the tofu mixture in oil until browned. Makes 2-4 servings.

# ZOE AND ANDY'S SESAME TOFU

This recipe rocks ... almost as much as all the *music @ acherecords.com*

> **4 tsp Braggs**
> **2 tsp Asian chili sauce**
> **2 tsp nutritional yeast**
> **4 tsp sesame seeds**
> **½ lb firm tofu, sliced *or* cubed**
> **1 tsp olive oil**

In a small bowl, combine the Braggs, chili sauce, yeast, and sesame seeds. Stir in the tofu and let marinate for 5 minutes. In a medium saucepan on medium-high heat, sauté the tofu and sauce in oil until the tofu is browned. Makes 1-2 servings.

# BARBECUE TOFU

Who said that vegans can't enjoy a good barbecue dish? Temp your taste buds with a mouth-watering dish good for all seasons.

> **1 lb firm tofu, sliced *or* cubed**
> **½ cup barbecue sauce (pg. 141)**
> **1 tbsp olive oil**

In a small bowl, combine the tofu and barbecue sauce and stir together until tofu is well coated. Let marinate for 5 minutes. In a medium saucepan on medium-high heat, sauté the tofu and sauce in oil until the tofu is browned. Makes 2-4 servings.

# MO-MO'S FALAFELS

Shhhh, don't tell Mo that we stole her delicious falafel recipe ... serve with Tahini Sauce (pg. 141)!

> **2 cups cooked *or* canned chickpeas**     **2 tbsp fresh parsley**
> **2 cloves garlic, roughly chopped**          **2 tbsp water**
> **1 tsp turmeric**                                      **1 ½ tsp lemon juice**
> **½ tsp salt**                                            **2 ½ tbsp flour**
> **¼ cup onion, roughly chopped**              **1 tbsp olive oil**

In a blender or food processor, blend the chickpeas, garlic, turmeric, salt, onion, parsley, water, and lemon juice until well mixed. Add the flour and blend until well mixed. Roll mixture with wet hands into balls. In a medium frying pan on medium-high heat, sauté balls in oil until browned on all sides. Makes 10 large or 18 small balls.

# MEGADARRA

This lovely and very simple dish comes from Ruthie in Boston. Garnish with flax oil ... yum!

> **1 large onion, roughly chopped**
> **1 tbsp dark sesame oil**
> **2 cups cooked *or* canned brown lentils**
> **1 tbsp Braggs**
> **¼ tsp black pepper**
> **1 tsp cumin**
> **1 large tomato, chopped**
> **1 ½ cups cooked basmati rice**

In a large saucepan on medium heat, sauté the onions in oil until translucent. Stir in lentils, Braggs, pepper, cumin, and tomato, and sauté for an additional 4-6 minutes. In a large bowl, toss lentils with cooked rice. Makes 2-4 servings.

# SWEE'S ROSEMARY MOCK CHICKEN

This is from the lovely *RandomGirl.com*!

> **3 cups seitan (pg. 208)**
> **1 tbsp dark sesame oil**
> **2 tsp dried rosemary**
> **1 tsp dried thyme**
> **½ tsp dried sage**
> **3 cloves garlic, minced**
> **1 tbsp Braggs**

In a large saucepan on medium-high heat, sauté the seitan in oil until it starts to brown. Add the rosemary, thyme, sage, garlic, and Braggs and sauté for an additional 3 minutes. Makes 2-4 servings.

# COCONUT CURRY VEGETABLE BAKE

A real treat for us lazy vegans, this is an incredible dish that is a snap to make.

**1 14-oz (398-ml) can coconut milk**
**1 tbsp Braggs**
**2 tsp curry powder**
**1 tsp turmeric**
**1 tsp black pepper**
**2 medium potatoes, chopped**
**2 small yams, chopped**
**1 medium onion, chopped**

Preheat oven to 350°F. In a small bowl, whisk together the coconut milk, Braggs, curry, turmeric, and pepper. In a lightly oiled 8x8 baking dish, lay alternating layers of potatoes, yams, and onions. Pour coconut milk mixture over layers. Bake uncovered for 45-50 minutes. Makes 2-4 servings.

# JEN'S VEGGIE RICE BALLS

"I serve these with a nice crisp salad, with pesto or gravy on the side for dipping. These balls are great served up cold, and they freeze well too. Make a big batch on the weekend, so you'll have something for those days when you just don't feel like cooking." – Jen, Kingston, Ontario

**¼ lb firm tofu, crumbled**
**½ cup vegetable stock**
**2 tbsp rolled oat flakes**
**1 ½ tbsp Braggs**
**½ cup fresh parsley**
**1 tsp dried basil**
**¼ tsp black pepper**
**½ cup bread crumbs**
**½ cup black olives, chopped**
**1 stalk celery, finely chopped**
**1 small onion, finely chopped**
**1 clove garlic, finely chopped**
**1 ½ cups cooked rice**
**½ cup bread crumbs (for coating)**

Preheat over to 400°F. In a blender or food processor, blend the tofu, stock, oat flakes, Braggs, and parsley until well mixed. Transfer mixture to a large bowl and add the basil, pepper, bread crumbs, olives, celery, onion, garlic, and cooked rice, and mix well. Place bread crumbs for coating on a large plate. Form mixture into balls and roll in the bread crumbs. Lay on a lightly-oiled cookie sheet and bake for 20 minutes or until browned. Makes 10-15 balls, depending on size.

Dips &
Spreads

*Need a dip that delights? Look no further. These recipes are fast, easy, and delicious. Dress up those raw veggies, crackers, and chips with our assortment of dips and salsas. Choose any recipe that suits your fancy as all are definite crowd pleasers. Be warned, these recipes will having you and your guests double and triple dipping in no time, although we don't advocate it!*

# BABA GANOUSH

Maybe the reason why eggplant is so delicious is because it falls into the category of fruit. Specifically, it's a berry. As you know, berries are usually sweet, but the eggplant is known to be quite bitter at times.That is why it's recommended that you cut and dash them with salt before using. (You need to wait 20 minutes before rinsing the salt off.) This dip is especially delicious when dipped in pita bread and served beside Quinoa Tabouli (pg. 95).

**1 medium eggplant (about 4 cups), peeled and roughly chopped**
**1 tbsp olive oil**
**3 tbsp lemon juice *or* apple cider vinegar**
**1 tsp salt**
**3 cloves garlic, roughly chopped**
**4 tbsp tahini**
**4 tbsp pine nuts, dry roasted (pg. 209)**
**2 tbsp olive oil**
**2 tbsp fresh parsley**
**1 tbsp water**

Preheat over to 400°F. Place eggplant in a large baking dish and toss with oil. Bake 25-30 minutes, or until tender. In a blender or food processor, blend together the baked eggplant, lemon juice, salt, garlic, tahini, pine nuts, oil, parsley, and water until smooth. Makes approx. 1½ cups.

# DILL PICKLE CHIP DIP

I've been working hard on creating just the right dip for the ripple potato chips that I so selfishly indulge in. I think anyone would agree that potato chips are extra scrumptious after an encounter with this creamy pickle dip. Indulge; you deserve it! (T)

**¾ cup soft *or* silken tofu**
**2 tbsp apple cider vinegar**
**1 tbsp maple syrup**
**1 tsp dried dill**
**½ tsp salt**
**⅛ tsp pepper**
**2-3 medium dill pickles, roughly chopped**

In a blender or food processor, blend together the tofu, vinegar, maple syrup, dill, salt, and pepper until smooth and creamy. Add pickles and pulse until pickles are chunky. Served chilled. Makes approx. 1 cup.

# ROASTED GARLIC CHIP DIP

Although it's tempting to limit this dip to potato chips, this is a great raw veggie dip too.

**¾ cup soft *or* silken tofu**
**2 tbsp apple cider vinegar**
**1 tbsp maple syrup**
**½ tsp salt**
**pinch of pepper**
**6 cloves garlic, roasted (pg. 207)**
**½ small onion, chopped**
**1-2 tsp olive oil**

In a blender or food processor, blend together the tofu, vinegar, maple syrup, salt, pepper, roasted garlic, and onion, and oil until smooth and creamy. Serve chilled. Makes approx. 1 cup.

# SPICY PEANUT DIP

This dip is great for dipping chips, veggies, or fried tofu (pg. 121). Or you can stir this into warm noodles or over rice.

> **1 ½ cups soft *or* silken tofu**
> **3-4 tbl peanut butter (*or* other nut butter)**
> **2 tbsp lime juice**
> **¼ tsp cayenne pepper**
> **¼ tsp pepper**
> **1 tbsp Braggs**
> **2 cloves garlic, roughly chopped**

In a blender or food processor, blend together all the ingredients until smooth. Serve chilled.
Makes approx. 1 cup.

# ARTICHOKE & BLACK BEAN DIP

All legumes are high in protein, and black beans are no exception. This wonderful dip has a double identity as it also works great as a sandwich spread.

> **1-½ cups cooked *or* canned black beans**
> **1 clove garlic, roughly chopped**
> **2 tsp apple cider vinegar**
> **1 tbsp olive oil**
> **½ tsp salt**
> **¼ tsp pepper**
> **1 6-oz (156-ml) jar artichoke hearts, chopped**

In blender or food processor, blend together the beans, garlic, vinegar, oil, salt, and pepper until coarse. Stir in the artichoke hearts. Serve chilled. Makes approx 2 cups.

# PINEAPPLE SALSA

Talk about salsa with a twist! This is a sweet and tangy salsa which makes a nice alternative to tomato-based ones. There's nothing better to serve as a dip for tortilla chips or as a condiment for your favorite food, like veggie burgers (pg. 165). Feel free to substitute orange juice in place of the pineapple juice if you are using fresh pineapple in this one.

**1 small red bell pepper, chopped**
**1 cup pineapple, chopped**
**1 cup cooked** *or* **canned black beans**
**1 small onion, minced**
**¼ cup pineapple juice**

**2 tbsp fresh cilantro, chopped**
**1 tbsp lemon juice**
**1 tsp cumin**
**⅛ tsp salt**
**⅛ tsp pepper**

In a large bowl, stir together all the ingredients until well combined. Serve chilled. Makes approx. 3 cups.

# FABULOUS FRUIT SALSA

This multi-talented salsa can be used in countless ways: over pancakes (pg. 40), in crepes (pg. 41), on cereal (pg. 37-38), or as a dip with Cinnamon Chips (pg. 213).

**1 kiwi, diced**
**1 small Granny Smith apple (***or*** apple of your choice), diced**
**½ cup raspberries**
**½ cup strawberries, finely chopped**
**1 tbsp dry sweetener**
**2 tbsp jam (pg. 215)**

In a large bowl, stir together all the ingredients until well combined. Serve chilled. Makes approx. 2 cups.

# GORGEOUS GREEN SALSA

Tomatillos look like small green tomatoes, probably because they come from the same nightshade family. They usually come wrapped in a thin paper-like covering that should be removed before using. They eventually turn yellow, but should be used while they are still green and firm. Available at most supermarkets and health food stores, they add interesting flavor to whatever dish they are in.

- **8 tomatillos, roughly chopped**
- **3 shallots, roughly chopped**
- **2 cloves garlic, roughly chopped**
- **1 4-oz (120-ml) can chopped green chili peppers**
- **¼ cup fresh cilantro**
- **1 fresh jalapeno pepper, seeded**
- **⅛ tsp salt**

In a blender or food processor, blend together all the ingredients until coarse. Serve chilled. Makes approx. 2 cups.

# BECKY'S PICO DE GALLO

"This adds Mexican flavor to anything, and is good with tortilla chips." – Becky, Austin, Texas

- **2 large tomatoes, diced**
- **1 small onion, diced**
- **½ cup fresh cilantro, chopped**
- **1 hot pepper (e.g., serrano, jalapeno, etc.)**
- **½ tsp garlic powder**
- **½ tsp salt**
- **½ fresh lime, squeezed for juice**

In a medium bowl, stir together all the ingredients and mix well. Serve chilled. Makes approx. 2 cups.

# AVOCADO SALSA

The real trick to this great salsa is to use good avocados. Make sure they are ripe and the skin unblemished. Avocados contain a fair amount of vitamin C, thiamine, and riboflavin, so eat up! Serve this dip with corn chips, fresh veggies, or on top of burgers.

½ cup cooked *or* canned corn niblets
¼ cup olives (your choice), chopped
½ small red bell pepper, chopped
½ small onion, chopped
1 clove garlic, minced
1 tbsp olive oil
1 tbsp lemon juice or apple cider vinegar
½ tsp dried oregano
⅛ tsp salt
⅛ tsp pepper
1 avocado, diced

In a large bowl, combine the corn, olives, red pepper, and onion. In a small bowl, whisk together the garlic, oil, lemon juice, oregano, salt, and pepper. Pour the dressing over the salsa. Stir in the avocado just before serving. Makes approx. 2 cups.

# SPREADS

*Spreads aren't just for sandwiches; they can be a versatile part of any meal. Used as an appetizer on top of crackers or bread, added to noodles, or instead of pizza sauce.... Wherever you use them, you'll be glad that you did, as they add a little kick to everything they touch.*

# OLIVADA

These two olive spreads can be served with crackers or bread as an appetizer or you can use it as a pizza topping or tossed in with noodles.

1 cup olives, pitted (Italian olives are best)
⅓ cup olive oil
1-2 cloves garlic, minced
⅛ tsp black pepper

In a blender or food processor, blend together all the ingredients until coarse. Makes approx. ¾ cup.

# TAPENADE

> **1 cup Kalamata olives, pitted**
> **2 cloves garlic, chopped**
> **10-12 sun-dried tomatoes, rehydrated (pg. 208)**
> **¼ cup capers**
> **1 cup olive oil**
> **2 tbsp Braggs**

In a blender or food processor, blend together all the ingredients until coarse. Makes approx. 1 cup.

# PUMPKIN SEED PARMESAN SPREAD

This spread combines the delicate flavors of pumpkin seeds with the complexities and granular texture of soy Parmesan. Pumpkins seeds are available in most supermarkets and health food stores. Don't limit this recipe as a spread; try it over pasta, too.

> **1 cup pumpkin seeds**
> **2 cups spinach, chopped**
> **3 tbsp lemon juice or apple cider vinegar**
> **¼-⅓ cup olive oil**
> **2-3 cloves garlic, roughly chopped**
> **½ cup soy Parmesan cheese**
> **1 tbsp balsamic vinegar**
> **½ tsp salt**
> **½ tsp pepper**

In a blender or food processor, blend together all the ingredients until smooth. Makes approx. 1 ½ cups.

# SUN-DRIED TOMATO HUMMUS

Sometimes known as garbanzo beans or ceci, the chickpea is quite a versatile legume. It's a staple food in some countries because it contains vitamin B, carbohydrates, and minerals. The sun-dried tomatoes add a rich, sweet flavor to this dip.

> **2 cups cooked** *or* **canned chickpeas**
> **¾ cup tahini**
> **¼ cup olive oil**
> **3 garlic cloves, roughly chopped**
> **2 tbsp lemon juice** *or* **apple cider vinegar**
> **1 tbsp Braggs**
> **1 tsp cumin**
> **½ tsp salt**
> **⅛-¼ tsp cayenne pepper**
> **6-8 sun-dried tomatoes, rehydrated (pg. 208)**

In a blender or food processor, blend together all the ingredients until smooth. Make approx. 2 cups.

# SUN DRIED TOMATO "BUTTER"

The ingredients of margarine vary from brand to brand, and some contain animal products. Read the label to be sure. There are 100% vegan spreads out there; check at your local health food store.

> **½ cup margarine**
> **2 tbsp fresh parsley, chopped**
> **1 garlic clove, minced**
> **4-6 sun-dried tomatoes, rehydrated (pg. 208) and chopped**
> **¼ tsp salt**
> **¼ tsp pepper**

In a small bowl, combine all the ingredients and stir together. Serve chilled. Makes approx. ½ cup.

# BLACK BEAN SPREAD

This sweet and sassy spread complements everything it touches. This wonderful spread also works great as a dip.

**2 cups cooked *or* canned black beans**
**1 small red onion, chopped**
**3 tbsp fresh cilantro**
**1 garlic clove, roughly chopped**
**1 tbsp all-purpose spice (pg. 210)**
**1 tsp cumin**
**2 tbsp lime juice**
**⅛ tsp salt**

In a blender or food processor, blend together all the ingredients until smooth. Makes approx. 2 cups.

Sauces

*It's been suggested that sauce was developed in the early days before refrigeration, when food spoiled quickly and people needed to mask food past its prime. Nowadays, sauces are used to add seasoning, zest, and piquancy. Even though the French are credited with refining the sophisticated art of sauce-making, these sauce recipes definitely give them a run for their money. Happy saucing!*

# OLIVE BASIL PESTO

Basil is a lovely, versatile herb that grows easily in any garden or flower pot. This is great on your favorite pasta.

**1 large clove garlic**
**1 cup fresh basil**
**½ cup parsley**
**15 kalamata olives, pitted**
**¼ dark sesame oil**
**⅓ cup pine nuts, dry roasted (pg. 209)**

In a blender or food processor, blend together the garlic, basil, parsley, olives, oil, and ½ of the pine nuts until coarsely mixed. Stir in the remaining pine nuts. Makes approx. ¾ cup.

# SUN-DRIED TOMATO PESTO

Yum yum yummy!

**2 cups fresh basil**
**6-8 sun-dried tomatoes, rehydrated (pg.208)**
**3 cloves garlic**
**¼ tsp salt**
**¼ cup olive oil**
**¼ cup pine nuts, dry roasted (pg.209)**

In a blender or food processor, blend together the basil, tomatoes, garlic, salt, oil, and ½ of the pine nuts until coarsely mixed. Stir in the remaining pine nuts. Makes approx. 1 cup.

# PIZZA SAUCE

Tomatoes are generally acidic, and a tomato-based paste is even more so. The maple syrup in this recipe helps nip that in the bud.

> **4 tbsp tomato paste**
> **1 tbsp all-purpose spice (pg. 210)**
> **1 tbsp maple syrup**

In a small bowl, stir together all the ingredients until well mixed. Makes approx. ⅓ cup.

# NO-COOK ALL-PURPOSE TOMATO SAUCE

This recipe is great for pizza, over noodles, or added to beans or rice. Get creative!

> **14-oz (420-ml) can tomato sauce**
> **1 5.5-oz (156-ml) can tomato paste**
> **1 tsp salt**
> **1 tsp dry sweetener**
> **2 tsp dried oregano**
> **½ tsp black pepper**

In a bowl or jar, combine all the ingredients and mix together well. Cover and refrigerate overnight. Store in a container with a tight-fitting lid. Will keep for 5-7 days. Makes approx. 2 cups.

# "CHEESE" SAUCE

This "cheese" sauce is for those of you, who like me, have a yeast intolerance. Ⓢ

> **12 oz soft *or* silken tofu**
> **½ tsp salt**
> **½ tsp black pepper**
> **½ tsp all-purpose spice (pg. 210)**
> **¼ tsp turmeric**
> **2 tsp Dijon mustard**
> **1 tsp water**
> **1 tbsp flour**
> **1 tbsp olive oil**

In a blender or food processor, blend together all the ingredients until smooth. Makes 1 ½ cups.

# RANDOMGIRL.COM "CHEESE" SAUCE

Says Miki in Los Angeles: "It's good cold as salad dressing, or warm over baked potatoes or vegatables."

> **12 oz soft or silken tofu**
> **¼ cup olive oil**
> **¼ cup Braggs**
> **¼ tsp dried basil**
> **⅛ tsp dried garlic**
> **2 tbsp nutritional yeast**
> **¼ tsp salt**
> **1 ½ tsp lemon juice *or* apple cider vinegar**

In a blender or food processor, blend together all the ingredients until smooth. Makes 1 ½ cups.

# BASIC SWEET & SOUR SAUCE

This is from Jane in Ann Arbor, Michigan, who says, "This can be a blend of your favorite vegetables." The only thing missing in this recipe is that it's not hot pink! We suggest you serve this over a stir fry with your favorite veggies and "mock meat" products.

> **⅓ cup pineapple juice (*or* juice of your choice)**
> **3 tbsp apple cider vinegar**
> **3 tbsp dry sweetener**
> **1 tbsp Braggs**
> **2 tsp arrowroot powder *or* 1 tbsp cornstarch**
> **½ medium red bell pepper, chopped**
> **½ medium green bell pepper, chopped**
> **½ medium onion, chopped**
> **1 tbsp olive oil**
> **½ cup pineapple, chopped**

In a small bowl, whisk together the juice, vinegar, sweetener, Braggs, and arrowroot powder. Set aside. In a large saucepan on medium heat, sauté the peppers and onions in oil until the onions are translucent. Add the pineapple and sauté for an additional minute. Stir in the juice mixture and stir continually until the sauce begins to thicken. Makes approx. 2 cups.

# SIMPLE SHALLOT GRAVY

Shallots, while a member of the onion family, are more like garlic. Their mild flavor, combined with the nutritious miso, makes this a tasty and healthy dish.

**2 tbsp miso**
**2 tbsp hot water**
**¼ cup shallots, minced**
**1 tbsp olive oil**
**¼ cup flour**
**2 cup vegetable stock**
**1 tbsp maple syrup**
**½ tsp salt**

In a small bowl, combine the miso and hot water and mix well. Set aside. In a large saucepan on medium-high heat, sauté the shallots in oil until translucent. Add the flour and mix well; this will become pasty and dry. Slowly start adding the stock while stirring continually; add a little bit at a time until everything becomes well mixed and there are no lumps. Stir in the maple syrup and salt. Lower heat to medium-low and simmer until the sauce is thickened, stirring often. Remove from heat. Stir in the miso and serve. Makes approx. 2 cups.

# SPICY ORANGE SAUCE

This sauce isn't thick, but it's spicy! Use in stir fries, noodles, or any recipe that needs a little kick.

**¼ cup maple syrup**
**¼ cup rice vinegar**
**3 tbsp orange juice**
**2 tbsp fresh ginger, grated**
**2 tbsp fresh cilantro, chopped**
**1 tbsp Braggs**
**2 tsp Asian chili sauce**
**1 tsp dark sesame oil**
**1 tbsp orange rind (optional)**

In a small saucepan on medium heat, whisk together all the ingredients. Cook until heated thoroughly. Makes approx. ¾ cup.

# BARBECUE SAUCE

Everyone and their dog has their own "top secret" barbecue sauce, and here's ours. This recipe has a lot of sweetness and spice, and can be made quickly with ingredients found in a well stocked cupboard. It's so tasty that it'll leave you licking your plate.

¼ cup apple cider vinegar
3 tbsp tomato paste
3 tbsp maple syrup
2 tbsp molasses
1 tbsp Braggs
1 tbsp Dijon mustard
½ tsp garlic powder
½ tsp liquid smoke
½ tsp Worchestershire sauce (pg. 207)

In a small saucepan, combine all the ingredients and bring to a boil while continually whisking. Reduce heat to medium low and simmer until desired thickness. Makes approx. ¾ cup.

# MO'S TAHINI SAUCE

We stole this recipe from our friend Mo. Don't tell her!

¾ cup tahini
5 tbsp lemon juice
2-4 cloves garlic, roughly chopped
½ - 1 tsp salt
¾ - 1 cup water

In a blender or food processor, combine the tahini, lemon juice, garlic, and salt. Slowly pour in water and blend until smooth. Makes approx. 1 ½ cups.

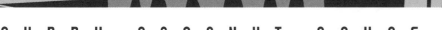

# CURRY COCONUT SAUCE

This lovely sauce is great over almost everything – veggies, noodles, rice – except maybe waffles ... mmm, curried waffles...

| | |
|---|---|
| 1 small onion, chopped | ½ tsp salt |
| 1 tbsp olive oil | 2 tbsp curry powder |
| 3 cloves garlic, minced | 2 tbsp flour |
| 1 cups vegetable stock (pg. 217) | 1 14-oz (398-ml) can coconut milk |
| ½ tsp cumin | 1 small tomato, chopped |

In a medium saucepan on medium-high heat, sauté the onions in oil until translucent. Add the garlic and sauté for an additional minute. Add the vegetable stock and whisk in the cumin, salt, curry, and flour until there are no lumps. Add the coconut milk and tomato. Reduce heat to low and simmer for 6-8 minutes.
Makes approx. 3 cups.

# PERFECT PEANUT SAUCE

You can use any type of peanut butter in this recipe, crunchy or smooth. Combine this sauce with noodle dishes or stir fries with veggies.

| | |
|---|---|
| 1 cup coconut milk | 2 tsp chilli sauce |
| ½ cup peanut butter, your choice | 1 tbsp liquid sweetener |
| 1 tbsp Braggs | ½ tsp dried red pepper flakes |
| 1 tsp rice vinegar | 1-2 tbsp water (optional) |

In a blender or food processor, blend together all the ingredients until smooth. Add optional water if too thick. Transfer to a medium saucepan on medium-low heat and warm thoroughly before serving.
Make approx. 2 cups.

Effortless, scrumptious, versatile – a few choice words to describe these next three recipes. These sauces can be used for dipping potstickers or veggies, as a marinade for tofu, or as a quick and easy noodle toss.

# MISO SESAME DIPPING SAUCE

| | |
|---|---|
| ¼ cup water | 1 tsp maple syrup |
| 1 tbsp miso | 1 tsp Asian chilli sauce |
| 1 tsp Braggs | 1 tbsp sesame seeds |
| 1 tsp rice vinegar | |

In a small saucepan, whisk together all ingredients. Warm on low heat before serving. Makes approx. ½ cup.

# SOY GINGER DIPPING SAUCE

¼ cup Braggs
2 tbsp rice vinegar
2 tsp fresh ginger, grated

2 tsp lime juice
2 tsp maple syrup
1 green onion, chopped

In a small saucepan, whisk together all ingredients. Warm on low heat before serving. Makes approx. ½ cup.

# PEANUT DIPPING SAUCE

½ cup coconut milk
2 tbsp rice vinegar
2 tbsp peanut butter, smooth
2 tbsp maple syrup
2 tbsp Braggs

2 cloves garlic, roughly chopped
1 tsp lime juice
1 tsp lime rind, grated
1 tsp dried mint
½ tsp dried red pepper flakes

In a blender or food processor, blend together all the ingredients until smooth. Warm on low heat before serving. Makes approx. 1 cup.

# CASHEW DIPPING SAUCE

This dipping sauce is thicker than others, but the same rules apply to this versatile recipe – use in or on anything you like.

1 cup dry roasted cashews (pg. 209), chopped
¾ cup soy yogurt (pg. 216)
1 tbsp dark sesame oil
1 tbsp lemon juice *or* apple cider vinegar
1 tbsp Braggs
2 cloves garlic, roughly chopped
½ tsp all-purpose spice (pg. 210)

In a blender or food processor, blend together all the ingredients until smooth. Transfer to a small saucepan and warm on low heat before serving. Makes approx. 1 cup.

Entrées

*There's nothing worse than crawling through the front door after a hard day at work and realizing that your work isn't over yet ... now you have to make dinner! These quick and nutritious recipes can be made in a flash so you can get on with relaxing.*

# RICE DISHES

*There are 7,000 different varieties of rice. Brown rice is one of our favorites because it's the most nutritious and has a mildly nutty flavor and chewy texture. It takes a little longer to cook than some other varieties such as basmati or jasmine, but it is well worth the wait. Don't limit yourself to one type of rice; experiment and try what's out there. Here are some of our favorite recipes that either feature rice or go well with it.*

# TEMPEH TOSS

Tempeh is a fermented soybean cake, but don't let that freak you out. It has a lovely nutty flavor and is an excellent alternative to tofu.

**1 cup tempeh, cubed**
**1 tbsp olive oil**
**1 medium carrot, chopped**
**⅓ cup shallots, chopped**
**1 leek, chopped (pale green end only)**
**2-4 cloves garlic, minced**
**⅛ tsp red pepper flakes**
**2 tbsp Braggs**
**¼ cup water**
**1 tbsp red wine vinegar**
**1 small red bell pepper, chopped**
**1 cup zucchini, chopped**
**1 medium tomato, chopped and seeded**

In a large saucepan on medium-high heat, sauté the tempeh in oil until lightly browned. Add the carrot, shallots, leek, garlic, red pepper flakes, and Braggs. Sauté until carrots are tender but firm to the bite. Add water, vinegar, red pepper, zucchini, and tomato. Cover and simmer for 3-4 minutes until zucchini is tender. Serve on a bed of rice. Makes 2-4 servings.

# DRAGON BOWL

This recipe is a meal in a bowl. Every veggie restaurant and veggie cookbook seems to have their own version of a Dragon Bowl; this is ours. Top it with any dressing you like. We suggest Sarah & Tanya's You-Must-Make-This Dressing (pg. 99), or Mo Kelly's (Pat Kelly's Sister) Dressing (pg. 101).

**1 cup uncooked brown rice**
**2 cups kale, chopped**
**2 medium carrots, grated**
**2 green onion, chopped**
**½ lb firm tofu, cubed**

Cook rice in a large pot (you'll need the extra space). When rice is done, turn off heat and place kale, carrots, onion, and tofu on top of rice. Cover and let sit for 5 minutes. Prepare your dressing. Assemble bowl with equal parts rice, kale, carrots, onion, and tofu. Top with dressing. Makes 2 servings.

# SEITAN VEGGIE KABOBS

Seitan is made from wheat gluten and has a chewy meaty texture, but with its mellow taste – much like tofu – it will pick up whatever flavors it's cooked in. You can easily make it yourself or substitute it with firm tofu. This simple recipe can be made for impromptu backyard barbecues or can be cooked in your oven. Serve over a bed of brown rice or quinoa and enjoy the simple things in life. Soak skewers in a bowl of water before adding veggies so the wood doesn't burn.

**1 cup vegetable stock**
**⅛ cup Braggs**
**1 tbsp olive oil**
**1 tbsp red wine vinegar**
**1 tsp dried basil**
**1 tsp dried oregano**
**1 tsp all-purpose seasoning**

**2 cups seitan, cut into bite-sized pieces (pg. 208)**
**1 small onion, cut into quarters**
**½ - 1 green/red/yellow bell pepper, cut into bite-sized pieces**
**6 large mushrooms, cut in half**
**1 cup zucchini cut into bite-sized pieces**
**12 cherry tomatoes**
**12 cloves garlic, skin removed**

Preheat oven to 350°F. In a large bowl, stir together the stock, Braggs, oil, vinegar, basil, oregano, and all-purpose seasoning. Place seitan and veggies in bowl and toss. Let sit for 15-30 minutes. Place a cooling rack on a baking sheet. Spear the seitan, veggies, and garlic on wooden skewers and place on rack. Cook in oven until slightly browned, approx. 15 minutes. Turn kabobs occasionally and brush with remaining marinade. Don't let them get too dry. Makes 6-8 kabobs.

# PORTOBELLO MUSHROOM BAKE

Many friendships have been cultivated and nurtured because of this dish. It's one of my favorite recipes to serve when guests come over for dinner. Sometimes I double up on the sauce because it's so incredibly delicious. Serve this one over rice and teamed up with Swiss Chard & Garlic (pg. 118). (T)

- ½ **cup almonds**
- ¼ **cup olive oil**
- ¼ **cup Braggs**
- ¼-½ **cup water**
- 2 **tbsp balsamic vinegar**
- 3 **cloves garlic, roughly chopped**
- 1 **tsp dried rosemary**
- 1 **tsp dried oregano**
- 4 **large Portobello mushrooms, stems removed**
- 1 **medium onion, sliced**

Preheat oven to 350°F. In a blender or food processor, blend the almonds until powdered. Add oil, Braggs, water, vinegar, garlic, rosemary, and oregano, and blend until well combined. In a large baking dish, place the mushrooms upside down and top with onions. Pour sauce over top and bake for 20-25 minutes. Makes 2-4 servings.

# CHICKPEA TOSS

"I created this recipe because I'm a chickpea-aholic and just can't get enough of them." – Amanda, Calgary, Alberta. This simply delicious dish is best served over a rice and garnished with flax oil, Braggs, and gomashio (pg. 209).

- 1 **small onion, chopped**
- 2 **cloves garlic, minced**
- 2 **tsp dark sesame oil**
- ¼ **cup olives (your choice), chopped**
- 2 **cups chickpeas, cooked or canned**
- ½ **tsp salt**
- ½ **tsp black pepper**
- 1 **tsp curry powder**

In a large saucepan on medium-high heat, sauté the onion and garlic in oil until the onions are translucent. Reduce heat to medium. Add the olives, chickpeas, salt, pepper, and curry and simmer for 5 minutes. Makes 2 servings.

# GINGER, POTATO & CAULIFLOWER TOSS

A enchanting recipe served over rice that will have you reaching for seconds.

2 medium potatoes, cubed
1 tbsp fresh ginger, minced
1 tbsp dark sesame oil
2 cups cauliflower, cut into bite-sized pieces
½ cup coconut milk
½ tsp salt

½ tsp black pepper
½ tsp turmeric
¼ tsp chili powder
¼ tsp paprika
½ cup peas, frozen *or* fresh

In a large saucepan on medium-high heat, sauté the potatoes and ginger in oil until potatoes start to brown. Add the cauliflower, coconut milk, salt, pepper, turmeric, chili powder, and paprika. Toss well, reduce heat to medium, and simmer for 5-7 minutes or until veggies are tender. Remove from heat. Stir in peas and let sit covered for 5 minutes. Makes 2-4 servings.

# CHRISTINA'S VEGETABLE CURRY

This quick and delicious dish comes from Christina in Chicago, Illinois.

1 cup uncooked jasmine rice
½ tsp cinnamon
2 cloves garlic, minced
1 cup broccoli, chopped
1 cup cauliflower, chopped
1 large carrot, chopped
½ tsp mustard seeds

1 tbsp dark sesame oil
1 14-oz (398-ml) can diced tomatoes
2 tsp curry powder
½ tsp cumin
½ tsp turmeric
3 tbsp shredded coconut

In a medium pot, cook the rice by boiling it with the cinnamon. In a large saucepan on medium-high heat, sauté the garlic, broccoli, cauliflower, carrots, and mustard seeds in oil for 2 minutes. Stir in the tomatoes, curry, cumin, turmeric, and coconut. Reduce heat to low and simmer for 5-10 minutes or until vegetables become tender. Serve over rice. Makes 2 servings.

# OYSTER MUSHROOM SAUTÉ

I work for this awesome company that delivers organic produce right to your door. Due to the nature of the business, there so much food around that we get to cook ourselves a delicious, organic, vegan lunch every day. This recipe came about from me messing around in the work kitchen. I hope you like it as much as my workmates did! I serve it over rice or noodles. (T)

⅛ cup orange juice
1 tbsp Braggs
1 tbsp maple syrup
½ tsp Asian chili sauce
½ tsp cumin
1 small onion, chopped
2 cloves garlic, minced

1 tbsp dark sesame oil
1 medium carrot, chopped
1 cup oyster mushrooms, sliced
1 cup spinach, chopped
1 cup bok choy, chopped
2 tbsp gomashio (pg. 209)

In a small bowl, whisk together the orange juice, Braggs, maple syrup, chili sauce, and cumin. Set aside. In a large saucepan on medium heat, sauté the onion and garlic in oil until the onions become translucent. Add the carrots and mushrooms. Cook until carrots are tender but firm to the bite. Reduce heat to medium-low and add spinach, bok choy, and orange juice mixture. Cook for 5-10 minutes or until liquid has reduced. Serve topped with gomashio. Makes 2-4 servings.

# NOODLE DISHES

*Noodles are not just made out of wheat anymore – there's buckwheat, rice, corn, and so on. Don't limit yourself to what your local supermarket carries; visit Asian markets and heath food stores and try something new. Live a little!*

## HOT 'N' SPICY RICE NOODLES WITH OYSTER MUSHROOMS

This delightful dish can be served hot or cold and with any kind of noodles you like. Rice noodles are a quick-cooking, light alternative to other noodles.

> **dry rice noodles (enough for 2 people)**
> **3 cloves garlic, minced**
> **1 hot red pepper, minced**
> **1 tsp dark sesame oil**
> **½ lb oyster mushrooms, roughly chopped**
> **3 tbsp Braggs**
> **⅛ tsp salt**
> **1 cup fresh basil, roughly chopped**
> **1 tbsp dark sesame oil**

In a large pot of water, boil the rice noodles. While noodles are cooking, in a large saucepan on medium-low heat, sauté the garlic and hot pepper in oil until garlic begins to soften. Be careful not to burn garlic. Add the mushrooms, Braggs, and salt and simmer for 3-5 minutes. Remove from heat, stir in basil, and cover. Let stand for 5 minutes. Drain noodles and toss with sesame oil. Portion out noodles on plate and spoon out mushroom mixture on top. Makes 2 servings.

# NUTTY PASTA TOSS

A lovely and light pasta dish. Perfect for summer nights when cooking seems like an impossible task.

- **dry pasta, your choice (enough for 2 people)**
- **¼ cup nuts, your choice (peanuts, almonds, etc.)**
- **2 tbsp fresh parsley**
- **2 cloves garlic**
- **¾-1 cup vegetable stock (pg. 217)**
- **¼ tsp salt**
- **¼ tsp black pepper**
- **1 tbsp lemon juice**
- **½ small zucchini, sliced**
- **12 cherry tomatoes, halved**
- **1 tbsp flax oil, optional**

In a large pot of water, boil the pasta. While pasta is cooking, in a blender or food processor, blend together the nuts, parsley, and garlic until minced. Add the stock, salt, pepper, and lemon juice and blend until well combined. In large saucepan on medium-high heat, cook the zucchini, tomatoes, and nut sauce until zucchini is tender but firm to the bite. Drain pasta and toss with sauce and optional flax oil. Make 2 servings.

# ZUCCHINI & BROCCOLI TOSS

The zucchini commonly sold in grocery stores are about 4-8 inches in length, but homegrown zucchini can grow to be as big as 2 feet long. Just remember … size isn't important. It's the quality that counts!

- **dry rice noodles (enough for 2 people)**
- **1 medium zucchini, cubed**
- **1 cup broccoli, florets only**
- **2 cloves garlic, minced**
- **3-4 tsp fresh ginger, grated**
- **2-3 tbsp Braggs**
- **2 tsp dark sesame oil**
- **¼ cup almonds, dry roasted (pg. 209)**

In a large pot of water, boil the rice noodles. While noodles are cooking, in a large saucepan on medium-high heat, sauté the zucchini, broccoli, garlic, ginger, and Braggs in oil until zucchini is tender. Drain noodles and toss with vegetables. Top with almonds. Serve hot or cold. Makes 2 servings.

# SPICY RICE NOODLE TOSS

You can find chili black bean sauce in most Asian markets. You might think that this sauce is made from turtle beans, the most common variety of black bean, but it's actually made from black soybeans. Be careful, though, as this bean sauce is very, very spicy.

**dry rice noodles (enough for 2 people)**
**1 medium zucchini, sliced**
**1 cup bean sprouts**
**2 stalks green onion, chopped**
**2 cloves garlic, minced**
**1 tbsp chilli black bean sauce**
**1 tbsp Braggs**
**1 tbsp dark sesame oil**
**2 tbsp fresh cilantro, chopped**

In a large pot of water, boil the rice noodles. While noodles are cooking, in a large saucepan on medium-high heat, sauté the zucchini, bean sprouts, onions, garlic, bean sauce, and Braggs in oil until zucchini is tender. Drain noodles and toss with vegetables. Top with cilantro. Serve hot or cold. Makes 2 servings.

# SPICY SZECHUAN NOODLES

Despite its well-deserved reputation for producing "mouth burners," at least of one-third of Szechuan dishes are not spicy at all. You can make this one hotter, if you dare, by adding more chili sauce. Hot foods like red chilies stimulate the palate, making it more sensitive to other flavors in the dish.

**dry rice noodles (enough for 2 people)**
**3 tbsp Braggs**
**2 tsp rice vinegar**
**1-2 tsp Asian chili sauce**
**1 tbsp peanut butter (or other nut butter)**
**½ cup vegetable stock (pg. 217)**

**½ lb medium tofu, chopped**
**1 medium carrot, chopped**
**1 tbsp dark sesame oil**
**1 cup bean sprouts**
**½ cup sugar snap peas, halved**
**2 cloves garlic, minced**

In a large pot of water, boil the rice noodles. While noodles are cooking, in a small bowl, mix together the Braggs, vinegar, chili sauce, peanut butter, and stock. Set aside. In a large saucepan over medium-high heat, sauté the tofu and carrots in oil until the carrots are tender but firm to the bite. Reduce heat to low and add the bean sprouts, peas, garlic, and Braggs mixture. Simmer for 3-5 minutes. Drain noodles and toss with vegetables. Serve hot or cold. Makes 2 servings.

# GREEN GODDESS BOWL

Perfect and lovely, just like a woman!

> dry buckwheat noodles (enough for 2 people)
> ½ cup Sarah's Sesame Dressing (pg. 101)
> 1 tbsp dark sesame oil
> 1 cup snow peas, ends removed and cut into thirds
> 1 small cucumber, seeded and diced
> 2 stalks green onion, chopped
> 2 tbsp gomashio (pg. 209)

In a large pot of water, boil the buckwheat noodles. While noodles are cooking, make Sarah's Sesame Dressing. Drain noodles, and toss with sesame oil and snow peas. Cover and set aside 5 minutes. Assemble bowls with equal parts noodles, dressing, cucumber, green onions, and gomashio. Makes 2 servings.

# HAYLEY & IAN'S PEANUT BUTTER PASTA

When Hayley first gave us this recipe to test, we thought it sounded disgusting, but since she was our friend we decided to try it. Wowzers! Were we ever wrong. What a great recipe! It's perfect for when money is tight and your tummy is growling.

> dry pasta (enough for 2 people)
> ⅓ cup peanut butter
> ¼ cup hot water
> 1 tbsp Braggs
> 1 tsp vegan Worcestershire sauce (pg. 207)
> 2 cloves garlic, minced
> ½ tsp cayenne
> ½ tsp salt
> ½ tsp black pepper
> 1 tsp dry sweetener
> 3 cups broccoli, cut into bite-sized pieces
> ½ cup peanuts, dry-roasted (pg. 209)

In a large pot of water, boil the pasta. While pasta is cooking, in a small bowl, whisk together the peanut butter and hot water until smooth. Stir in the Braggs, Worcestershire, garlic, cayenne, salt, pepper, and sweetener. Set aside. When pasta is almost done, add the broccoli to the pasta and cook for an additional 3-4 minutes. Drain and return to pot. Pour in peanut sauce and toss well. Garnish with chopped peanuts. Makes 2 servings.

# COCONUT SPICED VEGETABLES

Chinese cabbage has many different names: Napa cabbage, hakusai, celery cabbage, wong bok. Most grocery stores carry it, or you can find it in Asian markets. Serve over rice, udon, buckwheat noodles, or any other noodles you like.

¼ cup almonds
1-2 tsp Asian chili sauce
1 tsp coriander
1 tbsp fresh ginger, grated
1 small onion, roughly chopped
1 tbsp Braggs
1 tbsp dark sesame oil

1 carrot, chopped
1 cup cauliflower, chopped
1 cup broccoli, chopped
6 mushrooms, chopped
1 14-oz (398-ml) can coconut milk
1 cup Chinese cabbage, chopped
½ red bell pepper, chopped

In a blender or food processor, blend together the almonds, chili sauce, coriander, ginger, onion, and Braggs. In a large saucepan on medium heat, sauté the almond mixture in oil for 3-4 minutes, stirring often. Stir in the carrot, cauliflower, broccoli, mushrooms, and ½ the coconut milk and simmer for 5-6 minutes. Add the remaining coconut milk, cabbage, and red pepper, turn off heat, and let sit covered for 5 minutes. Makes 2 servings.

# LINGUINE WITH SUN-DRIED TOMATO PESTO SAUCE

This makes a exquisite dish, especially if you want to impress your friends. Just make sure to check each other's teeth before you smile, 'cause otherwise it could be embarrassing!

dry pasta (enough for 2 people)
1 12-oz pkg soft or silken tofu
¼ cup olive oil
1 ½ cups fresh basil
½ cup fresh parsley
10 sun-dried tomatoes (pg. 208)
3 cloves garlic, roughly chopped
¼ tsp salt
3 tbsp pine nuts, dry-roasted (pg. 209)

In a large pot of water, boil the pasta. While pasta is cooking, in a blender or food processor, blend together the tofu, oil, basil, parsley, tomatoes, garlic, and salt until smooth. Pour into saucepan and add pine nuts. Heat until warmed. Toss with cooked pasta. Makes 2-4 servings.

# TANYA'S ASIAN DELIGHT

What can I say? I was in Asia over five years ago, and I still can't get enough of the flavors and dishes from that region. Some things leave an impression that last a long, long time. (T)

dry buckwheat noodles (enough for 2 people)

| | |
|---|---|
| 1 small onion, chopped | 1 tsp liquid sweetener |
| 2 cloves garlic, minced | 1 tsp Asian chili sauce |
| 2 tbsp fresh ginger, grated | 1 ½ cups broccoli, chopped |
| ½ lb firm tofu, chopped | 1 cup bok choy, chopped |
| 1 tbsp sesame oil | 1 medium bell pepper (your choice), chopped |
| ¼ cup Braggs | ½ cup snow peas, halved |
| 2 tbsp lime juice | 4 tbsp almonds, dry roasted (pg. 209) |

In a large pot of water, boil the buckwheat noodles. While noodles are cooking, in a large saucepan on medium-low heat, sauté the onion, garlic, ginger, and tofu in oil until the onions become translucent. Add the Braggs, lime juice, sweetener, and chili sauce, and sauté for an additional minute. Add the broccoli, bok choy, bell pepper, and snow peas. Reduce heat to medium-low and simmer until veggies are tender but firm to the bite. Serve topped with almonds. Make 2 servings.

# MARC'S MAGNIFICENT NOODLES

Marc was our "driver" when we went down to Louisville, Kentucky for a cooking demo. We had so much fun with him. He took us thrift store shopping and to all his favorite stores. Marc rules!

dry soba noodles (enough for 2 people)
3 cloves garlic, minced
2 tbsp miso
3 tbsp flax oil or hemp oil
4 cups baby spinach
4 stalks green onion, chopped

In a large pot of water, boil the soba noodles. While noodles are cooking, in a small bowl, stir together the garlic, miso, and oil. Set aside. When noodles are almost cooked, add spinach to pot and let simmer with noodles 15-30 seconds. Drain and return noodles and spinach to pot. Stir in sauce and toss well. Garnish with green onions. Makes 2 servings (or one Marc serving!).

# MISCELLANY

## BAKED STUFFED EGGPLANT

"I make this recipe in bulk whenever eggplants are plentiful. It freezes well and I can have a quick dinner fixed in no time. Make sure you don't eat the shell in this recipe!" – Jane, Ann Arbor, Michigan

**1 medium eggplant, halved lengthwise, flesh scooped out, and chopped (reserve shells)**
**1 small onion, chopped**
**1 small green bell pepper, chopped**
**4-6 brown mushrooms, chopped**
**1 tbsp olive oil**
**½ cup cooked rice (your choice)**
**½ tsp dried oregano**
**½ tsp dried basil**
**1 tsp salt**
**2 tbsp tomato paste**
**4 tbsp soy Parmesan cheese (optional)**

Preheat oven to 350°F. In a large saucepan on medium heat, sauté the eggplant, onions, pepper, and mushrooms in oil until the onions are translucent. Add the rice, oregano, basil, salt, and tomato paste and let simmer for 5 minutes. Place the eggplant shells in a lasagna pan or baking sheet, and stuff with the vegetable mixture. Sprinkle top with soy parmesan. Cover with foil or lid, and bake for 30 minutes, uncovered for last 10 minutes. Makes 2-4 servings.

# DINNER CREPES

Crepes for dinner? Why not? You can fill them with anything you like, but here's a sure-fire hit that will have you wishing your stomach would stretch to fit more.

¼ cup shallots, minced
3 cloves garlic, minced
8 small brown mushrooms, chopped
¼ tsp salt
¼ tsp pepper
1 tbsp olive oil

1 large tomato, roughly chopped
¼ cup dried red lentils
1 tbsp Braggs
1 cup green beans, cut into 1-inch pieces
¼ cup walnuts, chopped
crepes (pg. 41)

In a large saucepan on medium heat, sauté the shallots, garlic, mushrooms, salt, and pepper in oil until onions are translucent. Reduce heat to medium-low, add the tomato, lentils, and Braggs, and simmer covered for approx. 10 minutes or until lentils are cooked. Remove lid and add green beans and walnuts. Let simmer uncovered until liquid has reduced. Set aside. Spoon 1-2 tbsp of filling into center of each prepared crepe. Roll up and lay on plate. If you have leftover filling, pour over top of the crepes as a garnish. Makes 8-12 crepes.

# BALSAMIC GRILLED VEGGIES WITH COUSCOUS

Couscous is a versatile grain in that it can be used for not only entrees, but also served for breakfast such as in Claire's Porridge (pg. 38).

1 red bell pepper, chopped
1 medium zucchini, chopped
1 small eggplant, chopped
1 medium onion, chopped
1 tbsp olive oil
1 cup vegetable stock (pg. 217)
1 cup couscous

1 14-oz (398-ml) can diced tomatoes
1 ½ tbsp balsamic vinegar
1 tbsp tomato paste
1 tbsp dry sweetener
1 tsp dried basil
2 tbsp capers (optional)

Preheat oven to 450°F. On a baking sheet or lasagna pan, lay out the peppers, zucchini, eggplant, and onions. Drizzle with oil and stir. Roast for 15-20 minutes, or until veggies are browned. In a small saucepan over high heat, bring the vegetable stock to a boil. Remove from heat, stir in couscous, and cover for 5 minutes. With a fork, fluff the couscous to prevent sticking. Set aside. In a large pot on medium heat, stir together the tomatoes, vinegar, tomato paste, sweetener, basil, capers, and roasted veggies and cook for 5-8 minutes, or until heated thoroughly. Serve over couscous. Makes 2-4 servings.

# WENDY'S BLACK BEAN CHILI

"I like to serve this chili with some brown rice to make a complete protein." – Wendy, Victoria, BC

| | |
|---|---|
| 1 medium onion, chopped | ¼ cup water |
| 1 medium carrot, chopped | 1 tbsp Braggs |
| 1 stalk celery, chopped | 1 tbsp apple cider vinegar |
| 1 tbsp olive oil | 1 tsp dry sweetener |
| 2 cups cooked or canned black beans | 1 tsp chili powder |
| 1 5.5-oz (156-ml) can tomato paste | ½ tsp salt |
| 1 cup corn | ½ tsp black pepper |

In a medium pot on medium-high heat, sauté the onion, carrot, and celery in oil until onions are translucent. Add the beans, tomato paste, corn, water, Braggs, vinegar, sweetener, chili powder, salt, and pepper. Reduce heat to medium and simmer for approx. 15 minutes or until veggies are tender. Makes 4-6 servings.

# CURRIED VEGETABLE PIE WITH CHICKPEA CRUST

Our gal-pal Becky from the Portland scooter club *HellsBelles.org* passed on this scrumptious recipe.

| | |
|---|---|
| ½ cup cooked or canned chickpeas | 2 cups cauliflower, chopped |
| 1 ½ cups flour | 1 cup peas, fresh *or* frozen |
| 1 tsp salt | 1/2 cup cooked *or* canned chickpeas (for filling) |
| ½ tsp cumin | 2 cloves garlic, minced |
| ⅓ cup vegetable shortening or margarine | 2-3 tsp curry powder |
| 3 tbsp water | 2 small tomatoes, chopped |
| 2 medium carrots, chopped | ½ cup vegetable stock (pg. 217) |
| 1 small onion, chopped | 1 ½ tsp salt |
| 2 stalks celery, chopped | ½ tsp black pepper |
| 1 large bell pepper, chopped (your choice) | 2 tbsp peanut butter |
| 2 tbsp olive oil | |

Preheat over to 375°F. In a blender or food processor, purée the chickpeas and set aside. In a large bowl, sift together the flour, salt, and cumin. Add the chickpeas, shortening, and water. Mix together until a dough forms. Knead the dough on a lightly floured surface for 3-5 minutes. Cut dough into two pieces. Roll out both pieces to fit an 8-inch pie plate. Place one on the bottom of a pie plate and reserve the other for the top. In a large saucepan on medium heat, sauté the carrots, onion, celery, and pepper in oil until onions are translucent. Add the cauliflower, peas, chickpeas, garlic, and curry. Stir and cook for 5 minutes. Add the tomatoes, stock, salt, and pepper. Reduce heat and simmer until cauliflower is tender, about 10 minutes. Remove from heat and stir in peanut butter. Pour mixture into crust and lay reserved crust dough on top. Bake for 30-45 minutes or until golden brown. Makes 1 pie.

# TOFU QUICHE

Tofu was developed more that 2,000 years ago in China and is now more popular than ever; you have to marvel at its greatness. Bask in the joy of another great tofu recipe.

| | |
|---|---|
| 1 small onion, chopped | ½ tsp pepper |
| 2 cloves garlic, minced | 2 cups spinach, chopped |
| 5 mushrooms, sliced | 1 lb medium-firm tofu |
| 1 tbsp olive oil | ⅓ cup soy milk |
| 2 tbsp Braggs | 1 cup soy cheese |
| 1 tsp dried oregano | 5-10 sun-dried tomatoes, chopped (pg. 208) |
| ½ tsp turmeric | 1 9-inch pie crust (pg. 195) |

Preheat to 350°F. In a medium saucepan on medium heat, sauté the onions, garlic, and mushrooms in oil until the onions are translucent. Add the Braggs, oregano, turmeric, and pepper. Mix well. Remove from heat, add the spinach on top of onion mixture, cover, and set aside. In a blender or food processor, blend the tofu and soy milk until well combined. In a large bowl, mix together the vegetable mixture, tofu mixture, soy cheese, and tomatoes. Pour mixture into pie crust. Bake for 40-45 minutes or until top is golden brown. Let cool and set for 10 minutes before serving. Makes 1 pie.

# CURRIED LENTILS

This delish recipe comes from someone in London, Ontario. Unfortunately, we lost their name somewhere in the mix and can't give them credit ... so if it's you, let us know at *iwrotethatrecipe@govegan.net.* Garnish this dish with Braggs and flax oil. Yum.

| | |
|---|---|
| 1 medium onion, chopped | ½ tsp turmeric |
| 2 cloves garlic, minced | 2 cups cooked *or* canned lentils |
| 1 medium carrot, chopped | 1 cup peas, fresh *or* frozen |
| 2 cups cauliflower, chopped | 1 tsp salt |
| 1 tbsp olive oil | ⅓ cup vegetable stock (pg. 217) |
| 2 tsp curry powder | ¼ cup fresh cilantro, chopped |
| 1 tsp cumin | |

In a large saucepan on medium-high heat, sauté the onions, garlic, carrots, and cauliflower in oil until the onions are translucent. Add the curry, cumin, turmeric, lentils, peas, salt, and stock. Stir and reduce heat to medium-low. Simmer for 10-15 minutes until the cauliflower is tender but firm to the bite. Serve over rice and top with cilantro. Makes 4-6 servings.

# CHRISTINE'S BLACK BEAN & TOMATO CHILI

Christine from Winnipeg, Manitoba sent us her recipe for black bean soup, but we think it's more of a chili than a soup. Christine and her daughter, Rachel, are the ones who thought up the title for this cookbook. Prairie people are the bomb! Christine says you can add any other veggies you have laying around, like parsnips or celery. I like to throw in ¼ cup of couscous to this recipe for fun. ⓢ

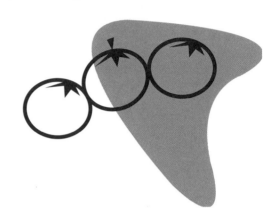

**1 small onion, chopped**
**2 cloves garlic, minced**
**1 carrot, chopped**
**1 tbsp olive oil**
**2 cups vegetable stock (pg. 217)**
**1 tsp chili powder**
**1 tsp cumin**
**½ tsp salt**
**½ tsp black pepper**
**1 tbsp dry sweetener**
**1 14-oz (398-ml) can of crushed tomatoes**
**½ cup corn**
**2 cups cooked or canned black beans**

In a large pot on medium-high heat, sauté the onions, garlic, and carrots in oil until onions are translucent. Add the stock, chili powder, cumin, salt, pepper, sweetener, tomatoes, corn, and ½ the beans. Purée the remaining beans in a blender or food processor and add to pot. Reduce heat to medium-low and simmer for 10-15 minutes. Makes 4-6 servings.

# STUFFED BELL PEPPERS

Serve this savory stuffed pepper recipe with Fragrant Fried Rice (pg. 118) and a nice green salad. You can use any color bell pepper to change the taste: green for more of a traditional taste, or red, orange, or yellow for a sweeter taste.

| | |
|---|---|
| 4 cloves garlic, minced | 4 tbsp tomato paste |
| 1 small onion, minced | 2 tbsp olive oil |
| 1 small carrot, chopped | 1 tbsp apple cider vinegar |
| 4 mushrooms, chopped | 2 tsp dried basil |
| 1 stalk celery, chopped | 1 tsp dried oregano |
| 1 tbsp olive oil | ½ tsp dried thyme |
| 1 cup spinach, chopped | ½ tsp salt |
| 1 cup cooked or canned chickpeas | 1 tsp pepper |
| 1 14-oz (398-ml) can diced tomatoes | 2 large bell peppers (your choice), halved and seeded |

Preheat oven to 375°F. In a medium saucepan on medium heat, sauté the garlic, onions, carrots, mushrooms, and celery in oil until vegetables become tender. Remove from heat, add spinach, and cover. Let sit for 5 minutes. In a large bowl, combine the vegetable mixture, chickpeas, tomatoes, tomato paste, oil, vinegar, basil, oregano, thyme, salt, and pepper and mix well. Lay out peppers on a large baking sheet or lasagna pan and spoon an even amount of mixture into each pepper. Cover and cook for 20-30 minutes.
Makes 2-4 servings.

# JESSE'S CUBAN SENSATION

"This recipe actually comes from my roommate, Jesse, who grew up next door to a Cuban family. When Jesse went vegan, she veganized their recipe. In honor of her I'll call it..." – Kevin, Bellevue, Washington

| | |
|---|---|
| 1 small onion, diced | 3 cups vegetable stock (pg. 217) |
| 2-4 cloves garlic, minced | ½ tsp dried thyme |
| 1 small green bell pepper, chopped | 1 tsp salt |
| 1 small red bell pepper, chopped | 1 tsp pepper |
| 2 jalapeno peppers, seeded and minced | 2 cups cooked *or* canned black beans |
| 1 tbsp olive oil | 2 tbsp lime juice |
| 1 cup uncooked jasmine rice | |

In a large saucepan on medium-high heat, sauté the onion, garlic, peppers, and jalapenos in oil until onions are translucent. Add the rice, vegetable stock, thyme, salt, pepper, and beans. Bring to a boil, reduce heat to low, and simmer for 10-15 minutes or until vegetables and rice are cooked. Stir in lime juice and let stand 5 minutes before serving. Makes 4-6 servings.

# T O F U   C H I M I C H A N G A S

This recipe came to us from Joel, who lives in Guelph, Ontario. Serve these with guacamole, salsa (pg. 131), and a side salad.

¼ cup Braggs
3 tbsp nutritional yeast
½ tsp onion powder
½ tsp garlic powder
1 cup water
1 lb firm tofu, diced
2 cloves garlic, minced
1 small onion, chopped

1 tbsp olive oil
¼ tbsp chili powder
½ tsp cumin
6 tortilla shells
2 cups refried beans (pg. 114)
1 cup soy cheese (grated)
⅓ cup olives (your choice) (optional)

In a medium bowl, stir together the Braggs, nutritional yeast, onion powder, garlic powder, and water. Add the tofu and let marinate for 1-2 hours, or overnight in refrigerator. Preheat oven to 350°F. Drain the marinated tofu and set aside. In a medium saucepan on medium heat, sauté the garlic and onions in oil until onions are translucent. Add the tofu, chili powder, and cumin. Stir together and cook for an additional 8-10 minutes while mashing tofu with a wooden spoon. Set aside. Spread out the tortilla shells on a flat surface. In the middle of each shell, evenly divide out the tofu mixture, beans, soy cheese, and olives. Wrap up and place on a baking sheet or lasagna pan. Bake for 10-15 minutes, or until tortillas are browned. Makes 6 chimichangas.

# SPICY VEGETABLE HOT POT

This easy to make hot pot doesn't scrimp on taste. Serve over a bed of couscous, quinoa or rice.

1 small onion, chopped
2 tbsp olive oil
2 cups vegetable stock (pg. 217)
2 medium carrots, chopped
2 medium potatoes, chopped
2 cloves garlic, minced
1 tbsp curry powder
1 tsp cumin
¼ tsp cardamom
¼ tsp nutmeg

⅛ tsp allspice
1 small red chili pepper, seeded and minced
1 tbsp fresh ginger, grated
1 medium apple, chopped
1 cup green beans, cut into thirds
1 cup cauliflower, chopped
2 cups cooked *or* canned chickpeas
1 tbsp fresh cilantro
¼ cup cashews, dry roasted (pg. 209)

In a large saucepan on medium heat, sauté the onions in oil until they are translucent. Stir in the stock, carrots, potatoes, garlic, curry, cumin, cardamom, nutmeg, allspice, chili pepper, and ginger. Bring to a boil, reduce heat to low, and simmer for 8 minutes. Add the apple, green beans, cauliflower, and chickpeas and cook for an additional 3 minutes or until veggies are cooked. Stir in the cilantro. Remove from heat and let sit covered for 5 minutes before serving. Garnish with cashews. Makes 4-6 servings.

# SIMPLY LOVELY QUINOA

"My daughter and I developed this recipe together. It's quick and makes for a good entrée and a great lunch for the next day if you have any left over. We serve it with corn chips and a nice green salad." – Sharon & Kandice, Saskatoon, Saskatchewan

1 small onion, chopped
2-3 cloves garlic, minced
2-3 stalks celery, chopped
6-8 mushrooms, chopped
1 tbsp olive oil
1 cup quinoa

1 28-oz (796-ml) can diced tomatoes
1 cup vegetable stock (pg. 217)
1 tsp dried thyme
½ tsp salt
½ tsp pepper

In a large saucepan on medium-high heat, sauté the onion, garlic, celery, and mushrooms in oil until the onions are translucent. Add the quinoa and sauté for an additional minute. Stir in the diced tomatoes (do not drain), stock, thyme, salt, and pepper. Mix together, reduce heat to medium-low, cover and simmer for 25-30 minutes, or until liquid has reduced. Makes 4-6 servings.

# VEGETABLE JUMBLE WITH CORNMEAL CRUST

Non-vegans always seem to ask why vegans like to use mock-meat products. We say, why not? They are cruelty-free, delicious, and are good for us. There are all different brands out there to try. Shop around and find the brand you like best.

**1 medium onion, chopped**
**1 medium bell pepper (your choice), chopped**
**1 tbsp olive oil**
**1 12-oz (340-g) pkg mock ground beef**
**1 12-oz (250-ml) can tomato sauce**
**2 tbsp tomato paste**
**1 cup corn**
**1 tbsp Worcestershire sauce (pg. 207)**
**2 tsp chili powder**
**1 tsp cumin**
**1 tsp hot sauce (your choice)**
**½ tsp allspice**
**½ tsp salt**
**½ cup flour**
**1 cup cornmeal**
**2 tbsp dry sweetener**
**2 tsp baking powder**
**3 tbsp olive oil**
**¾ cup soy milk**
**1 4-oz (120-ml) can green chilies**

Preheat oven to 375°F. In a large saucepan on medium-high heat, sauté the onions and peppers in oil until the onions are translucent. Add the mock ground beef, tomato sauce, tomato paste, corn, Worcestershire sauce, chili powder, cumin, hot sauce, allspice, and salt and sauté for an additional minute. Transfer mixture to a 9-inch casserole dish. In a medium bowl, stir together the flour, cornmeal, sweetener, and baking powder. Add the oil, soy milk, and chilies. Mix together until "just mixed." Spoon batter on top of vegetable mixture. Bake for 25-30 minutes, or until top is golden brown. Make 4-6 servings.

# KURSTIN'S WALNUT BURGERS

This recipe came from a old co-worker of mine. Not only is she a first-rate artist, she's also incredible in the kitchen. This recipe freeze well, so make a bunch and save them for a rainy day. (T)

- ¼ lb medium tofu
- ¼ cup hazelnuts
- ¼ cup Braggs
- 1 tbsp flour
- ¼ cup water
- 1 cup bread crumbs
- 1 cup cooked rice (your choice)
- 2-3 cup walnuts, ground
- ½ small onion, diced
- 1 small carrot, grated
- 1 small beet, grated
- ½ cup rolled oat flakes

In a blender or food processor, blend the tofu, hazelnuts, and Braggs, until smooth. Add the flour, and water. Blend until well mixed and set aside. In a large bowl, mix together the bread crumbs, rice, walnuts, onions, carrots, beets, and rolled oats. Add the tofu mixture and mix well. Divide and shape into 10 patties. Lay down each patty in flour, coating each side. On a lightly oiled frying pan on medium-high heat, fry patties for 5-10 minutes or until browned on both sides. Makes 10 patties.

Breads
& Muffins

*We occasionally get letters from people having problems with their vegan baking. Here are some easy tips that may help you:*

· It may be a urban myth, but we find that metallic bowls hinder the rising ability of baked goods. Get a nice, big ceramic bread bowl and use wooden spoons when stirring.

· Don't overmix! When a recipe asks you to stir gently until "just mixed," you want to mix "just" enough to blend all the ingredients together. Avoid mixing too vigorously as your baking will end up flat and heavy. Unless you're making something with yeast; then you can work out all your frustrations and stir to your heart's content.

· Sifting or whisking your dry ingredients before adding wet ingredients can help to keep your baking light.

· Check for readiness by inserting a toothpick or a clean knife into your baked goods before taking them out of the oven. If it comes out clean, it's ready; if it's still gooey, wait another 3-5 minutes and test again.

· Keep your ingredients fresh. Stale baking soda, baking powder, yeast etc. can sometimes be the reason for mishaps in your baking. We suggest you buy small amounts and replenish them often.

# BREADS

## FRENCH BAGUETTE

A baguette is bread that's been formed into a long, narrow cylindrical loaf. It has a crisp crust and light, chewy interior that will make your friends say, "Ooh la la."

**2 ¼ tsp *or* one packet dry active yeast**
**1 ½ cups warm water**
**1 tsp dry sweetener**
**4 cups flour**
**2 ½ tsp salt**

In a large bowl, stir together the yeast with warm water and sweetener. Let sit for 10 minutes. Stir in 2 cups of the flour until well combined. Stir in the remaining flour, ½ cup at a time, and salt. On a lightly floured surface, knead the dough until smooth and elastic. Transfer dough to a large, lightly oiled bowl, turning dough until covered with oil. Cover with cloth and set aside in a warm, non-drafty spot and let rise until doubled in size (approx. 1-1 ½ hours). Preheat oven to 475°F. Punch down dough and form a long slender loaf or two mini-loaves. Place loaf on lightly oiled cookie sheet, cover and let rise for 30 minutes. Make 4 diagonal slashes on loaf with knife and lightly brush top of loaf with water. Bake loaf for 20-25 minutes or until golden and sounds hollow when tapped. Let cool before serving. Makes 1 large or 2 small baguettes.

# CORIANDER BREAD

A beautiful, subtle bread that is perfect for all things bread-like, especially sandwiches.

| | |
|---|---|
| **1 tbsp dry active yeast** | **1 tsp salt** |
| **¼ cup warm water** | **¾ tsp coriander** |
| **½ tsp dry sweetener** | **¼ tsp ground ginger** |
| **¾ cup soy milk** | **½ tsp cinnamon** |
| **¼ cup olive oil** | **⅛ tsp cloves** |
| **¼ cup maple syrup** | **3 ¼ cups flour** |
| **egg replacer, equal to 1 egg** | |

In a large bowl, stir together the yeast with warm water and sweetener. Let sit for 10 minutes. Stir in the soy milk, oil, maple syrup, egg replacer, salt, coriander, ginger, cinnamon and cloves, and 1 cup of flour. Slowly stir in remaining flour ½ cup at a time. On a lightly floured surface, knead dough until smooth and elastic; add a little extra flour if it's too sticky. Transfer dough to a large, lightly oiled bowl, turning dough until covered with oil. Cover with cloth and set aside in a warm, non-drafty spot and let rise until doubled in size (approx. 1-1½ hours). Preheat oven to 350°F. Punch down dough, knead out air bubbles, and place in a lightly oiled bread pan. Lightly brush top of loaf with oil. Cover and let rise again for 15 minutes. Bake for 30-35 minutes. Cool on rack before serving. Makes 1 loaf.

# SESAME ANISE BREAD

Anise seeds have a distinctive, sweet licorice flavor, but don't let that freak you out. They add a subtle taste to this delicious bread.

| | |
|---|---|
| **1 tbsp dry active yeast** | **1 tbsp maple syrup** |
| **½ cup warm water** | **1 tsp salt** |
| **½ tsp dry sweetener** | **1 tsp anise seed** |
| **⅓ cup soy milk** | **1 tbsp sesame seeds** |
| **1 tbsp olive oil** | **2 ¼ cups flour** |

In a large bowl, stir together the yeast with warm water and sweetener. Let sit for 10 minutes. Add the soy milk, oil, maple syrup, salt, anise, sesame seeds, and 1 cup of flour. Slowly stir in remaining flour ½ cup at a time. On a lightly floured surface, knead dough until smooth and elastic; add a little extra flour if it's too sticky. Transfer dough to a large, lightly oiled bowl, turning dough until covered with oil. Cover with cloth and set aside in a warm, non-drafty spot and let rise until doubled in size (approx. 1-1½ hours). Preheat oven to 375°F. Punch down dough, knead out air bubbles, and place in a lightly oiled bread pan. Lightly brush top of loaf with oil. Cover and let rise again for 15 minutes. Bake for 30-35 minutes. Cool on rack before serving. Makes 1 loaf.

# RYE BREAD

A dark dense loaf ... but it's no dummy.

> ¾ tbsp dry active yeast
> 1 cup warm water
> 1 tbsp maple syrup
> 1 tsp olive oil
> 1 tsp salt
> ½ tbsp caraway seeds
> ½ tbsp poppy seeds
> 1 ½ cups rye flour
> 1 cup flour

In a large bowl, stir together the yeast with warm water and maple syrup. Let sit for 10 minutes. Add the oil, salt, and caraway and poppy seeds. Add the rye flour and stir together well. Slowly stir in the flour. On a lightly floured surface, knead until smooth and elastic; add a little extra flour if it's too sticky. Transfer dough to a large, lightly oiled bowl, turning dough until covered with oil. Cover with cloth and set aside in a warm, non-drafty spot and let rise until doubled in size (approx. 1-1½ hours). Preheat oven to 375°F. Punch down dough, knead out air bubbles, and place in a lightly oiled bread pan. Lightly brush top of loaf with oil. Cover and let rise again for 15 minutes. Bake for 30-35 minutes. Cool on rack before serving. Makes 1 loaf.

# PITA BREAD

This Middle Eastern flatbread travels well for lunch or picnics. Each pita round can split horizontally to form a pocket into which a wide variety of ingredients can be stuffed to make a sandwich (pg. 54), or can be rolled to make a wrap. They also can be sliced into wedges and are great for dipping in things like hummus (pg. 134). For extra zip, add 1 ½ tsp of your favourite herb (e.g., poppy seeds, anise, caraway).

> **2 ¼ tsp *or* one packet dry active yeast**
> **1 ⅛ cups warm water**
> **1 ½ tsp dry sweetener**
> **3 cups flour**
> **1 ½ tsp salt**

In a large bowl, stir together the yeast with warm water and sweetener. Let sit for 10 minutes. Stir in the flour 1 cup at a time. On a lightly floured surface, knead dough until smooth and elastic; add a little extra flour if it's too sticky. Transfer dough to a large, lightly oiled bowl, turning dough until covered with oil. Cover with cloth and set aside in a warm, non-drafty spot and let rise until doubled in size (approx. 1-1½ hours). Punch down dough, knead out air bubbles, and divide dough into 8. Shape with your hands or roll into 6-inch circles. Set aside on a lightly floured counter, cover with cloth, and let rise 30 minutes. Preheat oven to 500°F. Place 1 or 2 pitas on a wire cake rack. Place cake rack directly on oven rack. Bake for 4-5 minutes or until puffed and top begins to brown. Remove from oven and place in a sealed paper bag or cover with a damp cloth to keep from drying out. Let cool. Makes 8 pitas.

# OAT BREAD

A tasty cake-like bread that goes perfectly with a steaming bowl of chili or hot soup.

> **2 ½ cups flour**
> **1 ½ tsp baking powder**
> **⅛ tsp baking soda**
> **½ tsp salt**
> **¾ cup rolled oat flakes**
> **1 ¼ cups water**
> **¼ cup olive oil**
> **¼ cup maple syrup**

Preheat oven to 350°F. In a large bowl, sift together the flour, baking powder, baking soda, and salt. Stir in the oat flakes. Add the water, oil, and maple syrup, and stir together gently until "just mixed." Dough will be sticky but will pull away from the side of the bowl. Place into a lightly oiled bread pan and bake for 45-50 minutes or until toothpick comes out clean. Makes 1 loaf.

# OLIVE & SUN-DRIED TOMATO FOCACCIA BREAD

Focaccia is a traditional Italian flatbread which is drizzled with olive oil, sprinkled with coarse salt and coarsely chopped herbs, and baked. These days it comes soft or crisp, thick or thin. This is our version of a classic favorite.

**1 pizza dough, uncooked (pg. 176)**
**1 ½ tsp dried rosemary**
**1 ½ tsp dried oregano**
**1 tsp coarse sea salt**
**½ tsp coarse black pepper**
**2 tsp olive oil**
**⅓-½ cup olives (your choice), chopped**
**⅓-½ cup sun-dried tomatoes, rehydrated and chopped (pg. 208)**

Preheat oven to 400°F. In small bowl, mix together the rosemary, oregano, salt, and pepper. Set aside. Punch down dough and roll out to form a rectangle. Place loaf on lightly oiled cookie sheet and let rise for 30 minutes. Dimple surface of dough all over with fingertips and brush surface with olive oil. Sprinkle rosemary mixture evenly over dough and top with olives and sun-dried tomatoes. Bake for 15-20 minutes or until edge is browned. Makes 1 loaf.

# QUICK BREADS

## PEAR GINGER PECAN BREAD

Ginger adds a kick to this sweet little bread.

**2 cups flour**
**2 tsp baking powder**
**½ tsp baking soda**
**⅛ tsp salt**
**½ cup dry sweetener**
**¾ cup apple juice**

**⅓ cup olive oil**
**1 banana, mashed**
**1 large pear, cored and cubed**
**½ cup pecans, chopped**
**3 tbsp fresh ginger, grated**

Preheat oven to 350°F. In a large bowl, sift together the flour, baking powder, baking soda, and salt. Stir in sweetener, apple juice, oil, banana, pear, pecans, and ginger. Stir together gently until "just mixed." Pour batter into a lightly oiled bread pan and bake for 45-50 minutes or until a toothpick comes out clean. Let cool on a rack for 10 minutes before removing from pan. Makes 1 loaf.

## BOSTON BROWN BREAD

A dark and delicious bread that goes well served with chili or soup.

**1 cup rye flour**
**1 ¼ cups flour**
**¼ cup rolled oat flakes**
**⅓ cup cornmeal**
**¾ tsp baking powder**

**1 ½ tsp baking soda**
**½ tsp salt**
**½ cup currants**
**2 cups soy milk**
**⅓ cup molasses**

Preheat oven to 300°F. In a large bowl, stir together the rye flour, flour, oat flakes, cornmeal, baking powder, baking soda, salt, and currants. In a small bowl, whisk together the soy milk and molasses. Add to flour and stir together gently until "just mixed." Pour batter into a lightly oiled bread pan and bake for 1 ¼ hours. Let cool on a rack for 10 minutes before removing from pan. Makes 1 loaf.

# ENGLISH SCONES

"A slightly altered version of the one my mom has been making since I was knee high to a grasshopper!"
– Wendy, Victoria, BC

**1 ½ cups flour**
**2 tsp baking powder**
**½ tsp baking soda**
**1 tsp salt**
**½ cup dry sweetener**
**½ cup margarine**
**½ cup currants**
**½ cup soy milk**

Preheat oven to 400°F. In a large bowl, sift together the flour, baking powder, baking soda, and salt. Stir in the sweetener, margarine, currants, and soy milk. Stir together gently until "just mixed." Once mixed, evenly separate dough into 6. Place on a lightly greased baking sheet, pressing down with fingers. Bake for 12-15 minutes or until biscuits are golden brown. Makes 6 scones.

# APPLESAUCE RAISIN SPICE LOAF

This lovely loaf is from Tracy in Victoria, BC. It goes perfectly with friends and a spot of tea.

**2 cups flour**
**2 tsp baking powder**
**1 tsp baking soda**
**½ tsp dried ginger**
**2 tsp cinnamon**
**½ tsp nutmeg**
**½ tsp allspice**
**½ tsp salt**

**1 cup raisins**
**½ cup margarine**
**¾ cup dry sweetener**
**egg replacer, equal to 2 eggs (pg. 212)**
**⅔ cup applesauce**
**½ cup soy milk**
**2 tsp vanilla extract**

Preheat oven to 350°F. In a large bowl, sift together the flour, baking powder, and baking soda. Stir in the ginger, cinnamon, nutmeg, allspice, and salt. Stir in the raisins, margarine, sweetener, egg replacer, applesauce, soy milk, and vanilla extract. Stir together gently until "just mixed." Pour into a lightly oiled loaf pan and bake for 55-60 minutes or until a toothpick comes out clean. Let cool on a rack for 10 minutes before removing from pan. Makes 1 loaf.

# BISCUITS 'N' OTHER THINGS

## BISCUITS

This dough freezes well, but cannot be refrozen after it's been thawed. It can also be used for recipes such as NOT Pigs in a Blanket (pg. 105) as well as biscuits.

> **2 cups flour**
> **3 tsp baking powder**
> **1 tsp salt**
> **¼ cup margarine**
> **¾ cup soy milk**

Preheat oven to 475°F. In a large bowl, stir together the flour, baking powder, and salt. Add the margarine and incorporate into the flour. Add the soy milk, ¼ of a cup at a time, and gently knead the dough together. (Don't knead too much, or the biscuits won't be fluffy.) Once kneaded, separate dough into 2 balls and shape each ball into a rectangle. Cut 6 biscuits from each rectangle. Lay out on a lightly greased baking sheet and bake for 12-15 minutes or until biscuits are golden brown. Makes 12 biscuits.

## SAVOURY ONION & PEPPER BISCUITS

A delicious alternative to an old stand-by.

> **2 stalks green onion, chopped**
> **½ small red bell pepper, chopped**
> **1 tsp olive oil**
> **2 cups flour**
> **1 tbsp baking powder**
>
> **1 tbsp dried oregano**
> **½ salt**
> **⅓ cup margarine**
> **⅔ cup soy milk**
> **2 tbsp soy Parmesan cheese (optional)**

Preheat oven to 400°F. In a small saucepan, sauté the green onions and bell peppers in oil on medium-high heat until peppers are tender but firm to the bite. Set aside. In a medium bowl, stir together the flour, baking powder, oregano, and salt. Add the margarine and incorporate into the flour. Add the green onion/bell pepper mixture and soy milk, ¼ of a cup at a time, and gently knead the dough together. (Don't knead too much, or the biscuits won't be fluffy.) Once kneaded, separate dough into 2 balls and shape each ball into a rectangle. Cut 6 biscuits from each rectangle. Lay out on a lightly greased baking sheet and sprinkle with optional soy Parmesan. Bake for 15-18 minutes or until biscuits are golden brown. Makes 12 biscuits.

# CINNAMON RAISIN BISCUITS

A sweet cinnamon treat that goes great with breakfast.

**2 cups flour**
**2 tsp baking powder**
**1 tsp salt**
**1 tsp cinnamon**
**⅓ cup dry sweetener**
**¼ cup margarine**
**1 cup raisins**
**1 cup soy milk**

Preheat oven to 400°F. In a large bowl, stir together the flour, baking powder, salt, cinnamon, and sweetener. Add the margarine and incorporate into the flour. Add the raisins and soy milk, ¼ of a cup at a time, and gently knead the dough together. (Don't knead too much, or the biscuits won't be fluffy.) Once kneaded, separate dough into 2 balls and shape each ball into a rectangle. Cut 6 biscuits from each rectangle. Lay out on a lightly greased baking sheet and bake for 15-18 minutes or until biscuits are golden brown. Makes 12 biscuits.

# CALZONE DOUGH

Check out our calzone filling recipe on page 59.

**1 ½ tsp dry active yeast**
**1 cup warm water**
**1 tbsp dry sweetener**
**2 ½ cups flour**
**1 ½ tsp salt**

In a large bowl, stir together the yeast with warm water and sweetener. Let sit for 10 minutes. Preheat oven to 450°F. Stir in 2 cups of the flour until well combined. Stir in the remaining flour and salt. On a lightly floured surface, knead the dough for 6 minutes or until smooth and elastic. Transfer dough to a large lightly oiled bowl, turning dough until covered with oil. Cover with a cloth and set aside in a non-drafty spot and let rise until doubled in size (approx. 1-1½ hours). Divide dough into 6. On a lightly floured surface, roll out ball into a 6-inch circle. Place one cup of filling in middle of circle and fold over and press edges with finger, then crimp edge with fork. Arrange on baking tray and bake for 15-20 minutes. Makes 6 calzones.

# PIZZA DOUGH

Why get store-bought when it's just as easy to make it yourself?

> **2 tsp dry active yeast**
> **1 ½ cups warm water**
> **1 tsp dry sweetener**
> **3 cups flour**
> **1 tsp salt**

In a large bowl, stir together the yeast, warm water, and sweetener. Let sit for 10 minutes. With a wooden spoon stir in 2 cups of the flour until well combined. Stir in the remaining flour and salt. On a lightly floured surface, knead the dough for 6-8 minutes or until smooth and elastic. Transfer dough to a large, lightly oiled bowl, turning dough until covered with oil. Cover with a cloth and set aside in a warm, non-drafty spot and let rise until doubled in size (approx. 1-1½ hours). Punch down dough and roll out to form a rectangle. Place loaf on a lightly oiled cookie sheet and let rise for 30 minutes. Preheat oven to 350°F. Add favorite toppings and bake for 30-40 minutes. Makes 1 pizza crust.

# MUFFINS

## ALMOND COCONUT MUFFINS

Delicious and tasty, with a hint of orange. Who could ask for anything more?

> **1 ½ cups flour**
> **1 cup shredded coconut**
> **½ cup dry sweetener**
> **1 ½ tsp baking powder**
> **½ tsp baking soda**
> **¼ tsp salt**

> **¾ cup coconut milk**
> **egg replacer, equal to 2 eggs (pg. 212)**
> **¼ cup olive oil**
> **1 tsp vanilla extract**
> **zest of 1 small orange**
> **⅓ cup dry roasted almonds, chopped (pg. 209)**

Preheat oven to 400°F. In a large bowl, stir together the flour, coconut, sweetener, baking powder, baking soda, and salt. Stir in the coconut milk, egg replacer, oil, vanilla, orange zest, and almonds, and stir gently until "just mixed." Spoon into lightly oiled muffin tins and bake for 12-15 minutes or until toothpick comes out clean. Makes 6 muffins.

# CARROT GINGER MUFFINS

Who can resist the tastes of carrots and ginger? These muffins are moist, tender, and taste almost like carrot cake.

| | |
|---|---|
| 2 cups flour | ½ cup pecans, chopped |
| ½ cup dry sweetener | 2 medium carrots, grated |
| 1 tsp baking soda | ¾ cup soy milk |
| 1 tsp baking powder | egg replacer, equal to two eggs (pg. 212) |
| ½ tsp salt | ¼ cup olive oil |
| ½ tsp cinnamon | 2 tbsp fresh ginger, grated |

Preheat oven to 400°F. In a large bowl, stir together the flour, sweetener, baking soda, baking powder, salt, cinnamon, and pecans. Add the carrots, soy milk, egg replacer, oil, and ginger. Stir gently until "just mixed." Spoon into lightly oiled muffin tins and bake for 12-15 minutes or until a toothpick comes out clean. Makes 6 muffins.

# APPLE STREUSEL MUFFINS

My mom gave us this recipe. She loves to eat these for breakfast and so should you! It's the perfect combination of apples and cinnamon with a sweet topping. (T)

| | |
|---|---|
| 2 tbsp dry sweetener | 1 tsp cinnamon |
| ¼ tsp cinnamon | ¼ tsp salt |
| ¼ tsp nutmeg | 1 apple, finely chopped |
| 1 ¾ cups flour | 1 cup soy milk |
| ½ cup oat bran | ¼ cup water |
| ½ cup dry sweetener | ¼ cup olive oil |
| 1 tbsp baking powder | egg replacer, equal to two eggs (pg. 212) |

Preheat oven to 400°F. In a small bowl, stir together the sweetener, cinnamon, and nutmeg. Set aside. In a large bowl, stir together the flour, oat bran, sweetener, baking powder, cinnamon, and salt. Stir in the apples, soy milk, water, oil, and egg replacer. Stir gently until "just mixed." Spoon into lightly oiled muffin tins and sprinkle with cinnamon sugar. Bake for 12-15 minutes or until a toothpick comes out clean. Makes 6 muffins.

# NANA MARG'S BRAN MUFFIN MIX IN A JAR

My nana keeps this mixture around so when guests come by unexpectedly she can quickly make these and serve them with tea. This dry mixture stays fresh in the refrigerator for 2 months. This recipe makes enough for 3 batches of muffins. (T)

- **3 cups flour**
- **3 cups bran**
- **2 tbsp cinnamon**
- **2 tbsp baking powder**
- **1 tbsp baking soda**
- **1 ½ tsp salt**
- **1 tsp nutmeg**
- **1 tsp allspice**
- **1 tsp cloves**
- **1 ½ cup dry sweetener**
- **1 ½ cup raisins**

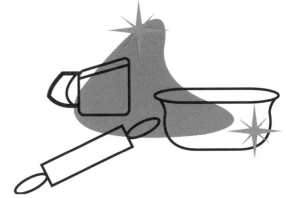

In a large bowl, mix together all the ingredients. Transfer mixture to a large, air-tight container. Store in refrigerator.

# NANA MARG'S QUICK MIX BRAN MUFFINS

- **2 cups Bran Muffin Mix (above)**
- **¼ cup olive oil**
- **1 banana, mashed**
- **¼ cup applesauce**
- **¼ cup water**

Preheat oven to 400°F. In a large bowl, mix together all the ingredients. Stir together gently until "just mixed." Spoon into lightly oiled muffin tins and bake for 12-15 minutes or until a toothpick comes out clean. Makes 6 muffins.

# BLUEBERRY MUFFINS

A wonderful muffin recipe from our friend Wendy in Victoria, BC. Throw some pecans into the mix and get nutty!

**1 cup soy milk**
**1 cup rolled oat flakes**
**1 cup flour**
**1 tsp baking powder**
**½ tsp baking soda**
**½ tsp salt**
**egg replacer, equal to 1 egg (pg. 212)**
**¼ cup olive oil**
**½ cup dry sweetener**
**1 cup fresh *or* frozen blueberries**

Preheat oven to 400°F. In a medium bowl, stir together the soy milk and oat flakes. Set aside for 10 minutes. In a large bowl, stir together the flour, baking powder, baking soda, and salt. Stir in the egg replacer, oil, sweetener, and oat mixture. Gently stir in the blueberries and spoon into lightly oiled muffin tins and bake for 20-25 minutes or until a toothpick comes out clean. Makes 6 muffins.

# COFFEE BREAK MUFFINS

Everyone needs a pick-me-up in the afternoon. While we don't usually recommend you supplement your energy with sugar, sometimes a sweet treat is exactly what you need.

**1 ½ cups flour**
**2 tsp baking powder**
**½ tsp salt**
**¼ cup margarine**
**½ cup dry sweetener**
**egg replacer, equal to 1 egg (pg. 212)**
**¾ cup soy milk**
**½ tsp vanilla extract**
**2 tbsp cinnamon sugar (pg. 213)**

Preheat oven to 400°F. In a large bowl, stir together the flour, baking powder, and salt. Stir in the margarine, sweetener, egg replacer, soy milk, and vanilla. Stir together gently until "just mixed." Spoon into lightly oiled muffin tins and sprinkle with cinnamon sugar. Bake for 20-25 minutes or until a toothpick comes out clean. Makes 6 muffins.

Desserts

*Desserts are high on the list of things that make vegans fall off the wagon. They can be a vegan's worst nightmare because inside every tempting, mouth-watering non-vegan dessert lurks eggs, butter, lard, milk, beef tallow ... but never fear, Sarah and Tanya are here to save the day. These desserts are not only delicious, delectable, and satisfying but animal friendly too. We use olive oil for all our cooking/baking; if you find you don't like the taste, just switch to an oil you prefer.*

# KATHLEEN'S CHOCOLATE COOKIES

"Hey guys, I just wanted to tell you I think your book is great, especially all the desserts. I have one of my own I wanted to share with you. Thanks again!" – Kathleen, Danville, California

> **½ cup margarine**
> **1 cup dry sweetener**
> **1 ½ tsp vanilla extract *or* mint extract**
> **egg replacer, equal to 1 egg (pg. 212)**
> **1 tsp baking soda**
> **½ tsp salt**
> **1 cup rolled oat flakes**
> **¼ cup cocoa**
> **½ cup flour**

Preheat oven to 350°F. In a large bowl, stir together the margarine, sweetener, vanilla, egg replacer, baking soda, and salt. Stir in the rolled oats, followed by the cocoa, and then the flour. Stir until well mixed. Spoon a heaping tablespoon of dough onto a cookie sheet and press flat with your fingers. Bake for 8-10 minutes or until edges are browned. Let cool on the sheet before moving them. Makes 12 cookies.

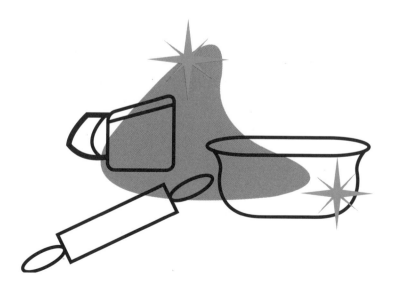

# MUM'S SUGAR COOKIES

"This is a twist on my mum's recipe. We used to have such fun making these every holiday." – Christina, Corvallis, Oregon

For a twist, add ¼ cup of pecans to the batter. Then ice, decorate, or sprinkle with sugar before you bake them. Anyway you do it, they are going to be yum!

**¾ cup dry sweetener**
**1 cup margarine**
**egg replacer, equal to 1 egg (pg. 212)**
**1 tsp vanilla extract**
**½ tsp salt**
**2 ¼ cups flour**
**¼ tsp baking soda**

Preheat oven to 375°F. In a large bowl, stir together the sweetener, margarine, egg replacer, and vanilla. Stir in the salt, flour, and baking soda and mix until well combined. Divide dough in half and roll out each half on a lightly floured surface. Cut into desired shapes and bake for 8-10 minutes or until edges are browned. Makes 25-50 cookies, depending on size.

# LEMON POPPY SEED SHORTBREAD COOKIES

Don't save this delightful recipe for Christmas time, make it all year round. Use your favorite cookie cutter to make fun shapes, or if you're in a pinch, use the open end of a drinking glass.

**1 cup flour**
**2 tbsp poppy seeds**
**2 tbsp arrowroot powder**
**¼ tsp nutmeg**
**⅛ tsp salt**
**½ cup margarine**
**⅓ dry sweetener**
**1 ½ tbsp lemon juice**
**1 tbsp lemon zest, grated**
**1 tsp vanilla extract**

Preheat oven to 350°F. In a medium bowl, stir together the flour, poppy seeds, arrowroot powder, nutmeg, and salt. In a small bowl, mix together the margarine, sweetener, lemon juice, lemon zest, and vanilla. Add the margarine mixture to the flour mixture and stir until "just mixed." Spoon a heaping tablespoon of dough onto a lightly oiled cookie sheet and press flat with your fingers, or roll dough out and use a cookie cutter. Bake for 10-12 minutes or until edges are browned. Make 12-18 cookies.

# MAUREEN'S OATMEAL CHOCOLATE CHIP COOKIES

After years of begging and pleading, Maureen finally caved and gave us her top secret and most amazing cookie recipe. Lucky you, lucky us! Make these for all occasions.

**¾ cup flour**
**½ cup dry sweetener**
**2 cups rolled oat flakes**
**½ tsp baking soda**
**½ tsp baking powder**
**½ tsp salt**
**⅓ cup soft tofu** *or* **½ banana**
**⅓ cup olive oil**
**½ cup maple syrup**
**1 tbsp vanilla extract**
**1 - 1 ½ cups chocolate chips (*or* carob chips)**

Preheat oven to 350°F. In a large bowl, stir together the flour, sweetener, rolled oats, baking soda, baking powder, and salt. In a blender or food processor, blend together the tofu, oil, maple syrup, and vanilla. Pour tofu mixture into flour mixture and stir. Add the chocolate chips and stir until well incorporated. Spoon a heaping tablespoon of dough onto a cookie sheet and press flat with your fingers. Bake for 12-15 minutes or until edges are browned. Makes 10-14 cookies, depending on size.

# RACHEL'S LOUISVILLE COOKIES

When we were in Louisville, Kentucky doing a cooking demo for Earthsave, a lovely woman came up to our table and handed us a piece of paper with a handwritten recipe. The recipe was for these wonderful cookies. So get baking, and thank Rachel out loud while you chomp down on them. Thanks, Rachel!

½ cup margarine
1 banana, mashed
¼ cup applesauce
1 tsp vanilla extract
½ cup dry sweetener
1 cup flour
¼ tsp salt
1 tsp baking powder
2 ½ cups rolled oat flakes
¼ cup shredded coconut
1 cup chopped walnuts (*or* nuts of your choice)
½ cup dried apricots (*or* dried fruit of your choice)

Preheat oven to 350°F. In a large bowl, stir together the margarine, banana, applesauce, vanilla, and sweetener. Add the flour, salt, baking powder, rolled oat flakes, coconut, walnuts, and apricots. Spoon a heaping tablespoon of dough onto a cookie sheet and press flat with your fingers. Bake for 12-15 minutes or until edges are browned. Makes 10-14 cookies, depending on size.

# NUT BUTTER COOKIES

Nothing takes you back to when you were a kid and says, "Come here and give your gramma a kiss" like these cookies. These are from Nina in Ottawa, Ontario. We suggest to add ½ cup of chocolate or carob chips if you feel the need.

1 ⅓ cups flour
¾ cup dry sweetener
½ tsp baking soda
½ tsp salt
½ cup margarine
1 ¼ cups nut butter, your choice (e.g., peanut, almond)
1 tsp vanilla extract

Preheat oven to 350°F. In a large bowl, stir together the flour, sweetener, baking soda, and salt. Add the margarine, nut butter, and vanilla and stir together until well mixed. Spoon a heaping tablespoon of dough onto a cookie sheet and press flat with your fingers. Use a fork to make a criss-cross pattern on top of each cookie. Bake for 12-15 minutes or until edges are browned. Let cool before removing from cookie sheet. Makes 10-18, cookies depending on size.

# CRANBERRY ALMOND COOKIES

A graceful, lovely cookie that goes great with tea. The cranberries make them tart, so even if you don't have much of a sweet tooth, you can also take pleasure in these.

| | |
|---|---|
| 2 ¼ cups flour | ¼ cup olive oil |
| ¾ cup dry sweetener | ¼ cup margarine |
| 1 tsp baking soda | 1 tsp almond extract |
| ¼ tsp salt | egg replacer, equal to 2 eggs (pg. 212) |
| ½ tsp cinnamon | 1 cup almonds, chopped |
| ⅓ cup soy milk | ¾ cup cranberries |

Preheat oven to 350°F. In a large bowl, stir together the flour, sweetener, baking soda, salt, and cinnamon. Add the soy milk, oil, margarine, almond extract, egg replacer, almonds, and cranberries and stir together until well mixed. Spoon a heaping tablespoon of dough onto a lightly oiled cookie sheet and press flat with your fingers. Bake for 10 minutes or until edges are browned. Makes 12-16 cookies, depending on size.

# BROWNIE COOKIES

Dark, lovely, and oh so delectable.

| | |
|---|---|
| 1 ¼ cups flour | ⅓ cup olive oil |
| ½ cup dry sweetener | egg replacer, equal to 2 eggs (pg. 212) |
| ¼ cup cocoa powder | ¾ cup soy milk |
| ½ tsp baking powder | 1 tsp vanilla extract |
| ½ tsp baking soda | ⅓ cup walnuts, chopped |
| ¼ tsp salt | ⅓ cup chocolate chips |

Preheat oven to 350°F. In a large bowl, stir together the flour, sweetener, cocoa, baking powder, baking soda, and salt. Add the oil, egg replacer, soy milk, vanilla, walnuts, and chocolate chips. Stir together until well mixed. Spoon a heaping tablespoon of dough onto a lightly oiled cookie sheet and press flat with your fingers. Bake for 10-12 minutes or until edges are browned. Makes 12-16 cookies, depending on size.

# CHOCOLATE ORANGE HAZELNUT COOKIES

Hazelnuts have a sweet, mild flavor and can be found in most grocery stores. They are rich in protein, complex carbohydrates, dietary fiber, iron, calcium, and vitamin E. So these cookies are practically guilt free!

**1 ¼ cups flour**
**½ tsp baking soda**
**⅛ tsp salt**
**¾ cup dry sweetener**
**½ cup margarine**
**zest of 1 large *or* 2 medium oranges**
**1 tsp vanilla extract**
**½ cup soy milk**
**½ cup chocolate chips**
**½ cup hazelnuts, chopped**

Preheat oven to 375°F. In a large bowl, sift together the flour, baking soda, and salt. Add the sweetener, margarine, orange zest, vanilla, soy milk, chocolate chips, and hazelnuts, and stir together until well mixed. Spoon a heaping tablespoon of dough onto a lightly oiled cookie sheet and press flat with your fingers. Bake for 12-15 minutes or until edges are browned. Makes 12 cookies.

# HERMAN'S NO-BAKE COOKIES

This easy and delectable recipe comes from Herman in Walla Walla, Washington. You can substitute chocolate/carob chips for raisins if you're feeling crazy.

**½ cup soy milk**
**½ cup liquid sweetener**
**1 tbsp peanut butter**
**3 cups rolled oat flakes**
**½ cup raisins**
**1 tsp vanilla extract**

In a small saucepan, bring the soy milk, sweetener, and peanut butter to a boil, stirring until smooth. Remove from heat and set aside. In a large bowl, combine the oat flakes, vanilla, raisins, and soy milk mixture and mix well. Spoon a heaping tablespoon of dough onto a cookie sheet and press flat with your fingers. Chill in refrigerator before serving. Makes 12 cookies.

# ANNE'S MOLASSES COOKIES

"This is an old family recipe; my dad will kill me for sharing it. I use this cookie every year for our traditional family 'cookie exchange' and no one can tell that the cookies are vegan." – Anne, London, Ontario

½ cup margarine
½ cup dry sweetener
½ cup molasses
1 ½ tsp baking soda
⅓ cup hot water
½ tbsp vanilla extract
½ tsp salt
½ tsp powdered ginger
½ tsp ground cloves
2 ½ cups flour

Preheat oven to 375°F. In a large bowl, stir together the margarine, sweetener, molasses, baking soda, hot water, and vanilla. Stir in salt, ginger, and cloves. Stir in flour until well mixed. Spoon a heaping tablespoon of dough onto a lightly oiled cookie sheet and press flat with your fingers. Bake for 8-10 minutes. Makes 15 large or 30 small cookies.

# BANANA WALNUT BARS

Dreamy bars with rich banana and walnut flavors. Easy and delicious, they are perfect for parties or just as a snack.

1 ½ cups flour
1 cup dry sweetener
1 ½ tsp baking powder
½ tsp salt
½ cup soy milk
¼ cup olive oil
½ tsp vanilla extract
½ tsp lemon juice
1 banana, mashed well
½ cup chopped walnuts, *or* nuts of your choice
¼ cup cinnamon sugar (pg. 213)

Preheat oven to 350°F. In a large bowl, sift together the flour, sweetener, baking powder, and salt. Add the soy milk, oil, vanilla, lemon juice, banana, and walnuts. Stir gently until "just mixed." Pour into a lightly oiled 8x8 cake pan, sprinkle with cinnamon sugar, and bake for 30 to 35 minutes. While still warm, cut into bars and remove from pan. Makes 8 large bars.

# KELLY'S DATE SQUARES

"I made up this recipe in my product development course. I hope you like it." – Kelly, from somewhere in cyberspace

| | |
|---|---|
| 1 cup pitted dates, chopped | ½ cup wheat bran |
| 1 cup water | ½ tsp baking powder |
| ½ cup dry sweetener | ½ tsp baking soda |
| 1 tsp vanilla extract | ¼ tsp nutmeg |
| 1 tsp lemon juice | ¼ tsp cinnamon |
| 1 cup flour | ½ cup margarine |
| 1 ½ cups rolled oat flakes | ½ cup applesauce |
| ⅔ cup dry sweetener | |

Preheat oven to 350°F. In a small saucepan, combine the dates, water, sweetener, vanilla, and lemon juice and bring to a boil. Reduce heat to low and let simmer for 15 minutes or until liquid is absorbed. In a large bowl, stir together the flour, oat flakes, sweetener, wheat bran, baking powder, baking soda, nutmeg, and cinnamon. Stir in the margarine and applesauce until well mixed. Pat half of the oat mixture on the bottom of a lightly oiled 8x8 cake pan. Spoon date mixture over top, spread out evenly, and pat remaining oats over date mixture. Bake for 20-25 minutes. Makes 8-16 bars, depending on size.

# DEAN DEAN THE SEX MACHINE'S SPICED BAKED DONUTS

This recipe comes for an e-mail buddy I had for a while. We lost track of each other, so Dean, if you're out there, write me! (S)

For this delicious recipe you need four 4-inch mini-bundt pans, or put the dough into 6 muffin tins and call them muffins!

| | |
|---|---|
| 1 ½ cups flour | ½ cup soy milk |
| ½ cup dry sweetener | ¼ cup olive oil |
| 1 ½ tsp baking powder | ½ banana, mashed |
| 1 tsp cinnamon | ½ tsp vanilla extract |
| ½ tsp ground nutmeg | 2 tbsp cinnamon sugar (pg. 213) |
| ¼ tsp salt | |

Preheat oven to 350°F. In a large bowl, sift together the flour, sweetener, baking powder, cinnamon, nutmeg, and salt. Add the soy milk, oil, banana, and vanilla. Stir gently until "just mixed." Cut dough into 4 and roll each section into a tube. Place into a lightly oiled bundt pan and press down with fingers. Repeat with remaining dough. Sprinkle each donut with ½ tbsp of cinnamon sugar and bake for 10-12 minutes or until a toothpick comes out clean. Remove from pan immediately. Makes 4 donuts.

# MAUREEN'S COFFEE CAKE

My husband is going to leave me one day for my friend Maureen, all because of her coffee cake. He can't get enough of it; he dreams about it. Oh dear, what's a girl to do? I guess I'd better start baking. (S)

- **⅓ cup soft tofu**
- **1 cup soy milk**
- **1 tbsp apple cider vinegar**
- **2 ½ cups flour**
- **1 ¼ cups dry sweetener**
- **3 tsp cinnamon**
- **1 ½ tsp ground ginger**
- **½ tsp salt**
- **¾ cup olive oil**
- **¾ cup walnuts, chopped**
- **1 tsp baking powder**
- **1 tsp baking soda**

Preheat oven to 350°F. In a blender or food processor, blend the tofu, soy milk, and vinegar until smooth. Set aside. In a large bowl, stir together the flour, sweetener, cinnamon, ginger, salt, and oil. Take 1 cup of this mixture and place in a medium bowl, stir in walnuts, and set aside. Add the baking soda and baking powder to the remaining flour mixture, then add the tofu mixture and stir together well. Spread the mixture in a lightly oiled 9x13 baking dish and sprinkle the reserved walnut mixture on top. Bake for 30-40 minutes. Makes 4-6 servings or enough for 1 husband.

# SAVORY CINNAMON BUNS

"I came up with this recipe by adapting it from other cinnamon bun recipes. I hope you like it." – Johnathan, Vancouver, BC

**1 ¼ cups warm water**
**2 tsp baking yeast**
**3 tbsp dry sweetener**
**¼ cup margarine**
**1 tsp cinnamon**
**¼ tsp nutmeg**
**3 cups flour**
**1 tsp salt**
**2 tbsp dry sweetener**
**¼ cup raisins**
**¼ cup nuts (your choice; e.g., pecans, walnuts, etc.), chopped**
**cream cheese icing (pg. 199)**

In a large bowl, stir together the warm water, yeast, and sweetener. Cover and let stand for 10 minutes. In a medium bowl, mix together the margarine, cinnamon, and nutmeg, and set aside. Add the flour and salt to the yeast and stir until a dough forms. On a lightly floured surface, knead the dough for 3-5 minutes. Roll out the dough on a lightly floured surface, until approx. the size of a cookie sheet. Spread the margarine mixture on dough and top evenly with the sweetener, raisins, and nuts. Roll up the dough, and cut into rolls about ½ inch thick. Place buns in a 9x13 baking dish, or lightly oiled cookie sheet. Cover with cloth and let rise in a non-drafty area for 2 hours. Preheat oven to 350°F. Bake for 25-30 minutes or until golden brown. Let cool and crown with cream cheese icing. Makes 8-10 buns.

# DECADENT BROWNIES

For a truly sinful treat, frost these with chocolate mint icing (pg. 198). You can substitute carob for cocoa in this recipe.

> **1½ cups flour**
> **½ cup cocoa powder**
> **¾ cup dry sweetener**
> **1 ½ tsp baking soda**
> **¾ tsp baking powder**
> **½ tsp salt**
> **1 ½ cups soy milk**
> **⅓ cup olive oil**
> **½ cup nuts (your choice; e.g., pecans, walnuts, etc.), chopped**

Preheat oven to 350°F. In a large bowl, sift together the flour, cocoa, sweetener, baking soda, baking powder, and salt. Add the soy milk, oil, and nuts. Stir gently until "just mixed." Pour mixture into a lightly oiled 8x8 baking pan, and bake for 30-35 minutes or until a toothpick comes out clean. Makes 8-16 brownies, depending on how you cut them.

# APPLE CIDER BAKED PEARS WITH CRANBERRY STUFFING

A combination of sweet and tangy ingredients make for a perfect dessert. Serve with ice cream (pg. 204-205) or Tanya's decadent chocolate sauce (pg. 42) if you want to get wicked.

> **2 tbsp margarine**
> **2 tbsp dry sweetener**
> **½ cup dried cranberries, chopped**
> **½ tsp cinnamon**
> **2 pears**
> **½ cup apple cider**

Preheat oven to 350°F. In a small bowl, stir together the margarine, sweetener, cranberries, and cinnamon. Cut pears in half and carefully scoop out center. Slice off a tiny piece of the bottom of each pear so it will sit flat in the pan. Stuff ¼ of the cranberry mixture in each half and set in a 8x8 baking pan. Pour in apple cider, cover with tin foil, and bake for 35-40 minutes or until pears are tender. Makes 4 servings.

# STICKY RICE WITH MANGO

A sticky sweet dessert that is satisfying on so many levels.

> **1 cup sushi rice**
> **1 cup coconut milk (for sauce)**
> **2 tbsp dry sweetener**
> **¼ tsp salt**
> **⅓ cup coconut milk**
> **2 tbsp sweetener**
> **2 large mangos, peeled, pitted and sliced into thin slices**
> **1 tbsp sesame seeds, dry roasted (pg. 209)**

In a pot or rice cooker, cook rice. When rice is almost done, in a small saucepan bring 1 cup of coconut milk to a boil. Reduce heat to low and stir in sweetener and salt. Keep warm. Once rice is done, remove from heat, stir in coconut mixture, and let stand covered for 30 minutes, or until rice has absorbed most of the milk. In a small saucepan, bring ⅓ cup coconut milk and sweetener to a boil. Reduce heat and let simmer for a few minutes, stirring constantly until sauce begins to thicken a little. To serve: mold ¼ of sticky rice onto a dessert plate. Top with ¼ of sliced mangos, sesame seeds, and warm coconut sauce. Makes 4 servings.

# MO-MO'S APPLE CRUMBLE

Our friend Maureen has graciously agreed to part with her much beloved apple crumble recipe. So now when Lisa has a craving in the middle of the night, she can use the cookbook instead of waking up Mo. You can use any fruit you like in this crumble: pears, peaches, etc. Just remove one apple for each cup of fruit you add in.

> **6 apples, your choice, cored and chopped**
> **1 tsp cinnamon**
> **½ cup margarine**
> **½ cup flour**
> **½ cup dry sweetener**
> **1 cup rolled oat flakes**

Preheat oven to 350°F. Place the apples in a 9-inch baking dish. Sprinkle cinnamon on top. In a large bowl, stir together the margarine, flour, sweetener, and oat flakes. Sprinkle on top of apples and bake for 40-45 minutes or until top is golden brown. Makes 4-6 servings.

# RHUBARB CRUNCH

This tart and mouthwatering recipe, served with a homemade sorbet (pg. 201-203), will have you unbuttoning the top of your pants to eat more.

- **6 cups rhubarb, chopped**
- **¾ cup dry sweetener**
- **3 tbsp flour**
- **½ cup dry sweetener**
- **1 cup rolled oat flakes**
- **1 cup flour**
- **½ cup margarine**

Preheat oven to 375°F. In a large bowl, stir together the rhubarb, sweetener, and 3 tbsp flour and place in a 9-inch baking dish. In a large bowl, stir together the sweetener, oat flakes, flour, and margarine. Sprinkle on top of rhubarb and bake for 35-40 minutes or until top is golden brown. Makes 4-6 servings.

# APRICOT AND CRANBERRY NUT PIE

Yummy-licious!

- **1 cup dry sweetener**
- **egg replacer, equal to two eggs**
- **1 tsp vanilla extract**
- **¼ cup soy milk**
- **3 tbsp margarine**
- **1 tsp cinnamon**
- **¼ tsp salt**
- **1 ½ cups walnuts, chopped**
- **1 ½ cups dried apricots, chopped**
- **½ cup dried cranberries**
- **1 pie crust (pg. 195)**

Preheat oven to 375°F. In a large bowl, mix together the sweetener, egg replacer, and vanilla. Add the soy milk, margarine, cinnamon, and salt, and stir until well mixed. Stir in the nuts, apricots, and cranberries. Pour into pie crust and bake for 30-35 minutes, or until filling is set. Let cool before serving. Makes 1 pie.

# PEAR GINGER PIE

There are many, different types of pears – almost 5,000 varieties – but any one will do for this recipe. Just make sure that they are still quite firm, for most favorable results.

**4 pears, cored and sliced**
**½ cup dry sweetener**
**3 tbsp fresh ginger, grated**
**2 tbsp lemon juice**
**1 tbsp agar agar *or* arrowroot powder**
**1 tsp vanilla extract**
**1 tsp lemon zest, grated**
**1 pie crust (pg. 195)**
**1 tbsp cinnamon sugar (pg. 213)**

Preheat oven to 375°F. In a large bowl, combine the pears, sweetener, ginger, lemon juice, agar, vanilla, and lemon zest and mix well. Pour into pie crust and top with cinnamon sugar. Bake for 40-45 minutes, or until filling is set. Let cool before serving. Makes 1 pie.

# DEATH BY CHOCOLATE PIE

"You've heard of the phrase 'death by chocolate'? Well, this is to die for." – Jennifer, Newark, Delaware

**2 cups chocolate chips**
**1 tbsp soy milk**
**2 12-oz packages soft *or* silken tofu**
**1 tsp vanilla extract**
**1 pie crust (pg. 196)**

In a double boiler, melt the chocolate chips and soy milk, stirring occasionally until smooth. In a blender or food processor, blend the tofu, vanilla, and chocolate mixture until smooth. Pour into pie crust and let chill for 3-4 hours before serving. Makes 1 pie.

# RAW FRESH FRUIT PIE

This raw fruit pie from Angie in Los Angeles can change with the seasons. Use strawberries, apples, nectarines; whatever's in season. Psyllium husks can be found at most health food stores and act to solidify the fruit in this recipe.

**2 cups strawberries, stemmed and thinly sliced**
**1 no-bake pie crust (pg. 196)**
**2 cups papayas, seeded and roughly chopped**
**2 bananas, roughly chopped**
**⅛ tsp cinnamon**
**1 tbsp psyllium husks**
**1 tbsp lemon juice**

Lay strawberries out evenly on top of the crust. In a blender or food processor, blend the papaya, bananas, cinnamon, psyllium husks, and lemon juice until very smooth. Pour over strawberries. Chill in refrigerator for at least 1 hour before serving. Makes 1 pie.

# BASIC FLAKY PIE CRUST

This is the easiest and most basic pie crust ever invented. The best way to get a pie crust into a pie plate is to roll out the dough on a lightly floured surface and then gently roll it onto the rolling pin. Then, gently lay it onto your pie plate. Don't forget to prick holes in the bottom with a fork. Voilà!

**1 ¼ cups flour**
**¼ tsp salt**
**½ cup vegetable shortening *or* margarine**
**3 tbsp cold water**

In a large bowl, stir together the flour and salt. Cut the shortening into the flour mixture and when well mixed, add the water. Mix together until a dough forms. Knead for a minute or two. Wrap the dough in wax paper and chill for 30 minutes. Roll the dough into a pie crust. Makes 1 crust.

# NUTTY PIE CRUST

A nutty spiced treat that adds flavor and depth to any pie.

> **1½ cups flour**
> **⅓ cup nuts (your choice; e.g., almonds, walnuts, etc.)**
> **1 tbsp dry sweetener**
> **1 tsp cinnamon**
> **½ tsp salt**
> **½ cup margarine**
> **2 tbsp vegetable shortening**
> **2 tbsp cold water**

In a blender or food processor, blend the flour, nuts, sweetener, cinnamon, and salt. Add the margarine and shortening, and blend until well combined. Transfer mixture to a large bowl, and add water. Mix together until a dough forms. Knead for a minute or two. Wrap the dough in wax paper and chill for 30 minutes. Roll the dough into a pie crust. Makes 1 crust.

# NO-BAKE PIE CRUST

This crust is for pies and desserts that you don't have to bake. You can just pour, let set, and serve. Use with the Death by Chocolate Pie (pg. 194) or the Raw Fresh Fruit Pie (pg. 195).

> **1½ cups pecans *or* walnuts**
> **8 pitted dates**
> **½ tsp vanilla extract**
> **¼ tsp cinnamon**
> **2 tbsp water**

In a food processor, blend the nuts until they are finely chopped. Add the dates, vanilla, cinnamon, and water, and blend until well combined. Spoon into an 8-inch pie plate and spread out evenly with fingers to cover bottom of plate. Fill with desired filling. For a crunchier crust, bake for 1 hour at 200°F before filling. Makes 1 crust.

# LEMON POPPY SEED CAKE

"I am a longtime devotee of your book. This recipe is adapted from the Lemon Cake recipe in *How It All Vegan!* (pg. 147). I double the cake recipe and make 2 layers and sometimes I add Amaretto. I am incapable of following a recipe to the letter! I hope you like it!" – Rebecca, Swarthmore, PA

Try icing this recipe with our Cream Cheese Icing (pg. 199).

> 1½ cups flour
> 2 tsp baking powder
> ¼ tsp salt
> 1½ tbsp poppy seeds
> ½ cup almonds, finely chopped
> ¾ cup dry sweetener
>
> ¾ cup soy milk
> 2 tsp lemon extract
> zest of 1 lemon
> ¼ cup olive oil
> egg replacer, equal to 1 egg
> 2 tbsp Amaretto (optional)

Preheat oven to 350°F. In a large bowl, stir together the flour, baking powder, salt, poppy seeds, and almonds. Add the sweetener, soy milk, lemon extract, zest, oil, egg replacer, and optional Amaretto and stir together gently until "just mixed." Pour into a lightly oiled 8-inch cake pan and bake for 25-30 minutes or until a toothpick comes out clean. Makes 1 cake.

# KENTUCKY VELVET 2-LAYER CAKE

This recipe comes from our lovely friend Holly in Louisville, Kentucky. Try it with the Chocolate Mint Icing (pg. 198).

> ½ cup chocolate chips
> ½ cup margarine
> 1½ cups flour
> 2 tsp baking soda
> 1 tsp baking powder
> 1½ cups dry sweetener
> 1 tbsp powdered egg replacer + 4 tbsp water
> ½ cup soy milk
> 1 tsp vanilla extract
> 1 cup boiling water
> 2 tsp apple cider vinegar

Preheat oven to 350°F. In a small saucepan, melt together the chocolate chips and margarine, stirring until smooth. Set aside. In a large bowl sift together the flour, baking soda, baking powder. Stir in the chocolate sauce, sweetener, egg replacer/water, soy milk, vanilla, boiling water, and vinegar. Stir together gently until "just mixed." Pour into 2 lightly oiled 8-inch cake pans and bake for 30-35 minutes or until a toothpick comes out clean. Makes 2 layers for 1 cake.

# SUZY SPOON'S 2-LAYER CHOCOLATE MUD CAKE

This scrumptious recipe is from Suzy Spoon Cakes in Sydney, Australia.

**1 cup margarine**
**1 cup chocolate chips**
**¾ cup water**
**½ cup cocoa powder**
**2 tbsp jam (pg. 215)**
**1½ cups flour**
**½ tsp baking soda**
**1 tsp baking powder**
**½ tsp salt**
**1½ cups dry sweetener**
**egg replacer, equal to 2 eggs (pg. 212)**
**2 tbsp olive oil**
**½ cup soy milk**

Preheat oven to 325°F. In a small saucepan over medium heat, melt the margarine, chocolate chips, water, cocoa, and jam together, stirring often. Remove from heat and set aside. In a large bowl, sift together the flour, baking soda, baking powder, and salt. Stir in the sweetener, egg replacer, oil, soy milk, and chocolate mixture. Stir gently until "just mixed." Pour into 2 lightly oiled 8x8 cake pans and bake for 25-30 minutes or until a toothpick comes out clean. Makes 2 layers for 1 cake.

# CHOCOLATE MINT ICING

Truly the most decadent and easiest icing recipe in the world! If you don't have a double boiler, just place a small pot in a larger pot holding water.

**1 cup chocolate chips**
**¼ cup soy milk**
**2 tbsp margarine**
**½ tsp mint extract**

In a double boiler on medium heat, melt together all ingredients, stirring occasionally until smooth. Place mixture in refrigerator until cool, and has reached a spreadable consistency. Makes approx. 1¼ cups.

# CREAM CHEESE ICING

You can find vegan cream cheese at most health food stores. It's sooooo worth the money!

> **1 cup vegan cream cheese**
> **2 tbsp margarine**
> **1 cup powdered sugar (pg. 212)**

In a blender or food processor, blend all the ingredients until smooth. Makes approx. 1 ¼ cups.

# "BUTTER" ICING

Throw in some chopped nuts or chocolate chips and add a twist to this classic icing.

> **¾ cup margarine**
> **2 cups powdered sugar (pg. 212)**
> **1 tbsp soy milk**
> **½ tsp vanilla extract**

In a medium bowl, cream the margarine and sugar together until light and fluffy. Add in soy milk and vanilla and stir until well mixed. Makes approx. 1½ cups.

# DECORATING ICING FOR COOKIES

This icing is perfect for decorating and painting your sugar cookies. It's shiny when it hardens, and when you mix it with different food coloring, the colors stay bright.

> **1 cup powdered sugar (pg. 212)**
> **2 tsp soy milk**
> **2-3 tsp corn syrup**
> **assorted food coloring**

In a small bowl, stir together the sugar and soy milk. Stir in the corn syrup (adding more corn syrup ½ tsp at a time if you want a thinner icing). Separate the frosting into small bowls and add colors. Dip cookies, or paint them with a brush and let harden. Makes approx. 1 cup.

# THE MOST AMAZING CHOCOLATE PUDDING

This is seriously delicious, and so simple to make too!

- **1 12-oz package of soft *or* silken tofu**
- **2 tbsp olive oil**
- **1 cup dry sweetener**
- **½ cup cocoa powder**
- **¼ tsp salt**

In a blender or food processor, blend tofu until smooth. Add the oil, sweetener, cocoa powder, and salt. Blend until well mixed. Serve chilled. Make approx. 1 ½ cups.

# CHOCOLATE MINT MOUSSE

A decadent and delicious taste of ecstasy with each spoonful. If you don't have a double boiler, just place a small pot in a larger pot holding water.

- **1½ cups chocolate chips**
- **2 tbsp soy milk**
- **1 12-oz package soft of silken tofu**
- **2-3 tsp mint extract**

In a double boiler on medium heat, melt the chocolate chips and soy milk, stirring occasionally until smooth. In a blender or food processor, blend the tofu, mint, and chocolate mixture until smooth. Pour into serving bowls and refrigerate at least one hour before serving. Makes 4 servings.

# HOLLY'S NAKED CHOCOLATE MOUSSE

"It's best if you get naked with someone fun and eat it off each other!" – Holly, Louisville, Kentucky

- **1½ cups chocolate chips**
- **2 tbsp soy milk**
- **1 12 oz package soft of silken tofu**
- **3-4 tbsp Amaretto**

In a double boiler on medium heat, melt the chocolate chips and soy milk, stirring occasionally until smooth. In a blender or food processor, blend the tofu, Amaretto, and chocolate mixture until smooth. Pour into serving bowls and refrigerate at least one hour before serving and getting freaky! Makes 4 servings.

# ICE CREAM SANDWICHES

Here we take two of the best treats from days gone by and combine them into one fabulous dessert. Get crazy and use different flavors of soy ice cream in this recipe.

½ cup chocolate chips
½ cup margarine
⅓ cup dry sweetener
egg replacer, equal to 1 egg
1 tsp vanilla extract
¾ cup flour
2 tbsp cocoa powder
½ tsp baking powder
3 cups soy ice cream, slightly softened (pg. 204-205)

Preheat over to 325°F. In a small sauce pan on medium heat, melt the chocolate chips and margarine until well combined, stirring constantly. Remove from heat and set aside. In a large bowl, stir together the sweetener, egg replacer, and vanilla. Add the chocolate mixture and mix well. Add the flour, cocoa, and baking powder, and stir together until "just mixed." Transfer batter to a cookie sheet lined with lightly oiled parchment paper. Spread evenly and bake for 12-15 minutes or until top looks "just" cooked. Let cool, carefully remove paper, and cut cookie in half. Spread ice cream over one half of cookie, and top with other half of cookie. Wrap in wax paper and freeze for 4 hours. Remove paper, and cut into sandwiches. Makes 8-12 sandwiches.

# SUGAR-FREE BANANA-STRAWBERRY SORBET

A wonderful and easy home-made dessert that will never have you paying for store bought ice cream again!

2 bananas, sliced into coins
2 tbsp lemon juice
1½ cups strawberries, stemmed and roughly chopped
¼-½ cup apple juice
¼ cup maple syrup

On a large plate or cookie sheet, arrange banana slices and brush with lemon juice. Freeze. In a separate container, freeze the strawberries. In a blender or food processor, blend the frozen bananas, apple juice, and maple syrup. Slowly add the frozen strawberries, a few pieces at a time. Blend until well incorporated and smooth. If the sorbet is too thick, add a little more apple juice until you reach the right consistency. Serve immediately, or freeze and let thaw 15-20 minutes before serving. Makes approx. 3 cups.

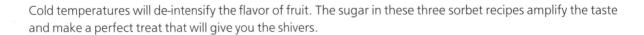

Cold temperatures will de-intensify the flavor of fruit. The sugar in these three sorbet recipes amplify the taste and make a perfect treat that will give you the shivers.

# STRAWBERRY SORBET

**2 cups fresh strawberries, stemmed and roughly chopped**
**1 cup water**
**¾ cup organic cane sugar**
**¼-½ cup apple juice (optional)**

Freeze the strawberries. In a small saucepan on high heat, bring the water and sugar to a boil. Reduce heat and let simmer for 5 minutes. Set aside to cool to room temperature. In a blender or food processor, blend ½ of the frozen strawberries with the sugar water. Slowly add the remaining strawberries, a few pieces at a time. Blend until well incorporated and smooth. If the sorbet is too thick, add apple juice until you reach the right consistency. Serve immediately, or freeze and let thaw 15-20 minutes before serving. Makes approx. 2 cups.

# SOUR APPLE SORBET

**2 large Granny Smith apples, cored and cubed**
**1 banana, sliced into coins**
**2 tbsp lime juice**
**1 cup apple juice**
**¾ cup organic cane sugar**
**¼-½ cup apple juice (for thinning) (optional)**

In a medium bowl, toss apples and banana with lime juice. Place in freezer and freeze. In a small saucepan over hight heat, bring the apple juice and sugar to a boil. Reduce heat and let simmer for 5 minutes. Set aside to cool to room temperature. In a blender or food processor, blend together the banana, ½ of the frozen apples, and apple juice mixture. Slowly add the remaining apples a few pieces at a time. Blend until well incorporated and smooth. If the sorbet is too thick, add apple juice until you reach the right consistency. Serve immediately, or freeze and let thaw 15-20 minutes before serving. Makes approx. 2 cups.

# PEAR GINGER SORBET

**2 large pears, cored and cubed**
**1 banana, sliced into coins**
**2 tbsp lime juice**
**1 cup apple juice**
**¾ cup organic cane sugar**
**2 tbsp fresh ginger, grated**
**¼-½ cup apple juice (for thinning) (optional)**

In a medium bowl, toss pears and banana with lime juice. Place in freezer and freeze. In a small saucepan over high heat, bring the apple juice, sugar, and ginger to a boil. Reduce heat and let simmer for 5 minutes. Set aside to cool to room temperature. (You can remove ginger pieces or keep them in.) In a blender or food processor, blend together the banana, ½ of the frozen pears, and the apple juice mixture. Slowly add the remaining pears, a few pieces at a time. Blend until well incorporated and smooth. If the sorbet is too thick, add apple juice until you reach the right consistency. Serve immediately, or freeze and let thaw 15-20 minutes before serving. Makes approx. 2 cups.

# CHOCOLATE ICE CREAM

This recipe is from *How It All Vegan!* It's so good that it bears repeating!

- **2 cups soft or silken tofu**
- **1 cup soy milk**
- **½ cup olive oil**
- **½-1 cup dry sweetener**
- **¼ cup cocoa powder**
- **1 tbsp vanilla extract**
- **⅛ tsp salt**

In a blender or food processor, blend all the ingredients until very smooth and creamy. Place in a sealable container and freeze. Remove from freezer and defrost for 20-40 minutes. Place back in food processor and blend again; you many need to add a titch more soy milk to help it along. Spoon back into container (at this point you can add chocolate chips or crumbled cookies if you like). Serve immediately or refreeze. Remove from freezer 15 minutes before serving. Makes approx. 3 cups.

# MAPLE PECAN ICE CREAM

Drizzle ice cream with chocolate sauce (pg. 42) for maximum "wow" factor.

- **2 cups soft or silken tofu**
- **½ cup soy milk**
- **½ cup olive oil**
- **½ cup maple syrup**
- **½ cup dry sweetener**
- **1 tbsp lemon juice**
- **2 bananas, roughly chopped**
- **1 tbsp vanilla extract**
- **⅛ tsp salt**
- **1 cup pecans, chopped**

In a blender or food processor, combine all the ingredients except for the pecans, and blend together until very smooth and creamy. Place in a sealable container and freeze. Remove from freezer and defrost for 20-40 minutes. Place back in food processor and blend again; you many need to add a titch more soy milk to help it along. Spoon back into container and stir in the pecans. Serve immediately or refreeze. Remove from freezer 15 minutes before serving. Makes approx. 4 cups.

# BLUEBERRY NECTARINE ICE CREAM

A perfect summertime treat that turns your tongue blue and your neighbors green with envy.

**2 cups soft or silken tofu**
**½ cup soy milk**
**½ cup olive oil**
**1 cup dry sweetener**
**1 tbsp lemon juice**
**1 tbsp vanilla extract**
**⅛ tsp salt**
**1-2 nectarines, pit removed**
**1 cup blueberries**

In a blender or food processor, blend the tofu, soy milk, oil, sweetener, lemon juice, vanilla, salt, nectarine and ½ cup of blueberries until very smooth and creamy. Place in a sealable container and freeze. Remove from freezer and defrost for 20-40 minutes. Place back in food processor and blend again until smooth; you many need to add a titch more soy milk to help it along. Spoon back into container and stir in the remaining blueberries. Serve immediately or refreeze. Remove from freezer 15 minutes before serving.
Makes approx. 4 cups.

DRAGON ALLEY

Odds
& Sods

*This is a hodgepodge collection of recipes that don't really fit in any specific category, but are fabulous nonetheless. Many are meal-making essentials that you can then use in other recipes. Behold ... the mighty and powerful Odds & Sods chapter!*

# WORCESTERSHIRE SAUCE

Most store-bought Worcestershire sauces contain anchovies, so here's a quick and easy recipe that has been veganized.

½ **cup apple cider vinegar**
2 **tbsp Braggs**
2 **tsp water**
1 **tsp dry sweetener**
¼ **tsp ground ginger**
¼ **tsp dry mustard**
¼ **tsp onion powder**
¼ **tsp garlic powder**
⅛ **tsp cinnamon**
⅛ **tsp pepper**

In a small saucepan over medium-high heat, combine all ingredients and whisk thoroughly. Bring to a boil, reduce heat, and simmer for 1 minute, stirring constantly. Set aside to cool. Store in the refrigerator in a clean container with a tight-fitting lid. Makes about ¾ cup.

# ROASTED GARLIC

In under a half hour, an entire head of slow-roasted garlic offers its rich, earthy essence to everything it comes in contact with. It's great when spread on crackers or bread, or mixed into hummus, pasta sauce, or just about anything else!

1 **whole bulb garlic**
1 **tsp olive oil**
**pinch of salt**

Preheat oven to 400°F. Peel off the loose layers of skin on the garlic bulb and slice off the top. Place in a small baking pan and drizzle with oil and sprinkle with salt. Cover with lid or foil and roast until garlic is soft, about 20-25 minutes. Set aside to cool. Squeeze out garlic cloves from bulb and serve.

Sun-dried tomatoes are just that: dried in the sun. The result is a dark, chewy, shriveled tomato that adds a lovely, intense flavor to whatever recipe you add them to. They come either packed in oil, dry-packed in cellophane or you can make your own (see below).

# HOW TO REHYDRATE SUN-DRIED TOMATOES

To rehydrate them, soak them in water, stock or vegetable juice; they usually rehydrate within 1-2 hours. If you're in a hurry, pour boiling water over them and they'll be ready in 15-20 minutes. You can also add the soaking liquid to your recipe for added flavor. If you're using them in soups or other recipes that involve a long cooking time, don't worry about rehydrating them; just throw them in and keep cooking.

# SUN-DRIED TOMATOES

Making your own sun-dried tomatoes is very simple and certainly is much less expensive than purchasing them at the grocery store. Technically, these are not "sun-dried" but more "oven-dried" but what-evah.

> **4-6 plum *or* Roma tomatoes, cut into ½-inch slices**

Preheat oven to 150°F. On a rack laid on top of a cookie sheet, spread out the tomato slices. Let bake for 15-20 hours, until tomatoes are leathery but pliable. Let tomatoes cool completely and store in a jar with a tight-fitting lid. They will keep for up to 6 months. If you want to store them longer, put them in the freezer. Makes approx. 1 cup.

# HOMEMADE SEITAN

Praise Seitan! Who knew it was so easy to make? Thanks to Fiona in Toronto, now we do! Seitan is made from wheat gluten and makes a great substitute for meat. It can be used in dishes like Mock Chicken (pg. 123) or veggie kabobs (pg. 146).

> **1 cup instant gluten flour**
> **1 cup water**
> **½ tsp Braggs**
> **6 cups vegetable stock (pg. 217)**

In a large bowl, stir together the flour, water, and Braggs. Mix quickly with your hands to avoid lumps. Knead gently until combined and slice into bite-sized chunks or strips, remembering that the Seitan will expand a little when you cook it. In a large pot over high heat, bring vegetable stock to a boil. Reduce heat to medium-low, add gluten pieces, and simmer for 30-45 minutes. Remove with slotted spoon and use accordingly. Makes approx. 3 cups.

# SPICED DRY ROASTED NUTS

Dry roasting nuts and seeds is a relatively simple task, but you have to be very attentive as they can quickly burn. Make sure to remove them when they turn golden because the fat in nuts keeps them "cooking" after you remove them from the heat. You can use most nuts and seeds, and even combine them to make unique mixtures. You add spices to the nuts while roasting for extra flavour, check out pages 110-111 for ideas. Use roasted nuts and seeds to top rice, most dishes, and all salads.

> **1 cup nuts *or* seeds, your choice**
> **1 tbsp Braggs (optional)**
> **½-1 tsp spice, your choice (optional)**

In a small saucepan stir the nuts or seeds and optional ingredients continually over medium heat for 2-5 minutes, or until they begin to look toasted. Remove and let cool completely. Store in a air tight jar. Makes approx. 1 cup.

# DRY ROASTED NUTS

Dry roasting nuts is similar to the Spiced Dry Roasting, except you're not adding any spices. Simply add the nuts to a dry frying pan on medium-high heat and roast for 2-5 minutes, or until they begin to look toasted. Shake the pan continually so they don't burn. Remove and let cool completely. Remember to keep an eye on them because they can burn quickly.

# GOMASHIO

Gomashio is a simple yet wonderful Japanese condiment. Very addictive and satisfying, use it as a topping for any recipe or in place of salt on cooked vegetables or in salads and soups. Yum!

> **1 cup raw sesame seeds**
> **1-2 tsp sea salt**
> **1 tsp kelp powder**

In a small, dry saucepan over medium-high heat, combine the sesame seeds, salt, and kelp, stirring continually for 3-5 minutes, until seeds start to pop and brown. Remove from heat and let cool completely. Place in food processor and grind for 3 seconds (you don't want the seeds to become powdery, just lightly ground). Store in an air-tight container. Makes 1 cup.

You can crush your spices with a mortar and pestle or use a coffee grinder (reserved only for grinding spices, not coffee) and go crazy. These three spices pack a powerful punch to whatever you add them to.

# ALL-PURPOSE SPICE

- 2 tbsp chili powder
- 2 tsp onion powder
- 2 tsp cumin
- 2 tsp garlic powder
- 2 tsp oregano
- 1 tsp paprika
- 1 tsp salt
- ½ tsp cayenne

Combine all the ingredients; store in an air-tight container. Makes approx. ¼ cup.

# FIVE SPICE POWDER

- 2 tsp anise seeds, crushed
- 2 tsp ground pepper
- 2 tsp fennel seeds, crushed
- 2 tsp ground cloves
- 2 tsp cinnamon
- 1 ½ tsp ground ginger
- ½ tsp allspice

Combine all the ingredients; store in an air-tight container. Makes approx. ¼ cup.

# GARAM MASALA

- 2 tbsp cumin
- 2 tbsp coriander
- 2 tsp black pepper
- 1 tsp ground cardamom
- 1 tsp ground ginger
- ⅛ tsp cinnamon
- ⅛ tsp ground cloves
- ⅛ tsp nutmeg

Combine all the ingredients; store in an air-tight container. Makes approx. ⅓ cup.

# MAYONNAISE

Quick and easy!

> **1 12-oz package silken *or* soft tofu**
> **1 tsp mustard**
> **2 tbsp cider vinegar**
> **1 tbsp dry sweetener**
> **½ tsp onion powder**
> **½ tsp salt**

In a blender or food processor, blend all the ingredients. Makes approx. 1 ½ cups.

# FAKE FETA

This delightfully tangy tofu masterpiece was in *How It All Vegan!* but it's worth repeating! Use in salads, on top of pizzas, or in the Greek Salad Pita Sandwiches on pg. 55.

> **¼ cup olive oil**
> **¼ cup water**
> **½ cup red wine vinegar**
> **2 tsp salt**
> **1 tbsp dried basil**
> **½ tsp pepper**
> **½ tsp dried oregano**
> **1 lb firm herb tofu, cubed *or* crumbled**

In a large bowl, mix together the oil, water, vinegar, salt, basil, pepper, and oregano. Marinate the tofu in the mixture for at least an hour or more. Makes approx. 1 ½ cups.

# CHEESY SHAKY-SHAKE

Our friend Trevor M. gave us the idea for this recipe. Use over popcorn, on top of baked potatoes, pasta or whereever a cheesy taste is required.

> **1 cup nutritional yeast**
> **½ cup almonds**
> **¼ tsp salt**

In a blender or food processor, blend all ingredients until finely ground. Makes approx. 1 cup.

# EGG SUBSTITUTES

Baking without eggs can be tricky, since eggs do several important things; they help recipes to rise as well as bind together, and they also provide extra liquid. So if you omit eggs, you need to replace it with something that will accomplish these same feats.

**Powdered egg replacer:** This stuff is great. It's what we used when we were testing our recipes, unless otherwise noted. Available in health food stores, you blend it with water to replace an egg in recipes. It may seem pricy, but a box lasts a long time, so it's worth it.

**Banana:** Use ½ a banana, mashed, to replace one egg in sweet baked goods.

**Applesauce:** Add about ¼ cup applesauce in place of an egg in sweet baked goods. It's a great binder but you might need to add a little extra baking powder (about ½ tsp) to help with the rising.

**Tofu:** Use about ¼ cup mashed silken tofu for one egg. Also add ¼-½ tsp extra baking powder.

**Soy flour:** Use 1 heaping tbsp of soy flour or cornstarch plus 2 tbsp of water to replace each egg in a baked product.

**Flax seeds:** Flax seeds are available at natural foods stores. They work great in pancakes, breads, and other baked goods. 3 tbsp flax eggs equals 1 egg (see below).

# FLAX EGGS

> **⅓ cup whole flax seeds**
> **1 cup water**

In a blender or food processor, blend the seeds until they have an even consistency. Slowly start adding the water while blending. Continue blending until mixture becomes thick. Transfer to an air-tight container. It will keep refrigerated for 3-6 days. Makes 6 "eggs."

# POWDERED SUGAR

This powdered sugar is perfect for any of the icing recipes (pg. 198-199).

> **2 cups sugar**
> **½ cup corn starch**

In blender or food processor, blend ingredients for 1 minute. Push mixture down sides of blender with a wooden spoon and blend for an additional 30 seconds. Makes approx. 2½ cups.

# CINNAMON CHIPS

These chips are perfect for dipping in the Fruit Salsa (pg. 130).

> **5 (10-in) flour tortillas**
> **Animal-friendly cooking spray *or* olive oil**
> **1 cup cinnamon sugar (see below)**

Preheat oven to 350°F. Spray or lightly coat bottom of large baking sheet with oil. Cut tortillas into wedges and arrange in a single layer on baking sheet. Spray or lightly coat with oil and sprinkle wedges with cinnamon sugar. Bake for 8 to 10 minutes. Repeat with any remaining tortilla wedges. Allow to cool for approximately 15 minutes before using.

# CINNAMON SUGAR

We figured everyone knows how to make cinnamon sugar, right? But we put this recipe in, just in case you were born in a cave.

> **1 cup dry sweetener**
> **1-2 tsp cinnamon**

In a small bowl, stir together all the ingredients. Makes approx. 1 cup.

# CRANBERRY RELISH

Relish is typically known as a condiment or a spread. This version is subtly sweet and lightly spiced. It's easy to make, and is a colorful and flavorful accompaniment to many dishes. This recipe was submitted by Mark, a cook turned glass-blowing artist!

> **1 small red onion, chopped**
> **2 tsp olive oil**
> **1 cup dried cranberries**
> **1 tbsp sweetener**
> **¼ tsp cinnamon**

In a medium saucepan on medium-high heat, sauté the onions in oil until translucent. Add the cranberries, sweetener, and cinnamon. Stir together and saute for 5-8 minutes over medium-low heat. Set aside to cool. In a blender or food processor, blend the cranberry mixture until coarse. Serve warm. Makes approx. 1 cup.

# PEAR RAISIN CHUTNEY

Chutneys are served with almost every meal in India. They are served on the side with curries, but are also used as sauces for hot, spicy dishes. They can be prepared in a variety of ways and are made from a wide variety of ingredients. They range in flavor from sweet or sour, to spicy or mild, or any combination thereof. They can be thin or chunky and can be made with fruits or vegetables or both. Make sure to use very ripe pears in this recipe, as it adds to the sweetness.

**⅓ cup raisins**
**2 tbsp balsamic vinegar**
**2 tbsp water**
**⅓ cup shallots, chopped**
**1 tbsp olive oil**
**1 tbsp dry sweetener**
**2-3 pears, finely chopped**
**2 tbsp balsamic vinegar**
**½-1 tbsp dried rosemary**
**½ tsp salt**
**½ tsp pepper**
**½ cup dry roasted nuts, your choice (pg. 209), chopped**

In a small saucepan over medium-high heat, stir together the raisins, 2 tbsp vinegar, and water. Bring to a boil. Reduce heat to medium-low and simmer for 10 minutes or until raisins are plump. Set aside. In a large saucepan over medium-high heat, sauté the shallots in oil until translucent. Add the sweetener, pears, vinegar, rosemary, salt, pepper, and raisins. Cook for 8-10 minutes or until chutney has thickened. Add optional nuts. Makes approx. 2 cups.

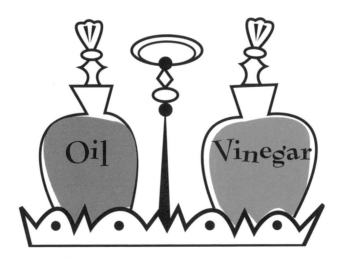

Fresh fruit is best for making jam, but you can used frozen fruit for these recipes. Let the frozen fruit thaw completely before proceeding with directions. Make sure you use powdered pectin or check the ingredients as most liquid pectins contain lactic acid which is derived from an animal product (see Vegan No-No's pgXX).

# STRAWBERRY FREEZER JAM

A classic. If you want to combine different fruits, add 1 cup of another fruit and remove an equal amount of strawberries.

**2 ½ cups strawberries**
**4 cups dry sweetener**
**1 2-oz (57-g) pkg powdered pectin**
**¾ cup water**

In a large bowl, crush the fruit with a potato masher. Stir in sweetener and let stand for about 20 minutes, stirring occasionally. In a small saucepan on medium-high heat, stir together the pectin and water; bring to a boil and boil rapidly for 1 minute, stirring constantly. Stir the pectin into the fruit, stirring constantly for 2 minutes. Spoon into warm, sterilized jam jars (leaving ¼ inch from rim). Cover with air-tight lids and let stand at room temperature for 24 hours or until jam has set. Store in freezer; if jam is used within 3 weeks, it may be stored in refrigerator (mark due date on jar so you don't forget). Makes 4 8-oz (250-ml) jars.

# BLUEBERRY FREEZER JAM

Berry-licious!

**3 cups blueberries**
**4 cups dry sweetener**
**1 2-oz (57-g) pkg powdered pectin**
**¾ cup water**

In a large bowl, crush the fruit with a potato masher. Stir in sweetener and let stand for about 20 minutes, stirring occasionally. In a small saucepan on medium-high heat, stir together the pectin and water; bring to a boil and boil rapidly for 1 minute, stirring constantly. Stir the pectin into the fruit, stirring constantly for 2 minutes. Spoon into warm, sterilized jam jars (leaving ¼ inch from rim). Cover with air-tight lids and let stand at room temperature for 24 hours or until jam has set. Store in freezer; if jam is used within 3 weeks, it may be stored in refrigerator (mark due date on jar so you don't forget). Makes 4 8-oz (250-ml) jars.

# SUGAR-FREE BERRY JUMBLE JAM

Perfect on toast, in a crepe, or stirred into ice cream ... a nice alternative to all things sugary.

> **2 cups strawberries**
> **2 cups blackberries**
> **2 cups blueberries**
> **1 cup frozen apple juice concentrate**

In a blender or food processor, purée half of the berries. Combine puréed berries with remaining whole berries into a large saucepan and cook on medium heat for 10-15 minutes. Add the apple juice concentrate and bring mixture to a boil for 15 minutes or until mixture reaches 220°F on a candy thermometer. Remove from heat and spoon into warm, sterilized jam jars (leaving ¼ inch from rim). Cover with air-tight lids and let stand at room temperature for 24 hours or until jam has set. Store in freezer; if jam is used within 3 weeks, it may be stored in refrigerator (mark due date on jar so you don't forget). Makes 4 8-oz (250-ml) jars.

# SOY YOGURT

Who knew making yogurt was so easy? It may not be as thick as you're used to, so if you want, add a titch of powdered agar-agar or cornstarch to thicken. For flavor, that's up to you; try maple syrup or vanilla extract, or stir in some cane sugar and some fresh fruit ... whatever tickles your fancy. Remember to set aside some of the yogurt before you add your flavor so you have a starter for your next batch. Acidophilus can be found in health food stores.

> **2 cups soy milk**
> **1 tsp active non-dairy powdered acidophilus** *or* **2 tbsp plain soy yogurt**
> **powdered agar-agar** *or* **cornstarch (optional)**

Preheat oven to minimum; temperature should be no more than 110°F. In a medium jar, combine the soy milk and acidophilus. Cover with lid and shake well. Remove lid and place jar in oven. Let sit 7-10 hours. Don't open oven, it acts as a nice womb for your yogurt. Makes approx. 2 cups yogurt.

# BASIC VEGETABLE STOCK

Most soups have stock as a main ingredient. Quite simply, stock is the strained liquid in which vegetables have been simmered. It adds pizzazz to any soup, gravy, or sauce.

**5 carrots, chopped**
**2 stalks celery with leaves, chopped**
**2 onions, roughly chopped**
**1 bulb garlic, unpeeled and roughly chopped**
**1 potato, chopped**
**1 turnip, chopped**
**any leftover veggies in the fridge, chopped (not rotten!)**
**1 bay leaf**
**1 handful fresh parsley**
**1 tsp salt**
**1 tsp peppercorns**
**12 cups water**

In a large pot, combine all the ingredients. Bring to a boil then lower heat and simmer for 45 minutes to one hour. Strain out ingredients and use stock accordingly. Makes approx. 8 cups.

Party

*Parties are one of the best ways to visit and hang out with friends and family. You're surrounded by people who love you, taste-testing new recipes they bring, and wowing them with your own amazing cooking abilities.*

*Parties also give you the excuse you need to use that Saturday Night Fever sleeping bag, or wear that Hawaiian muumuu. So get out your dress-up clothes, pull out your wigs, and let's throw a party!*

# SLUMBER PARTY

Slumber parties can be great fun. They take you back to the days when you thought you were a pimply loser and that everyone else was way cooler than you, only now you have all the grace and confidence of a grown-up, so you can really enjoy yourself.

Slumber parties don't necessarily have to involve sleeping over (although if there's drinking involved, it's probably a good idea). Whatever you decide, make sure you insist that everyone wear pajamas.

## MOVIES

No slumber party is complete without watching a trashy movie. Here's our list of perfect slumber party movies:

**Say Anything...:** Lloyd Dobler is the perfect man. Sigh....

**Grease:** There are worse things I could do....

**Bring It On:** A fun girly movie.

**Crossroads:** Britney's not that bad ... seriously!

**Fast Times at Ridgmont High:** A high school classic.

**The Rock:** A perfect action movie from start to finish.

**Saturday Night Fever:** A truly amazing movie once you get past the polyester shirts.

**Porky's:** A hilariously horrible film (not for kids).

**Sleep Away Camp:** Oooh, scary. The last shot of this movie is so amazing. It still gives Sarah nightmares.

**The Go-Go's Live in Central Park:** Turn up the TV and get on your feet. Have a dancing/singing party with the ladies!

## GAMES

**Ouija:** Apparently this game conjures up the devil, but is available at most toy stores ... hmm....

**Twister:** A fun game that finally puts all that yoga you do to good use.

**Spin the Bottle:** Nothing better than kissing people you don't normally kiss.

**Truth or Dare:** This game can get nasty, especially if people have been drinking. Make sure that everyone is comfortable about playing before you start. After all, you don't want to hurt anyone's feelings.

## MUSIC

Music can be a problem at parties. Everyone has different tastes, but since you'll want to go for old-school flavor, burn a bunch of mixed CDs with all your favorite songs from when you were in high school: not the angst-ridden, somber stuff from your "I only wear black" phase, but tunes that you were once embarrassed to admit that you liked, and got you dancing and excited when you were alone in your room pining for that classmate who wouldn't give you the time of day.

## TREATS

Junk food is a necessity at a slumber party; sugar is what starts all those giggle-fits. Check out Desserts (pg. 180) and Appetizers and Snacks (pg. 102) for ideas. Here's a list of our favorite snacks:

Hot Artichoke Dip & Chips (pg. 103)

Not Pigs in a Blanket (pg. 105)

Na-Na Marg's Nuts and Bolts (pg. 108)

Cracker Janes (pg. 108)

Maureen's Oatmeal Cookies (pg. 183)

Kelly's Date Squares (pg. 188)

Decadent Brownies (pg. 191)

Kentucky Velvet 2-Layer Cake (pg. 197)

## BREAKFAST

If your slumber party guests actually sleep over, make sure you have a wonderful breakfast ready for them. Coffee, tea, and fresh juice are a good start.

**Pancakes** are an easy way to fill up growling bellies (pg. 40-41).

**Waffles** are super, but not if you have impatient, hungry houseguests. Save time by making them the night before, storing them in the freezer, and toasting them in the toaster in the morning (pg. 39-40).

**Scrambled tofu** (pg. 44-45), mock bacon, toast, and jam (pg. 215) is a classic vegan breakfast.

If you're feeling lazy, a big pot of **Hot Cereal** (pg. 38) will always do the trick.

# DRESS-UP PICTURE-TAKING PARTY

So what do you do when you have a closet full of awesome thrift store outfits that you can't wear to your job or in your daily life? You invite your friends over and have a dress up party!

There's nothing more fun than running around the living room in your underwear with your friends. Make sure you've got lots of wigs, makeup, and polyester jumpsuits. It's the fastest way to bond and make lasting memories. Especially if you take pictures!

Remember, dress-up parties always start out slowly. Everyone is a little shy and feeling weird, so get the ball rolling and be the first to strip to your undies. Put on a wig, smear on some lipstick, and have some fun!

## CLOTHING & PROPS

Fill a suitcase full with your best dress-up clothes, wigs, shoes, and other apparel, then get your friends to bring a full suitcase of their own. The more outfits to choose from, the more fun you'll have! Don't forget accessories like hats, sunglasses, and jewelry.

## MAKEUP

Bring your own. Makeup is one thing you don't want to share (remember what you learned in Sex Ed about herpes)! At the end of the evening, remove each other's makeup and then enjoy a nice, soothing skin mask. It's a nice way to wrap up your party.

### FOOD

No party is complete without things to nibble on. It could be a party featuring hors d'oeuvres, fruit, hummus (pg. 134), chips and dip (pg. 126), popcorn (pg. 109), soda, or junk food (Cracker Janes, pop, cookies, cake). Pick whatever theme you want.

### MUSIC

Preferably The Go-Go's, the soundtrack from *Grease*, or old-school Madonna. Whatever brings out the silly in you.

### CAMERA

It's not a picture-taking party unless there are incriminating photos to tease your friends about. Have a tripod, camera with a self-timer, and a flash. Most importantly film – at least eight to ten rolls of film; it might seem excessive, but it's better to have too much film than not enough.

# PITY PARTY

There are days when you roll out of bed and you realize you should have stayed there. Life sucks sometimes, so get out the tissues and your pajamas and throw yourself a pity party.

Stress is hard on the body as well as the brain. Pampering your body and reducing stress can be a simple as slowing down creating a quiet place and taking a few moments for yourself. Here are a few simple ideas on how to give yourself some TLC that won't break your bank account.

## 23 WAYS TO PAMPER YOURSELF

1. Light some candles and draw a hot bath ... maybe ask someone to join you. Use your homemade bath oils or a bath bomb (pg. 224).

2. Turn off the TV, unplug the phone, and curl up with a good book.

3. Send yourself flowers.

4. Do something nice for your feet (pg. 226).

5. Make cookies and eat them all – guilt-free (pg. 181-187).

6. Take the day off work and do nothing – absolutely nothing.

7. Invite your favorite friend over and have a slumber party.

8. Forget about the housework and go to bed early.

9. Give your dog a belly scratch.

10. Go for a hike or a walk on the beach.

11. Call up an old friend you haven't talked to in years and chat as long as you want.

12. Do some yoga stretches by candlelight.

13. Burn an awesome mix-tape or CD, then go for a long walk with your new favorite tunes.

14. Go to a comedy club or improv night and laugh till you pee your pants.

15. Rent Sarah's all-time-favorite movie (*Say Anything...*) and curl up on the couch with Lloyd Dobler.

16. Do you have dark circles under the eyes from staying up too late watching movies? Raw potato slices contain potassium that will take them away. Place them over your eyes for ten to fifteen minutes.

17. Go for a picnic in the park and fall asleep in the grass. Watch out for park poo.

18. Put on your favourite CD, turn up the stereo, and dance and sing along as loudly as you can. Ignore the neighbors' protests.

19. Lay in the backyard or on your porch swing and breathe deeply.

20. Lay in bed with a big box of tissue and bawl your eyes out. Cry till you've got no more tears. Very cathartic.

21. Puffy eyes from crying too much? Place cool slices of cucumber over your eyes for ten to fifteen minutes.

22. Go to a massage school and get the students to practice on you. It's a cheap way to soothe your aching muscles.

23. Stay out of the sun! Suntans are icky. Not only will they make you wrinkly like a dried prune, but they increase your chances of getting skin cancer. If you're tattooed, the fastest way to fade your tattoo is to expose it to the sun. You paid big bucks for it, so cover it up. Pale is where it's at ... besides, punks don't tan!

# PAMPERING RECIPES

## FIZZING BATH BOMBS

Bath bombs are expensive to buy, but so cheap to make! Drop homemade bath bombs into a tub of warm water and fizz and bubble your bad mood away. Note: if the bomb breaks during unmolding, just place it back into the mold and try again.

> **1 cup baking soda**
> **½ cup dry citric acid (available at any pharmacy *or* craft store)**
> **½ cup cornstarch**
> **2 ½ tbsp olive oil**
> **¾ tbsp water**
> **2 tsp essential oils, your choice**
> **¼ tsp Borax**
> **a few drops of food coloring (optional)**

In a medium bowl, stir together the baking soda, citric acid, and cornstarch until well mixed. In a separate small bowl, stir together the oil, water, essential oil, Borax, and food coloring until well mixed. Add wet ingredients to the dry ingredients and mix thoroughly until a dough forms. Pack into candy or soap molds. Press down firmly. Turn them over and remove from molds. Lay on a plate or cookie sheet and allow to dry for 1-2 days. Wrap each bomb in wax paper or cellophane to keep them fresh and to prevent crumbling. Makes 6 soap-sized bombs.

## FIZZING BATH SALTS

Too lazy to make bath bombs? Throw this stuff in a jar, shake it up, and have a bath!

> **essential oil, your choice**
> **1 cup of cornstarch**
> **1 cup of dry citric acid (available at any pharmacy *or* craft store)**
> **2 cups of baking soda**
> **a few drops of food coloring (optional)**

Mix the essential oil and cornstarch until well blended. Add other ingredients. Mix well and store in an airtight container. Makes enough for 3 baths.

## COCOA BUTTER COOKIE BATH MELTS

Don't be tempted to eat these fragrant cookies! Throw one cookie into bath water and watch your worries melt away.

> **2 cups water**
> **¼ cup cocoa butter (available at health food stores)**
> **essential oil, your choice**
> **¼ cup baking soda**
> **¼ cup dry citric acid (available at any pharmacy *or* craft store)**
> **a few drops of food coloring (optional)**

In a medium saucepan, bring water to a boil and remove from heat. Place cocoa butter into a glass bowl and set into saucepan (making sure the water is 2 inches below the lip of the bowl). Let cocoa butter melt. Once melted, remove bowl from saucepan. Add essential oil, baking soda, and citric acid and stir until well mixed and a dough forms. Quickly shape into 4 large or 6 small balls. Place on wax paper, press down with fingers and let set for 1 hour. Wrap in cellophane paper. Makes 4-6 cookies.

## BATH & MASSAGE OILS

Bath and massage oils are made by adding essential oils to vegetable oil. Using essential oils in the bath is one of the nicest ways to enjoy their therapeutic benefits. Lighter oils, such as vegetable, disperse more readily in the water. Heavier oils, such as olive, lay on the top of the bath water and will cling to your skin when you leave the tub.

Massage oils can be made from many different oils. Choose one based on what you want it to do. Use a lighter oil if you want it to be absorbed readily into the skin; use a heavier one if you want it to stay on the top of the skin.

There are all sorts of essential oils out there. Here are a few of our favorite combinations:

> **Lavender:** wonderful for calming.
>
> **Rose geranium:** can be an anti-depressant and lift your spirits.
>
> **Eucalyptus:** will help relieve cold symptoms, especially when used in the bath. Excellent for muscular aches and pains.
>
> **Ginger:** anti-inflammatory and great for sore muscles.

Check out books about aromatherapy and make your own blend!

*To make your own bath or massage oil:*
Use one teaspoon of essential oil to ½ cup of oil. Use 2 tsp oil per bath; use as needed for massage. Be sure to store in an amber or dark-colored bottle away from heat.

## FOOT BATH

Your feet do so much for you, and you do nothing but suffocate them with socks that don't breathe, cram them into shoes that don't fit, and then you curse them when they complain. Take your feet out and do something nice for them; they deserve it.

Epsom salts in a warm footbath will reduce swelling and soothe aching feet. Add a few drops of essential oil – lavender oil to soothe, or rosemary to energize.

## FOOT SCRUB

Got nasty rough feet? Shame on you! Your feet deserve to be pampered and coddled as much as the rest of you.

> ¼ **cup oats**
> ¼ **cup cornmeal**
> **1 tbsp sea salt**
> **water**

In a food processor, combine the oats, cornmeal, and salt until well mixed. Combine the dry ingredients with enough water to form a creamy, gritty paste. Wet your feet, then apply paste and massage for 2-3 minutes, adding water as needed. Rinse feet with warm water and slather on your favorite lotion or massage oil. Your feet will thank you.

## FUNGUS FOOT RUB

Yikes ... garlic is a natural anti-fungal agent. Don't forget to wear your flip-flops in public showers.

> **1 whole bulb garlic**
> ¼ **cup vinegar**

Roast a head of garlic (pg. 207). Remove from the oven and let cool. Squeeze out the soft cloves into a bowl. Mash with a fork and combine with vinegar. Massage feet with paste for 2-3 minutes, then rinse.

## PEPPERMINT FOOT MASSAGE OIL

Are your dogs barking? Peppermint is an anti-inflammatory with cooling, soothing properties. Rub this into your tired puppies after you give them a bath.

> ½ **cup oil**
> **4 drops peppermint essential oil**

Combine oils and massage into tired feet and legs until absorbed. Store excess in a jar.

# STITCH & BITCH PARTY

A stitch & bitch party combines craft-making with friendly banter. It's a great way to meet new people and hang out with your friends. You get to relax and enjoy yourself, do a little bitching (and stitching), and learn something new.

## MEETING PLACE

Rotate the hosting duties for each party. During the course of each party, ensure that someone volunteers his or her house for the next one. This way no one gets stuck playing host(ess) all the time.

## CONTACT LIST

Once you have your group, make a phone and/or e-mail list and designate one person to send out party info. We have a webpage listing our own stitch & bitches; it's an easy way for everyone to check and see the where and when: *govegan.net/stitchnbitchindex.html*

## STITCHING SUPPLIES

No matter what stitching project you get into (knitting, sock monkeys, quilts, crocheting, etc.), you don't have to buy top-of-the-line stitching materials. A lot of your supplies can be found second-hand; alternatively, go halfers with someone to keep down costs.

## APPOINT A TEACHER

It's no good to have an S&B party and have no one there who knows what they are doing. Find someone with a reasonable amount of knowledge – either a friend, auntie, grandma or someone you met at the craft store – and ask them to come and show everyone the basics. You can also find information in books or on the Internet, but there's no better way to learn than hands-on with a teacher by your side giving you pointers.

## FOOD

You need nourishment to be creative. Get everyone to bring a little something-something to nosh on. If it's not vegan (there may be non-vegans at your S&B) ask them to label it so there's no confusion.

## STITCH & BITCH INSTRUCTIONS

### Knitting

Yes, knitting can be vegan. There is a lot of yarn out there that is made from wool, but like everything these days there are animal-free alternatives. Check the label of the yarn you're buying; it will indicate the content. Stick to acrylic or cotton. And start with thick yarn and large needles. Trust us … it's easier to learn that way.

There are lots of books and a ton of information on the Internet about knitting basics. It is way too complicated for us to explain how to knit ... we're just learning ourselves. So find someone to show you; it's way easier that way.

Remember, start off simply. Don't pressure yourself. Begin by knitting a square; use it as a washcloth or a coaster. Frame it and show everyone your first knitting project. Just relax and remember not to hold your shoulders too tightly. Enjoy yourself!

## SOCK MONKEYS

Sock monkeys are traditionally made out of wool socks, but like everything these days you can find a vegan alternative. A lot of socks are made from acrylic now. Don't worry if you can't find socks with a red heel or a red toe ... be different and make a blue monkey, or a monkey with a white mouth. It doesn't matter; they're all cute in the end.

You also don't have to limit yourself to monkeys. You can make sock cats, sock dogs, sock bunnies.... But here's an easy sock monkey pattern to get you started.

*Materials:*

> **1 pair socks (2 socks = 1 monkey)**
> **Stuffing: use scraps of cloth *or* get polyester fiber from the craft store**
> **1 small needle and thread**
> **1 large needle and colored yarn (for making the face)**

*Instructions:*
Turn your socks inside out and lay them down flat. Mark out your pattern with a felt pen and cut out your pieces (see pattern).

**BODY:** Sew up each side of the legs from the crotch to the toe. With your scissors, cut one inch up the crotch and turn your monkey inside out through the opening. Stuff the body and legs through the opening with your stuffing. Sew opening shut.

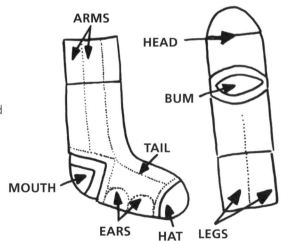

Drawings by GerryKramer.com

228

**ARMS:** Sew the arms together (right side in) and once sewn, turn right side out and stuff with stuffing. Attach to body.

**MOUTH:** It's easier to embroider the mouth before you fasten it to the body. This way, your yarn ends are tucked inside. You can give him big lips, a smile, or a toothy grin. Once embroidered, sew on the top half of the mouth, tucking in the edges. Fill mouth with stuffing and finish sewing around the bottom.

**TAIL:** You can sew your tail as you did the arms, or you can simply roll the tail up tight and sew it together. The tail is usually the part of the monkey that gets abused the most. If it's rolled, it is a lot sturdier. Attach to body.

**EARS:** Either sew on as is or stuff the ears as you did the arms and attach to the head.

**EYES:** You can sew on buttons for eyes, but if you're going to give your monkey to a small child, embroider with thread instead so they don't have anything to choke on.

**HAT:** (Optional) You'll have one toe left, so if you want you can stuff it and turn it into a hat.

Makes 1 monkey.

## EYE PILLOWS

Eye pillows can be make with any scent for any occasion; don't limit yourself to the old standby of lavender. Rosemary and chamomile are both said to relieve stress, stimulate relaxation, and ease insomnia and headaches. Try peppermint to tame a hangover. If you find your pillow lacks fragrance, give it a good squeeze to release the scent of the dried herbs.

> **5-10 drops essential oil (your choice)**
> **⅔ cup uncooked rice**
> **1 tbsp dried herbs (your choice)**
> **1 8"x8" piece of fabric**
> **1 needle and thread *and/or* sewing machine**

In a small bowl, stir together the essential oil, rice, and dried herbs. Let stand for 15 minutes. Meanwhile, fold the square of fabric in half, right sides facing one another, so the opposite side of what you want to show is on the outside. With a sewing machine or by hand, sew along the edges of fabric to form a pouch, but leave a small opening about ½-1 inch long. Use the hole to turn the pouch inside out, and place the mixture inside. Fold in the unfinished hole and sew up the opening. Makes 1 pillow.

## MENSTRUAL PADS

Why spend tons of money each year on bleached cotton menstrual pads that fill up our landfills when you can easily make your own reusable pads? Making your own is cost effective and sanitary, as long as you are. It's not as gross as you think! For an average period, you'll probably need about 10-12 cloth menstrual pads and liners on hand depending on your flow. If you do laundry every day, you may not need as many. Carry your cloth menstrual pads along with you in a plastic bag in case you need to do a quick change.

Pads with a wing design give the greatest protection. For material, we suggest using cotton flannel as it works best. It's soft and absorbent. Terry cloth is great for absorbency, but can make the pad quite thick; experiment and try different pads to see which fabric and shapes works best for you. Wash the fabric before you sew it so there will be no shrinking. It will also increase its absorbency.

*Note:*
If you don't want to sew your own pads, you can purchase cloth pads at most health food stores or at online stores (*happyperiod.com*). We also recommend The Keeper (*keeper.com*) instead of tampons. It is an amazing product that will change the way you feel about your period.

*Materials:*

> **Sewing machine *or* needle and thread (takes longer)**
> **fabric**
> **snaps**

**PAD:** You'll need a pattern. Take your favorite disposable pad (we all have a favorite shape and size that works for us) and lay it down on a piece of paper. Trace around the pad with a pen. Cut out the shape (adding 1/4 inch border for sewing), and voilà – you have a pattern to follow.

Cut out 2 pieces of fabric using this pattern. Straight stitch together (right side of fabric in), leaving a 2-inch hole. Fold the pad inside out, poking out the corners. Sew the remainder shut. Sew around the edges of the pad; it will help to flatten pad and keep its shape. Sew 2-3 snaps in succession on the wing flaps so you can adjust the size depending on how many liners you add. Makes 1 pad.

**LINERS:** The pad you just made may give you enough protection for light days, but there are times when flows are heavier. That's where liners come in. Making the liners is easy; all you have to decide is how much protection you need:

> **2-4 strips for medium**
> **2 strips flannel and 2 strips terrycloth for heavy**

Using your pad pattern, cut the fabric in the shape of your pad, without the wings. You want them to fit underneath your pad. Layer material strips one on top of another and pin together. Straight stitch around.

**To use:** Place liner under pad before snapping wings around panty. Makes 1 liner.

**To wash:** simply rinse out and toss in the laundry, no special care needed.

## IN A PINCH PAD

If you're in a pinch and don't have your cloth pads readily available, simply buy the cheapest terry facecloths you can find. Use a color separate from anything you would normally use as a facecloth. To use, simply fold in half, then half again – both length-wise. Place in the crotch of your panties, and you're all set! Fabric against fabric doesn't move. For more absorbency, simply fold two facecloths together. To wash, simply rinse out, and toss in the laundry, no special care needed.

# PET CRAFTS

If you have a cat, you'll know that fancy cat toys are a waste of money. Cats seem to enjoy play-things that are made from household materials. Here are a few easy cat toys that can be made with things you use around the house.

## CAT NIP TOY

Everyone has a stray sock or two that the washing machine ate. Instead of throwing them out make your cat a toy!

> **1 clean sock**
> **¼-½ cup dried catnip**

Fill toe end of sock with catnip. If there's a hole in the toe, tie the end in a knot and add catnip. Then tie the other end in a knot and cut off excess sock. Watch your cat get crazy.

## CAT CHASER

This cheap and easy to make cat toy is the best toy in the world.

> **Guitar string *or* bike cable**
> **4 1"x3" strips of cardboard**

Thread 1 of the cardboard strips to almost the end of the cable. With needle-nose pliers, bend the wire around the cardboard until end of wire is hidden. Add remaining cardboard and cut wire to appropriate length. Shake and shimmy cardboard end in front of your cat. Watch him (or her) get crazy.

## CAT BALL

It's a good thing cats don't have metal fillings. Ouch!

| **Tin foil**
| **1 tbsp catnip**

Spread out a small sheet of tin foil flat on table. Add catnip to center and crumple up foil into a loose ball. Watch your cat get crazy.

## DOG THROW

Dogs will play with just about anything, especially my dog Fergus. One of his favorite toys is a plastic water bottle filled ¼ of the way with rocks and/or pennies.

It's loud and it freaks him out, but he has the time of his life trying to play with it. Just make sure you check the bottle for sharp edges each time your dog plays with it. This is not a toy to be used unsupervised. Ⓢ

# CLOTHING SWAP PARTY

One of the easiest and cheapest ways to renew your wardrobe without spending any money is to have a clothing swap party. Here's how:

· Ask your friends to go through their closets and put the clothes they don't want anymore in garbage bags.

· Have everyone come over and place their unopened garbage bags in the middle of the living room floor. Once everyone has arrived, get everyone to open and dump out their bags at the same time.

· Get crazy! Grab all the items you want and make a pile behind you. Once the frenzy settles down and you've grabbed everything you want, start trying things on. Throw things you don't want or don't fit back into the pile.

· Put any leftover clothing back in the garbage bags and take it to a thrift store like the Salvation Army. This way your closet is lighter, you have new stuff to wear, and your old stuff becomes new again for someone else.

· Don't forget the food. You're going to be using up a lot of energy fighting for that pair of jeans at the bottom of the pile. Ask everyone to bring something to nosh on.

# DINNER PARTY

We keep hearing stories of people having *How It All Vegan!* potluck parties featuring recipes from the cookbook. How cool is that?

Here's an easy way to make sure that everyone enjoys a complete meal. Sometimes potlucks end up consisting of lots of salads and no dessert.

· Make a list of friends to invite.

· Make a list of what dishes you'd like for dinner.

· Ask each person you invite to choose from that list what they'd like to make and to bring a recipe card listing the ingredients and directions of their dish so that people with food sensitivities won't be worried about what they can eat. Plus if someone loves the recipe, they can copy it and take it home.

· Whether you have a disposable camera or a fancy schmancy one, take lots of photos. It's a nice way for you to remember the moment.

# COCKTAIL PARTY

The recipe for a successful cocktail party is simple: friends, music, cocktails, and most importantly, food.

### PLANNING

Your cocktail party can be intimate and small or large and raucous. It all depends on who and how many people you invite. If you make a list of guests, you'll know how much food and drinks you'll need.

### DRESS UP

Ask everyone to get as swanked up as possible. It's not a cocktail party unless everyone is looking sharp. Ya dig?

### BE RESPONSIBLE

When inviting your guests over, ask them to arrive and leave in a taxi, or at least appoint a designated driver.

## DRINKS

Plan on 3 drinks per person; it doesn't sound like much, but you don't want things getting out of control. Get a nice assortment of highball and martini glasses. Choose recipes for 3-4 different drinks and purchase what you need. Alternatively, write a list of what alcohol and mixers you need and ask each guest to pick something from the list to bring with them. Don't forget the mixers so people can also have non-alcoholic drinks.

## GARNISHES AND ICE

Garnishes dress up those fancy cocktails. Make sure you have maraschino cherries, olives, pickled onions, pickled green beans, lemon and lime slices, etc. on hand. And don't forget the ice. It's better to have too much than not enough.

## PREPARATIONS

Store away anything that you think you'll miss if they get broken. These are your friends, and you love them ... but you know how they get when they drink. Place plenty of napkins and coasters all over the house. Let's hope they use them.

## FOOD

It is your responsibility as host to make sure guests don't get too drunk. The solution? Food. Especially finger food that can be eaten with one hand while the other holds a drink. Check out Appetizers & Snacks (pg. 102) and Dips and Spreads (pg. 126). Here's our list of sure-fire hits for any party:

> Veggies & dip (pg. 126), Not Pigs in a Blanket (pg. 105)
>
> Artichoke Dip (pg. 103), Dolmades (pg. 106)
>
> Sarah Kramer's Stuffed Mushrooms (pg. 103)
>
> Millers Magnificent 5-Layer Dip (pg. 105)
>
> Nana Marg's Nuts and Bolts (pg. 108)
>
> Spicy Maple Nuts, All-Purpose Seasoning Nuts, Barbecue Nuts (pg. 110-111)

## MUSIC

Nothing can wreck the mood of a cocktail party more than the wrong music. Make some mixed CDs for your party; this way you won't be searching frantically for the perfect CD to keep the mood going. Stick with the classics. Anything jazzy and swingy, like Frank, Dean, Billie, or Ella. Or for full vintage effect, pull out your turntable and impress your friends with your vinyl collection.

# TIKI BARBECUE PARTY

Backyard barbecue parties are a great way to spend an afternoon and evening with friends and family, but why not spice it up a little and have a theme party! When do you ever get to wear any of your Hawaiian muumuus or dress your dog up in a coconut bra? Even if you don't have a backyard, you can still have a great party in your house; instead of an outdoor barbecue, use the oven instead!

## DECORATIONS

Find some Chinese paper lanterns and X-mas lights to decorate the yard. Cover the food table with grass skirts and brightly colored tablecloths. Get yourself to a thrift or party store and get crazy! Tiki torches, Hawaiian girl lamps ... the sky is the limit!

## DRINKS

Don't forget paper umbrellas for drinks. They add a festive look and you can use them to decorate your food as well. Fill a kiddy pool or a small blow-up raft with ice to keep your drinks cold.

## MUSIC

Make a few mixed CDs with some exotic Hawaiian music, or if you want to get really kitschy, set up a turntable and pull out all your Don Ho, *Elvis in Hawaii*, and *Hawaii is for Lovers* records and start hula dancing. Pull out a broom stick or bamboo stick and have a limbo contest!

## STUFF FOR YOUR GUESTS

Hula skirts, leis, and coconut and pineapple glasses can be easily found for cheap at dollar and party stores. Ask your friends to come dressed up in the tackiest Hawaiian garb they can find. If you're outside, don't forget to have bug spray and suntan lotion available as well as lawn chairs and blankets for people to sit on.

## FOOD IDEAS

Tropical Crunch (pg. 109)

Pineapple Salsa & Fabulous Fruit Salsa (pg. 130)

Amazing Grace Pasta Salad (pg. 96)

Exotic Fruit Salad with fresh mint sauce (pg. 96)

Kurstin's Walnut Burgers (pg. 165) cooked with Barbeque Sauce (pg. 141)

Tanya's Picnic Wraps (pg. 59)

Seitan Veggie Kabobs (pg. 146)

Balsamic Grilled Veggies over Couscous (pg. 157)

# INGREDIENTS GLOSSARY

We have tried our best to use ingredients that you can buy easily, but you may find your local supermarket doesn't carry so-called "specialty items." Having said that, some stores will try to keep your patronage by bringing in items that you request, so don't be afraid to ask! Check your local health food store, and if you can't find what you need in your town, there is always the Internet.

Here are a few ingredients that may have you guessing:

**Agar-agar:** A gelatin-like product derived from seaweed, available in powder, flakes, or bars. Use as a gelatin replacement.

**Acidophilus:** A "friendly" bacteria that assists in the digestion of proteins. It has antifungal properties, aids digestion, and enhances the absorption of nutrients. Look for Non-Dairy acidophilus at healthfood or vitamin stores.

**Arrowroot:** A starch flour processed from the root of an American native plant. Use as a thickening agent, similar to cornstarch or flour, for making sauces, stews, gravies, or desserts.

**Asian chili sauce:** Spicy sauce found in the condiment section of most Asian markets or grocery stores.

**Bok choy:** A mild, versatile vegetable with crunchy white stalks and tender, dark green leaves. Great source of vitamin C.

**Braggs:** A tamari/soy sauce alternative that is not heated, fermented, or salted. It is available in health food stores and some grocery stores. We love this stuff!

**Bran:** The outer layer of the grain kernel that is removed during milling. Common varieties of bran are wheat and oat. They are a good source of fibre.

**Brown rice:** Whole, unpolished rice. Comes in four main varieties – short-, medium-, long-grain, and basmati – and contains an ideal balance of minerals, protein, and carbohydrates.

**Buckwheat:** A staple food in many European countries, this cereal plant is eaten widely in the form of kasha, whole groats, and soba noodles.

**Capers:** Small, olive green flower buds picked from a bush native to the Mediterranean and parts of Asia. They have a delicate flavor, but are usually sold pickled in vinegar or brine. Can be found in most grocery stores.

**Chickpeas/garbanzo beans:** These legumes have two common names. They are good source of folic acid and potassium.

**Couscous:** Partially refined, cracked wheat. It can be consumed like rice or other cereal grains.

**Dulse:** A reddish-purple seaweed. Used in soups, salads, and vegetable dishes. Very high in iron.

**Egg replacer:** Healthy alternative to eggs. See more info on page 212.

**Flax oil:** Oil made from crushed flax seeds. It is a rich source of Omega-3, essential fatty acids.

**Galangal:** Used primarily as a seasoning and as a substitute for ginger. Can be found fresh or dried in most Asian or Thai markets and some grocery stores.

**Ginger:** A spicy, pungent, golden-coloured root, used as a condiment or for flavoring.

**Gluten (wheat):** The sticky substance that remains after the bran has been kneaded and rinsed from whole wheat flour. Used to make seitan.

**Gomashio:** A condiment made from roasted, ground sesame seeds and sea salt.

**Grape leaves:** Leaves from grapevines. Used by Greek and Middle Eastern cooks to wrap up foods for cooking. Can be found in most grocery stores.

**Kelp:** Dried seaweed. Found in health food stores, Japanese, or Korean markets.

**Lemongrass:** A long, thin, light green herb grown in subtropical countries. It grows to a height of two feet and has a subtle lemony flavor. Not only used to flavor dishes, it's also cultivated for aromatherapy use. Sometimes referred to as citronella.

**Lime leaves:** Leaves from the lime tree. They have a strong fragrance and flavor. Can be found fresh or dried in most Asian or Thai markets and some grocery stores.

**Millet:** This small, yellow grain, which comes in many varieties, can be eaten on a regular basis. It can be used in soups or vegetable dishes, or eaten as a cereal.

**Miso:** A thick paste make from fermented rice or soy beans. It is used as a flavoring agent and for soup stocks and gravies. Found in Japanese markets and some grocery stores.

**Nutritional yeast:** A yellow, non-leavening yeast used as a food supplement. It has a distinct, pleasant aroma and delicious cheesy taste. It's available in health food stores and some grocery stores.

**Oyster mushroom:** A fan-shaped mushroom. It comes in a variety of colors (white being most common), have a subtle taste, and sometimes a strong fragrance.

**Pearl barley:** One of the oldest cultivated grains. Pearl barley goes through a polishing process that removes the bran and germ. It is good in stews and mixed with other grains such as rice.

**Psyllium husks:** Psyllium seeds are ground to a powder and can be used as a thickener. They are a great source of fiber.

**Quinoa:** An ancient grain that was a staple food of the Incas. It's considered a complete protein because it contains all eight essential amino acids. It is higher in unsaturated fats and lower in carbohydrates than most grains, and it provides a rich and balanced source of vital nutrients.

**Sea salt:** Salt obtained from the ocean, as opposed to land salt. It is either sun-baked or kiln-baked. High in trace minerals, it contains no chemicals or sugar.

**Seitan:** Praise seitan! A protein-rich food made from wheat gluten. Seitan's firm texture is definitively chewy and meat like but its flavor is very mild and that allows it to act like a sponge and pick up what ever flavors it is surrounded by. It's available in the refrigerator section of health-food stores and Asian markets or you can make it yourself (pg 208).

**Serrano chili:** Small but very hot chili pepper. Can be found fresh or canned in most grocery stores.

**Shallot:** Part of the onion family. More aromatic and subtle in flavor than the onion, and less pungent than garlic.

**Shiitake:** A brown, almost flat-headed mushroom. It has a pleasant flavor and absorbs the taste of other ingredients.

**Soba:** Noodles made from buckwheat flour or a combination of buckwheat with whole-wheat flour.

**Tahini:** A thick paste made from ground sesame seeds. Popular condiment in Asia and the Middle East.

**Tamari:** Naturally made soy sauce, distinguishing it from the commercial, chemically processed variety. The original term tamari refers to a thick, condensed liquid that rises to the top during the process of making miso.

**Tofu:** A white, semi-solid product made from pressed soybean curds. It's high in protein and calcium, low in sodium and is cholesterol-free.

**Udon:** Japanese noodles made from wheat, whole-wheat, or whole-wheat and unbleached white flour.

**Wheat germ:** Located at the base of the wheat kernel, it's the embryo of the plant. It contains the most nutrients of the kernel, as it's high in vitamins, minerals, and protein. Wheat germ is also pressed to make oil.

## VEGAN NO-NOS, A TO Z

Trying to figure out what ingredients contain animal products can be a nightmare. We hope this A to Z listing of animal-product ingredients to avoid will help you on your journey to becoming a full-fledged vegan warrior. This list is used with the permission of People for the Ethical Treatment of Animals.

## A

**Adrenaline.** Hormone from adrenal glands of hogs, cattle, and sheep. In medicine. Alternatives: synthetics.

**Alanine.** (See Amino Acids.)

**Albumen.** In eggs, milk, muscles, blood, and many vegetable tissues and fluids. In cosmetics, albumen is usually derived from egg whites and used as a coagulating agent. May cause allergic reaction. In cakes, cookies, candies, etc. Egg whites sometimes used in "clearing" wines. Derivative: Albumin.

**Albumin.** (See Albumen.)

**Alcloxa.** (See Allantoin.)

**Aldioxa.** (See Allantoin.)

**Aliphatic Alcohol.** (See Lanolin and Vitamin A.)

**Allantoin.** Uric acid from cows, most mammals. Also in many plants (especially comfrey). In cosmetics (especially creams and lotions) and used in treatment of wounds and ulcers. Derivatives: Alcloxa, Aldioxa. Alternatives: extract of comfrey root, synthetics.

**Alpha-Hydroxy Acids.** Any one of several acids used as an exfoliant and in anti-wrinkle products. Lactic acid may be animal-derived (see Lactic Acid). Alternatives: glycolic acid, citric acid, and salicylic acid are plant- or fruit-derived.

**Ambergris.** From whale intestines. Used as a fixative in making perfumes and as a flavouring in foods and beverages. Alternatives: synthetic or vegetable fixatives.

**Amino Acids.** The building blocks of protein in all animals and plants. In cosmetics, vitamins, supplements, shampoos, etc. Alternatives: synthetics, plant sources.

**Aminosuccinate Acid.** (See Aspartic Acid.)

**Animal Fats and Oils.** In foods, cosmetics, etc. Highly allergenic. Alternatives:olive oil, wheat germ oil, coconut oil, flaxseed oil, almond oil, safflower oil, etc.

**Animal Hair.** In some blankets, mattresses, brushes, furniture, etc. Alternatives: vegetable and synthetic fibers.

**Arachidonic Acid.** A liquid unsaturated fatty acid that is found in liver, brain, glands, and fat of animals and humans. Generally isolated from animal liver. Used in companion animal food for nutrition and in skin creams and lotions to soothe eczema and rashes. Alternatives: synthetics, aloe vera, tea tree oil, calendula ointment.

**Arachidyl Proprionate.** A wax that can be from animal fat. Alternatives: peanut or vegetable oil.

**Aspartic Acid.** Aminosuccinate Acid. Can be animal or plant source (e.g., molasses). Sometimes synthesized for commercial purposes.

## B

**Bee Pollen.** Microsporic grains in seed plants gathered by bees then collected from the legs of bees. Causes allergic reactions in some people. In nutritional supplements, shampoos, toothpaste's, deodorants. Alternatives: synthetics, plant amino acids, pollen collected from plants.

**Bee Products.** Produced by bees for their own use. Bees are selectively bred. Culled bees are killed. A cheap sugar is substituted for their stolen honey. Millions die as a result. Their legs are often torn off by pollen-collection trapdoors.

**Beeswax.** Honeycomb. Wax obtained from melting honeycomb with boiling water, straining it, and cooling it. From virgin bees. Very cheap and widely used but harmful to the skin. In lipsticks and many other cosmetics (especially face creams, lotions, mascara, eye creams and shadows, face makeup's, nail whiteners, lip balms, etc.). Derivatives: Cera Flava. Alternatives: paraffin, vegetable oils and fats. Ceresin aka ceresine aka earth wax. (Made from the mineral ozokerite. Replaces beeswax in cosmetics. Also used to wax paper, to make polishing cloths, in dentistry for taking wax impressions, and in candle-making.) Also, carnauba wax (from the Brazilian palm tree; used in many cosmetics, including lipstick; rarely causes allergic reactions). Candelilla wax (from candelilla plants; used in many cosmetics, including lipstick; also in the manufacture of rubber, phonograph records, in waterproofing and writing inks; no known toxicity). Japan wax (Vegetable wax. Japan tallow. Fat from the fruit of a tree grown in Japan and China.). Benzoic Acid. In almost all vertebrates and in berries. Used as a preservative in mouthwashes, deodorants, creams, aftershave lotions, etc. Alternatives: cranberries, gum benzoin (tincture) from the aromatic balsamic resin from trees grown in China, Sumatra, Thailand, and Cambodia.

**Beer.** Most domestic beers use animal charcoal. Drink organic beer or make your own.

**Beta Carotene.** (See Carotene.)

**Biotin. Vitamin H. Vitamin B Factor.** In every living cell and in larger amounts in milk and yeast. Used as a texturizer in cosmetics, shampoos, and creams. Alternatives: plant sources.

**Blood.** From any slaughtered animal. Used as adhesive in plywood, also found in cheese-making, foam rubber, intravenous feedings, and medicines. Possibly in foods such as lecithin. Alternatives: synthetics, plant sources.

**Boar Bristles.** Hair from wild or captive hogs. In "natural" toothbrushes and bath and shaving brushes. Alternatives: vegetable fibers, nylon, the peelu branch or peelu gum (Asian, available in the U.S., its juice replaces toothpaste).

**Bone Char.** Animal bone ash. Used in bone china and often to make sugar white. Serves as the charcoal used in aquarium filters. Alternatives: synthetic tribasic calcium phosphate.

**Bone Meal.** Crushed or ground animal bones. In some fertilizers. In some vitamins and supplements as a source of calcium. In toothpastes. Alternatives: plant mulch, vegetable compost, dolomite, clay, vegetarian vitamins.

**Brown and White Sugar.** Most refineries use animal charcoal filters. Alternatives: Sucanat (brand name) sweetener, turbinado sugar, concentrated fruit sweetener, rice syrup, maple syrup (after checking up on company to make sure they don't use lard as a de-foamer)

## C

**Calciferol.** (See Vitamin D.)

**Calfskin.** (See Leather.)

**Caprylamine Oxide.** (See Caprylic Acid.)

**Capryl Betaine.** (See Caprylic Acid.)

**Caprylic Acid.** A liquid fatty acid from cow's or goat's milk. Also from palm and coconut oil, other plant oils. In perfumes, soaps. Derivatives: Caprylic Triglyceride, Caprylamine Oxide, Capryl Betaine. Alternatives: plant sources.

**Caprylic Triglyceride.** (See Caprylic Acid.)

**Carbamide.** (See Urea.)

**Carmine. Cochineal. Carminic Acid.** Red pigment from the crushed female cochineal insect. Reportedly 70,000 beetles must be killed to produce one pound of this red dye. Used in cosmetics, shampoos, red apple sauce, and other foods (including red lollipops and food colouring). May cause allergic reaction. Alternatives: beet juice (used in powders, rouges, shampoos; no known toxicity); alkanet root (from the root of this herblike tree; used as a red dye for inks, wines, lip balms, etc.; no known toxicity. Can also be combined to make a copper or blue colouring). (See Colours.)

**Carminic Acid.** (See Carmine.)

**Carotene. Provitamin A. Beta Carotene.** A pigment found in many animal tissues and in all plants. Used as a colouring in cosmetics and in the manufacture of vitamin A.

**Casein. Caseinate. Sodium Caseinate.** Milk protein. In "non-dairy" creamers, soy cheese, many cosmetics, hair preparations, beauty masks. Alternatives: soy protein, soy milk, and other vegetable milks.

**Caseinate.** (See Casein.)

**Castor.** Castoreum. Creamy substance with strong odour from muskrat and beaver genitals. Used as a fixative in perfume and incense. Alternatives: synthetics, plant castor oil.

**Castoreum.** (See Castor.)

**Catgut.** Tough string from the intestines of sheep, horses, etc. Used for surgical sutures. Also for stringing tennis rackets and musical instruments, etc. Alternatives: nylon and other synthetic fibers.

**Cera Flava.** (See Beeswax.)

**Cetyl Alcohol.** Wax found in spermaceti from sperm whales or dolphins. Alternatives: vegetable cetyl alcohol (e.g., coconut), synthetic spermaceti.

**Cetyl Palmitate.** (See Spermaceti.)

**Chitosan.** A fiber derived from crustacean shells. Used as a lipid binder in diet products. Alternatives: raspberries, yams, legumes, dried apricots, and many other fruits and vegetables.

**Chocolate.** Contains milk/milk products, white sugar eat carob or dark chocolate instead.

**Cholesterin.** (See Lanolin.)

**Cholesterol.** A steroid alcohol in all animal fats and oils, nervous tissue, egg yolk, and blood. Can be derived from lanolin. In cosmetics, eye creams, shampoos, etc. Alternatives: solid complex alcohols (sterols) from plant sources.

**Choline Bitartrate.** (See Lecithin.)

**Civet.** Unctuous secretion painfully scraped from a gland very near the genital organs of civet cats. Used as a fixative in perfumes. Alternatives: (See alternatives to Musk).

**Cochineal.** (See Carmine.)

**Cod Liver Oil.** (See Marine Oil.)

**Collagen.** Fibrous protein in vertebrates. Usually derived from animal tissue. Can't affect the skin's own collagen. An allergen. Alternatives: soy protein, almond oil, amla oil (see alternative to Keratin), etc.

**Colours.** Dyes. Pigments from animal, plant, and synthetic sources used to colour foods, cosmetics, and other products. Cochineal is from insects. Widely used FD? and D? colours are coal-tar (bituminous coal) derivatives that are continously tested on animals due to their carcinogenic properties. Alternatives: grapes, beets, turmeric, saffron, carrots, chlorophyll, annatto, alkanet.

**Cortisone. Corticosteroid.** Hormone from adrenal glands. Widely used in medicine. Alternatives: synthetics.

**Cysteine, L-Form.** An amino acid from hair which can come from animals. Used in hair care products and creams, in some bakery products, and in wound-healing formulations. Alternatives: plant sources.

**Cystine.** An amino acid found in urine and horsehair. Used as a nutritional supplement and in emollients. Alternatives: plant sources.

# D

**Dexpanthenol.** (See Panthenol.)

**Diglycerides.** (See Monoglycerides and Glycerin.)

**Dimethyl Stearamine.** (See Stearic Acid.)

**Down.** Goose or duck insulating feathers. From slaughtered or cruelly exploited geese. Used as an insulator in quilts, parkas, sleeping bags, pillows, etc. Alternatives: polyester and synthetic substitutes, kapok (silky fibers from the seeds of some tropical trees) and milkweed seed pod fibers.

**Duodenum Substances.** From the digestive tracts of cows and pigs. Added to some vitamin tablets. In some medicines. Alternatives: vegetarian vitamins, synthetics.

**Dyes.** (See Colours.)

## E

**Egg Protein.** In shampoos, skin preparations, etc. Alternatives: plant proteins.

**Elastin.** Protein found in the neck ligaments and aortas of cows. Similar to collagen. Can't affect the skin's own elasticity. Alternatives: synthetics, protein from plant tissues.

**Emu Oil.** From flightless ratite birds native to Australia and now factory farmed. Used in cosmetics, creams. Alternatives: vegetable and plant oils.

**Ergocalciferol.** (See Vitamin D.)

**Ergosterol.** (See Vitamin D.)

**Estrace.** (See Estrogen.)

**Estradiol.** (See Estrogen.)

**Estrogen. Estrace. Estradiol.** Hormones from cow ovaries and pregnant mares' urine. Considered a drug. Can have harmful systemic effects if used by children. Used for reproductive problems and in birth control pills and menopausal drugs. In creams and lotions. Has a negligible effect in the creams as a skin restorative; simple vegetable-source emollients are considered better. Alternatives: oral contraceptives and menopausal drugs based on synthetic steroids or phytoestrogens (from plants; currently being researched). Menopausal symptoms can also be treated with diet and herbs.

## F

**Fats.** (See Animal Fats.)

**Fatty Acids.** Can be one or any mixture of liquid and solid acids such as caprylic, lauric, myristic, oleic, palmitic, and stearic. Used in bubble baths, lipsticks, soap, detergents, cosmetics, food. Alternatives: vegetable-derived acids, soy lecithin, safflower oil, bitter almond oil, sunflower oil, etc.

**FD&C Colours.** (See Colours.)

Feathers. From exploited and slaughtered birds. Used whole as ornaments or ground up in shampoos. (See Down and Keratin.)

**Fish Liver Oil.** Used in vitamins and supplements. In milk fortified with vitamin D. Alternatives: yeast extract ergosterol and exposure of skin to sunshine.

**Fish Oil.** (See Marine Oil.) Fish oil can also be from marine mammals. Used in soap-making.

**Fish Scales.** Used in shimmery makeups. Alternatives: mica, rayon, synthetic pearl.

Fructose. From white sugar, even further refined. (see sugar)

**Fur.** Obtained from animals (usually mink, foxes, or rabbits) cruelly trapped in steel-jaw leghold traps or raised in intensive confinement on fur "farms." Alternatives: synthetics. (See Sable Brushes.)

## G

**Gelatin. Gel.** Protein obtained by boiling skin, tendons, ligaments, and/or bones with water. From cows and pigs. Used in shampoos, face masks, and other cosmetics. Used as a thickener for fruit gelatins and puddings (e.g., "Jello"). In candies, marshmallows, cakes, ice cream, yogurts. On photographic film and in vitamins as a coating and as capsules. Sometimes used to assist in "clearing" wines. Alternatives: carrageen (carrageenan, Irish moss), seaweeds (algin, agar-agar, kelp-used in jellies, plastics, medicine), pectin from fruits, dextrins, locust bean gum, cotton gum, silica gel. Marshmallows were originally made from the root of the marsh mallow plant. Vegetarian capsules are now available from several companies. Digital cameras don't use film.

**Glucose Tyrosinase.** (See Tyrosine.)

**Glycerides.** (See Glycerin.)

**Glycerin. Glycerol.** A byproduct of soap manufacture (normally uses animal fat). In cosmetics, foods, mouthwashes, chewing gum, toothpastes, soaps, ointments, medicines, lubricants, transmission and brake fluid, and plastics. Derivatives: Glycerides, Glyceryls, Glycreth-26, Polyglycerol. Alternatives: vegetable glycerin-a byproduct of vegetable oil soap. Derivatives of seaweed, petroleum.

**Glycerol.** (See Glycerin.)

**Glyceryls.** (See Glycerin.)

**Glycreth-26.** (See Glycerin.)

**Guanine. Pearl Essence.** Obtained from scales of fish. Constituent of ribonucleic acid and deoxyribonucleic acid and found in all animal and plant tissues. In shampoo, nail polish, other cosmetics. Alternatives: leguminous plants, synthetic pearl, or aluminum and bronze particles.

## H

**Hide Glue.** Same as gelatin but of a cruder impure form. Alternatives: dextrins and synthetic petrochemical-based adhesives. (See Gelatin.)

**Honey.** Food for bees, made by bees. Can cause allergic reactions. Used as a colouring and an emollient in cosmetics and as a flavoring in foods. Should never be fed to infants. Alternatives: in foods-maple syrup, date sugar, syrups made from grains such as barley malt, turbinado sugar, molasses; in cosmetics-vegetable colours and oils. Some Vegans choose to use honey.

**Honeycomb.** (See Beeswax.)

**Horsehair.** (See Animal Hair.)

**Hyaluronic Acid.** A protein found in umbilical cords and the fluids around the joints. Used as a cosmetic oil. Alternatives: plant oils.

**Hydrocortisone.** (See Cortisone.)

**Hydrolyzed Animal Protein.** In cosmetics, especially shampoo and hair treatments. Alternatives: soy protein, other vegetable proteins, amla oil (see alternatives to Keratin).

## I

**Imidazolidinyl Urea.** (See Urea.)

**Insulin.** From hog pancreas. Used by millions of diabetics daily. Alternatives: synthetics, vegetarian diet and nutritional supplements, human insulin grown in a lab.

**Isinglass.** A form of gelatin prepared from the internal membranes of fish bladders. Sometimes used in "clearing" wines and in foods. Alternatives: bentonite clay, "Japanese isinglass," agar-agar (see alternatives to Gelatin), mica, a mineral used in cosmetics.

**Isopropyl Lanolate.** (See Lanolin.)

**Isopropyl Myristate.** (See Myristic Acid.)

**Isopropyl Palmitate.** Complex mixtures of isomers of stearic acid and palmitic acid. (See Stearic Acid).

## K

**Keratin.** Protein from the ground-up horns, hooves, feathers, quills, and hair of various animals. In hair rinses, shampoos, permanent wave solutions. Alternatives: almond oil, soy protein, amla oil (from the fruit of an Indian tree), human hair from salons. Rosemary and nettle give body and strand strength to hair.

## L

**Lactic Acid.** Found in blood and muscle tissue. Also in sour milk, beer, sauerkraut, pickles, and other food products made by bacterial fermentation. Used in skin fresheners, as a preservative, in the formation of plasticizers, etc. Alternative: plant milk sugars, synthetics.

**Lactose.** Milk sugar from milk of mammals. In eye lotions, foods, tablets, cosmetics, baked goods, medicines. Alternatives: plant milk sugars.

**Laneth.** (See Lanolin.)

**Lanogene.** (See Lanolin.)

**Lanolin. Lanolin Acids. Wool Fat. Wool Wax.** A product of the oil glands of sheep, extracted from their wool. Used as an emollient in many skin care products and cosmetics and in medicines. An allergen with no proven effectiveness. (See Wool for cruelty to sheep.) Derivatives: Aliphatic Alcohols, Cholesterin, Isopropyl Lanolate, Laneth, Lanogene, Lanolin Alcohols, Lanosterols, Sterols, Triterpene Alcohols. Alternatives: plant and vegetable oils.

**Lanolin Alcohol.** (See Lanolin.)

**Lanosterols.** (See Lanolin.)

**Lard.** Fat from hog abdomens. In shaving creams, soaps, cosmetics. In baked goods, French fries, refried beans, and many other foods. Alternatives: pure vegetable fats or oils.

**Leather. Suede. Calfskin. Sheepskin. Alligator Skin. Other Types of Skin.** Subsidizes the meat industry. Used to make wallets, handbags, furniture and car upholstery, shoes, etc. Alternatives: cotton, canvas, nylon, vinyl, ultrasuede, other synthetics.

**Lecithin. Choline Bitartrate.** Waxy substance in nervous tissue of all living organisms. But, frequently obtained for commercial purposes from eggs and soybeans. Also from nerve tissue, blood, milk, corn. Choline bitartrate, the basic constituent of lecithin, is in many animal and plant tissues and prepared synthetically. Lecithin can be in eye creams, lipsticks, liquid powders, handcreams, lotions, soaps, shampoos, other cosmetics, and some medicines. Alternatives: soybean lecithin, synthetics.

**Linoleic Acid.** An essential fatty acid. Used in cosmetics, vitamins. (See alternatives to Fatty Acids.) Lipase. Enzyme from the stomachs and tongue glands of calves, kids, and lambs. Used in cheese-making and in digestive aids. Alternatives: vegetable enzymes, castor beans.

**Lipoids. Lipids.** Fat and fat-like substances that are found in animals and plants. Alternatives: vegetable oils. Marine Oil. From fish or marine mammals (including porpoises). Used in soap-making. Used as a shortening (especially in some margarines), as a lubricant, and in paint. Alternatives: vegetable oils.

## M

**Maple Syrup.** Most companies add lard as foam reducer. Buy organic or check with company

**Methionine.** Essential amino acid found in various proteins (usually from egg albumen and casein). Used as a texturizer and for freshness in potato chips. Alternatives: synthetics.

**Milk Protein.** Hydrolyzed milk protein. From the milk of cows. In cosmetics, shampoos, moisturizers, conditioners, etc. Alternatives: soy protein, other plant proteins.

**Mink Oil.** From minks. In cosmetics, creams, etc. Alternatives: vegetable oils and emollients such as avocado oil, almond oil, and jojoba oil.

**Monoglycerides.** Glycerides. (See Glycerin.) From animal fat. In margarines, cake mixes, candies, foods, etc. In cosmetics. Alternative: vegetable glycerides.

**Musk (Oil).** Dried secretion painfully obtained from musk deer, beaver, muskrat, civet cat, and otter genitals. Wild cats are kept captive in cages in horrible conditions and are whipped around the genitals to produce the scent; beavers are trapped; deer are shot. In perfumes and in food flavorings. Alternatives: labdanum oil (which comes from various rockrose shrubs) and other plants with a musky scent. Labdanum oil has no known toxicity.

**Myristal Ether Sulfate.** (See Myristic Acid.)
**Myristic Acid.** Organic acid in most animal and vegetable fats. In butter acids. Used in shampoos, creams, cosmetics. In food flavorings. Derivatives: Isopropyl Myristate, Myristal Ether Sulfate, Myristyls, Oleyl Myristate. Alternatives: nut butters, oil of lovage, coconut oil, extract from seed kernels of nutmeg, etc.
**Myristyls.** (See Myristic Acid.)

## N

**"Natural Sources."** Can mean animal or vegetable sources. Most often in the health food industry, especially in the cosmetics area, it means animal sources, such as animal elastin, glands, fat, protein, and oil. Alternatives: plant sources.
**Nucleic Acids.** In the nucleus of all living cells. Used in cosmetics, shampoos, conditioners, etc. Also in vitamins, supplements. Alternatives: plant sources.

## O

**Ocenol.** (See Oleyl Alcohol.)
**Octyl Dodecanol.** Mixture of solid waxy alcohols. Primarily from stearyl alcohol. (See Stearyl Alcohol.)
**Oleic Acid.** Obtained from various animal and vegetable fats and oils. Usually obtained commercially from inedible tallow. (See Tallow.) In foods, soft soap, bar soap, permanent wave solutions, creams, nail polish, lipsticks, many other skin preparations. Derivatives: Oleyl Oleate, Oleyl Stearate. Alternatives: coconut oil. (See alternatives to Animal Fats and Oils.)
**Oils.** (See alternatives to Animal Fats and Oils.)
**Oleths.** (See Oleyl Alcohol.)
**Oleyl Alcohol. Ocenol.** Found in fish oils. Used in the manufacture of detergents, as a plasticizer for softening fabrics, and as a carrier for medications. Derivatives: Oleths, Oleyl Arachidate, Oleyl Imidazoline.
**Oleyl Arachidate.** (See Oleyl Alcohol.)

**Oleyl Imidazoline.** (See Oleyl Alcohol.)
**Oleyl Myristate.** (See Myristic Acid.)
**Oleyl Oleate.** (See Oleic Acid.)
**Oleyl Stearate.** (See Oleic Acid.)

## P

**Palmitamide.** (See Palmitic Acid.)
**Palmitamine.** (See Palmitic Acid.)
**Palmitate.** (See Palmitic Acid.)
**Palmitic Acid.** From fats, oils (see Fatty Acids). Mixed with stearic acid. Found in many animal fats and plant oils. In shampoos, shaving soaps, creams. Derivatives: Palmitate, Palmitamine,
**Palmitamide.** Alternatives: palm oil, vegetable sources.
**Panthenol.** Dexpanthenol. Vitamin B-Complex Factor. Provitamin B-5. Can come from animal or plant sources or synthetics. In shampoos, supplements, emollients, etc. In foods. Derivative: Panthenyl. Alternatives: synthetics, plants.
**Panthenyl.** (See Panthenol.)
**Pepsin.** In hogs' stomachs. A clotting agent. In some cheeses and vitamins. Same uses and alternatives as Rennet.
**Placenta.** Placenta Polypeptides Protein.
**Afterbirth.** Contains waste matter eliminated by the fetus. Derived from the uterus of slaughtered animals. Animal placenta is widely used in skin creams, shampoos, masks, etc. Alternatives: kelp. (See alternatives for Animal Fats and Oils.)
**Polyglycerol.** (See Glycerin.)
**Polypeptides.** From animal protein. Used in cosmetics. Alternatives: plant proteins and enzymes.
**Polysorbates.** Derivatives of fatty acids. In cosmetics, foods.
**Pristane.** Obtained from the liver oil of sharks and from whale ambergris. (See Squalene, Ambergris.) Used as a lubricant and anti-corrosive agent. In cosmetics. Alternatives: plant oils, synthetics.
**Progesterone.** A steroid hormone used in anti-wrinkle face creams. Can have adverse systemic effects. Alternatives: synthetics.

**Propolis.** Tree sap gathered by bees and used as a sealant in beehives. In toothpaste, shampoo, deodorant, supplements, etc. Alternatives: tree sap, synthetics.

**Provitamin A.** (See Carotene.)

**Provitamin B-5.** (See Panthenol.)

**Provitamin D-2.** (See Vitamin D.)

## R

**Rennet.** Rennin. Enzyme from calves' stomachs. Used in cheese-making, rennet custard (junket), and in many coagulated dairy products. Alternatives: microbial coagulating agents, bacteria culture, lemon juice, or vegetable rennet.

**Rennin.** (See Rennet.)

**Resinous Glaze.** (See Shellac.)

**Ribonucleic Acid.** (See RNA.)

**RNA. Ribonucleic Acid.** RNA is in all living cells. Used in many protein shampoos and cosmetics. Alternatives: plant cells.

**Royal Jelly.** Secretion from the throat glands of the honeybee workers that is fed to the larvae in a colony and to all queen larvae.No proven value in cosmetics preparations. Alternatives: aloe vera, comfrey, other plant derivatives.

## S

**Sable Brushes.** From the fur of sables (weasel-like mammals). Used to make eye makeup, lipstick, and artists' brushes. Alternatives: synthetic fibers.

**Shark Liver Oil.** Used in lubricating creams and lotions. Derivatives:Squalane, Squalene. Alternatives: vegetable oils.

**Sheepskin.** (See Leather.)

**Shellac. Resinous Glaze.** Resinous excretion of certain insects. Used as a candy glaze, in hair lacquer, and on jewelry. Alternatives: plant waxes.

**Silk. Silk Powder.** Silk is the shiny fiber made by silkworms to form their cocoons. Worms are boiled in their cocoons to get the silk. Used in cloth. In silk-screening (other fine cloth can be and is used instead). Taffeta can be made from silk or nylon. Silk powder is obtained from the secretion of the silkworm. It is used as a coloring agent in face powders, soaps, etc. Can cause severe allergic skin reactions and systemic reactions (if inhaled or ingested). Alternatives: milkweed seed-pod fibers, nylon, silk-cotton tree and ceiba tree filaments (kapok), rayon, and synthetic silks.

**Snails.** In some cosmetics (crushed).

**Sodium Caseinate.** (See Casein.)

**Sodium Steroyl Lactylate.** (See Lactic Acid.)

**Sodium Tallowate.** (See Tallow.)

**Spermaceti. Cetyl Palmitate. Sperm Oil.** Waxy oil derived from the sperm whale's head or from dolphins. In many margarines. In skin creams, ointments, shampoos, candles, etc. Used in the leather industry. May become rancid and cause irritations. Alternatives: synthetic spermaceti, jojoba oil, and other vegetable emollients.

**Sponge** (Luna and Sea). A plant-like animal. Lives in the sea. Becoming scarce. Alternatives: synthetic sponges, loofahs (plants used as sponges).

**Squalane.** (See Shark Liver Oil.)

**Squalene.** Oil from shark livers, etc. In cosmetics, moisturizers, hair dyes, surface-active agents. Alternatives: vegetable emollients such as olive oil, wheat germ oil, rice bran oil, etc.

**Stearamide.** (See Stearic Acid.)

**Stearamine.** (See Stearic Acid.)

**Stearamine Oxide.** (See Stearyl Alcohol.)

**Stearates.** (See Stearic Acid.)

**Stearic Acid.** Fat from cows and sheep and from dogs and cats euthanized in animal shelters, etc. Most often refers to a fatty substance taken from the stomachs of pigs. Can be harsh, irritating. Used in cosmetics, soaps, lubricants, candles, hairspray, conditioners, deodorants, creams, chewing gum, food flavoring. Derivatives: Stearamide,Stearamine, Stearates, Stearic

Hydrazide, Stearone, Stearoxytri-methylsilane, Stearoyl Lactylic Acid, Stearyl Betaine, Stearyl Imidazoline. Alternatives: Stearic acid can be found in many vegetable fats, coconut.

**Stearic Hydrazide.** (See Stearic Acid.)

**Stearone.** (See Stearic Acid.)

**Stearoxytrimethylsilane.** (See Stearic Acid.)

**Stearoyl Lactylic Acid.** (See Stearic Acid.)

**Stearyl Acetate.** (See Stearyl Alcohol.)

**Stearyl Alcohol. Sterols.** A mixture of solid alcohols. Can be prepared from sperm whale oil. In medicines, creams, rinses, shampoos, etc. Derivatives: Stearamine Oxide, Stearyl Acetate, Stearyl Caprylate, Stearyl Citrate, Stearyldimethyl Amine, Stearyl Glycyrrhetinate, Stearyl Heptanoate, Stearyl Octanoate, Stearyl Stearate. Alternatives: plant sources, vegetable stearic acid.

**Steroids. Sterols.** From various animal glands or from plant tissues. Steroids include sterols. Sterols are alcohol from animals or plants (e.g., cholesterol). Used in hormone preparation. In creams, lotions, hair conditioners, fragrances, etc. Alternatives: plant tissues, synthetics.

**Sterols.** (See Stearyl Alcohol and Steroids.)

**Suede.** (See Leather.)

**Sugar.** Most refineries use animal charcoal filters. Alternatives: Sucanat (brand name)sweetner, turbinado sugar, concentrated fruit sweetener, rice syrup, maple syrup (after checking up on company to make sure they don't use lard as a de-foamer)

**Syrup, Maple.** Most companies add lard as foam reducer. Buy organic or check with company.

# T

**Tallow. Tallow Fatty Alcohol. Stearic Acid.** Rendered beef fat. May cause eczema and blackheads. In wax paper, crayons, margarines, paints, rubber, lubricants, etc. In candles, soaps, lipsticks, shaving creams, other cosmetics.

Chemicals (e.g., PCB) can be in animal tallow. Derivatives: Sodium Tallowate, Tallow Acid, Tallow Amide, Tallow Amine, Talloweth-6, Tallow Glycerides, Tallow Imidazoline. Alternatives: vegetable tallow, Japan tallow, paraffin and/or ceresin (see alternatives for Beeswax for all three). Paraffin is usually from petroleum, wood, coal, or shale oil.

**Triterpene Alcohols.** (See Lanolin.)

**Turtle Oil. Sea Turtle Oil.** From the muscles and genitals of giant sea turtles. In soap, skin creams, nail creams, other cosmetics. Alternatives: vegetable emollients (see alternatives to Animal Fats and Oils).

**Tyrosine.** Amino acid hydrolyzed from casein. Used in cosmetics and creams. Derivative: Glucose Tyrosinase. Urea. Carbamide. Excreted from urine and other bodily fluids. In deodorants, ammoniated dentrifices, mouthwashes, hair colorings, hand creams, lotions, shampoos, etc. Used to "brown" baked goods, such as pretzels. Derivatives: Imidazolidinyl Urea, Uric Acid. Alternatives: synthetics.

# V

**Vinegar distilled (white).** Use animal charcoal for filtering use rice, wine, or apple cider vinegar

**Vitamin A.** Can come from fish liver oil (e.g., shark liver oil), egg yolk, butter, lemongrass, wheat germ oil, carotene in carrots, and synthetics. It is an aliphatic alcohol. In cosmetics, creams, perfumes, hair dyes, etc. In vitamins, supplements. Alternatives: carrots, other vegetables, synthetics.

**Vitamin B-Complex Factor.** (See Panthenol.)

**Vitamin B Factor.** (See Biotin.)

**Vitamin B-12.** Usually animal source. Some vegetarian B-12 vitamins are in a stomach base. Alternatives: some vegetarian B-12-fortified yeasts and analogs available. Plant algae discovered containing B-12, now in supplement form (spirulina). Also, B-12 is normally produced in a healthy body.

**Vitamin D. Ergocalciferol. Vitamin D-2. Ergosterol. Provitamin D-2. Calciferol. Vitamin D-3.** Vitamin D can come from fish liver oil, milk, egg yolk, etc. Vitamin D-2 can come from animal fats or plant sterols. Vitamins D-2 and D-3 may be from fish oil. All the D vitamins can be in creams, lotions, other cosmetics, vitamin tablets, etc. Alternatives: plant and mineral sources, synthetics, completely vegetarian vitamins, exposure of skin to sunshine. Many other vitamins can come from animal sources. Examples: choline, biotin, inositol, riboflavin, etc.
**Vitamin H.** (See Biotin.)

# W

**Wax.** Glossy, hard substance that is soft when hot. From animals and plants. In lipsticks, depilatories, hair straighteners. Alternatives: vegetable waxes.
**Whey.** A serum from milk. Usually in cakes, cookies, candies, and breads. In cheese-making. Alternatives: soybean whey.
**White Sugar, Brown sugar.** Most refineries use animal charcoal filters. Alternatives: Sucanat (brand name) sweetner, turbinado sugar, concentrated fruit sweetener, rice syrup, maple syrup (after checking up on company to make sure they don't use lard as a de-foamer)
**Wool.** From sheep. Used in clothing. Ram lambs and old "wool" sheep are slaughtered for their meat. Sheep are transported without food or water, in extreme heat and cold. Legs are broken, eyes injured, etc. Sheep are bred to be unnaturally woolly, also unnaturally wrinkly, which causes them to get insect infestations around the tail areas. The farmer's solution to this is the painful cutting away of the flesh around the tail (called mulesing). "Inferior" sheep are killed. When shearing the sheep, they are pinned down violently and sheared roughly. Their skin is cut up. Every year, hundreds of thousands of shorn sheep die from exposure to cold. Natural predators of sheep (wolves, coyotes, eagles, etc.) are poisoned, trapped, and shot. In the U.S., overgrazing of cattle and sheep is turning more than 150 million acres of land to desert. "Natural" wool production uses enormous amounts of resources and energy (to breed, raise, feed, shear, transport, slaughter, etc., the sheep). Derivatives: Lanolin, **Wool Wax, Wool Fat.** Alternatives: cotton, cotton flannel, synthetic fibers, ramie, etc.
**Wool Fat, wool wax.** (See Lanolin.)

### People for the Ethical Treatment of Animals
There are many ways to make your life animal friendly. Reading labels is a good way to start. If you're interested in avoiding companies that test or use animal products, you can contact People for the Ethical Treatment of Animals (PETA)'s website:

www.peta-online.org/index.html

or

People for the Ethical Treatment of Animals
501 Front St., Norfolk, VA
USA 23510
(757) 622-7382

For a few bucks, they can also provide you with a booklet of animal-friendly and non-animal-friendly companies entitled Shopping Guide for Caring Consumers that you can carry with you while you shop. PETA is an excellent resource for books, products, and other information.

# APPENDIX

## MEASUREMENTS

*In elementary school, I was eight years old when we changed over from Imperial to Metric measurements. Needless to say I am a very confused person. I can't live without this chart.* (S)

28 grams: 1 ounce
100 grams: 3½ ounces
454 grams: 1 pound
1 teaspoon: 5 millilitres
1 quart: about 1 litre

1000 micrograms: 1 milligram
.001 gram: 1 milligram
.001 milligram: 1 microgram
1000 milligrams: 1 gram
1000 grams: 1 kilogram

3 teaspoons: 1 tablespoon
4 tablespoons: ¼ cup
5 ⅓ tablespoons: ⅓ cup
16 tablespoons: 1 cup
1 cup: 8 fluid ounces
1 cup: ½ pint
2 cups: 1 pint
4 cups: 1 quart
4 quarts: 1 gallon

100°F:    38° C
180° F:    82° C
250° F:   121° C
300° F:   149° C
325° F:   163° C
350° F:   177° C
375° F:   191° C
400° F:   204° C
425° F:   218° C
450° F:   232° C

# INDEX

# INDEX

# INDEX

# INDEX

# INDEX

# INDEX